Love and Forgiveness
in Yeats's Poetry

Studies in Modern Literature, No. 57

A. Walton Litz, General Series Editor

Professor of English
Princeton University

Richard J. Finneran

Consulting Editor for Titles on W.B. Yeats
Professor of English
Newcomb College, Tulane University

Other Titles in This Series

Love and Forgiveness in Yeats's Poetry

by
Catherine Cavanaugh

UMI RESEARCH PRESS
Ann Arbor, Michigan

Produced and distributed by
UMI Research Press
an imprint of
University Microfilms International
A Xerox Information Resources Company
Ann Arbor, Michigan 48106

Library of Congress Cataloging in Publication Data

Cavanaugh, Catherine, 1945-
Love and forgiveness in Yeats's poetry.

(Studies in modern literature ; no. 57)
Revision of thesis (Ph.D.)—State University of
New York at Binghamton, 1984.
Bibliography: p.
Includes index.
1. Yeats, W. B. (William Butler), 1865-1939—
Criticism and interpretation. 2. Love in literature.
3. Forgiveness in literature. 4. Yeats, W. B.
(William Butler), 1865-1939. Three bushes. I. Title.
II. Series.
PR5908.L65C38 1986   821'.8   85-20692
ISBN 0-8357-1728-3 (alk. paper)

For
my father, my brothers,
and my sisters, Joan and Kitty

W. B. Yeats, by Althea Gyles
(Reproduced by courtesy of the Trustees of the British Museum)

Contents

Acknowledgments

I thank John Vernon, State University of New York at Binghamton, under whose direction I began this study. I am grateful to my colleagues at the College of Saint Rose, Albany, New York, for their support, most especially to Katherine Hanley, C. S. J., and Joan Lescinski, C. S. J., for their faith in this project from its beginning and their patience in reading and rereading the manuscript. I also thank Maureen Elliot, who typed the original manuscript, and the following for allowing me time on various word processors: Sean Peters, C. S. J., and the Office of Graduate and Continuing Studies; Pat McAuley and Rooney Hall; and Kris Barber, Andrew Harnichar, and the Computer Center.

I gratefully acknowledge permission from Michael B. Yeats and Anne Yeats, A. P. Watt and Son, A. D. Peters, Ltd., Macmillan Publishers, Ltd., London, and Macmillan Publishing Company, Inc., New York, for permission to quote from the following works of W. B. Yeats: *The Autobiography* (copyright renewed 1963, Bertha Georgie Yeats); *Essays and Introductions* (copyright 1961, Mrs. W. B. Yeats); *Explorations* (copyright 1962, Mrs. W. B. Yeats); *Letters*, ed. Allan Wade (copyright 1954, Anne Butler Yeats); *Memoirs*, ed. Denis Donoghue (copyright 1972, M. B. Yeats and Anne Yeats); *Mythologies* (copyright 1959, Mrs. W. B. Yeats); *The Poems,* ed. Richard H. Finneran (copyright Anne Yeats); *A Critical Edition of Yeats's A VISION (1925)*, ed. George Mills Harper and Walter Kelly Hood (copyright 1978, George Mills Harper and Walter Kelly Hood); *A Vision,* 1937 (copyright 1937 by W. B. Yeats, renewed 1956 by Bertha Georgie Yeats and Anne Butler Yeats); *The Variorum Edition of the Plays*, ed. Russell K. Alspach and Catharine C. Alspach (copyright 1966, Russell K. Alspach and Bertha Georgie Yeats); *The Variorum Edition of the Poems*, ed. Peter Allt and Russell K. Alspach (copyright 1940, George Yeats). I thank Oxford University Press for permission to quote from *Letters on Poetry* by W. B. Yeats and Dorothy Wellesley (copyright 1940, Oxford University Press).

Sources of additional shorter quotations are acknowledged in notes.

List of Abbreviations

For bibliographical details see the Selected Bibliography.

A	*The Autobiography*
EI	*Essays and Introductions*
Ex	*Explorations*
JS	*John Sherman and Dhoya*, ed. Richard J. Finneran
L	*Letters*, ed. Allan Wade
LP	*Letters on Poetry*, by W. B. Yeats and Dorothy Wellesley
M	*Memoirs*, ed. Denis Donoghue
My	*Mythologies*
P	*Poems*, ed. Richard J. Finneran
UnP	*Uncollected Prose*, ed. John Frayne and Colton Johnson
V, 1925	*A Critical Edition of Yeats's A VISION (1925)*, ed. George Mills Harper and Walter Kelly Hood
V, 1937	*A Vision*, 1937
VP	*Variorum Edition of the Poems*, ed. Peter Allt and Russell K. Alspach
VP1	*Variorum Edition of the Plays*, ed. Russell K. Alspach and Catharine C. Alspach
YE-B	*The Works of William Blake—Poetical, Symbolic, and Critical*, ed. W. B. Yeats and Edwin Ellis

1

"The Three Bushes"

If ever Yeats followed Aristotle's advice to think like a philosopher but speak like a common person, as Lady Gregory often urged,[1] he did so in his late sequence "The Three Bushes." In this seemingly simple ballad with its six attendant songs, Yeats weaves a tightly woven tapestry of many of the figures, themes, questions, and convictions that he raveled and unraveled in his lifelong attempt to find unity of being, imaged both in the perfect union of two lovers and in the total integrity of the poet's psyche. This short sequence not only encapsulates Yeats's later vision of love and art, but also traces the difficult mental and emotional journey that brought him to these views.

The plot involves a love triangle among a chaste lady, a poet-lover, and a chambermaid:

THE THREE BUSHES

(An Incident from the 'Historia mei Temporis'
of the Abbé Michel de Bourdeille)

Said lady once to lover,
"None can rely upon
A love that lacks its proper food;
And if your love were gone
How could you sing those songs of love?
I should be blamed, young man."
O my dear, O my dear.

"Have no lit candles in your room,"
That lovely lady said,
"That I at midnight by the clock
May creep into your bed,
For if I saw myself creep in
I think I should drop dead."
O my dear, O my dear.

"I love a man in secret,
Dear chambermaid," said she.
"I know that I must drop down dead
If he stop loving me,
Yet what could I but drop down dead
If I lost my chastity?"
        O my dear, O my dear.

"So you must lie beside him
And let him think me there,
And maybe we are all the same
Where no candles are,
And maybe we are all the same
That strip the body bare."
        O my dear, O my dear.

But no dogs barked and midnights chimed,
And through the chime she'd say,
"That was a lucky thought of mine,
My lover looked so gay;"
But heaved a sigh if the chambermaid
Looked half asleep all day.
        O my dear, O my dear.

"No, not another song," said he,
"Because my lady came
A year ago for the first time
At midnight to my room,
And I must lie between the sheets
When the clock begins to chime."
        O my dear, O my dear.

"A laughing, crying, sacred song,
A leching song," they said.
Did ever men hear such a song?
No, but that day they did.
Did ever man ride such a race?
No, not until he rode.
        O my dear, O my dear.

But when the horse had put its hoof
Into a rabbit hole
He dropped upon his head and died.
His lady saw it all
And dropped and died thereon, for she
Loved him with her soul.
        O my dear, O my dear.

The chambermaid lived long, and took
Their graves into her charge,
And there two bushes planted
That when they had grown large
Seemed sprung from but a single root
So did their roses merge.
        O my dear, O my dear.

When she was old and dying,
A priest came where she was;
She made a full confession.
Long looked he in her face,
And O, he was a good man
And understood her case.
        O my dear, O my dear.

He bade them take and bury her
Beside her lady's man,
And set a rose-tree on her grave.
And now none living can
When they have plucked a rose there
Know where its roots began.
        O my dear, O my dear.   (P 296-98)

As the title indicates, everything in the ballad moves inexorably toward
an apparently traditional ballad ending—the intertwined rose bushes on the
lovers' graves. Yet Yeats's three bushes are not so clearcut a symbol of the
irrevocable union after death as two entwined bushes or a merged rose and
briar would be. The three bushes suggest a less easily resolved multiplicity.
Even this simple title implies a philosophic question in the context of Yeats's
later work. Do these three bushes symbolize that the dead lovers share the
eternal state of "God that is but three" (P 285), as Ribh describes in "Ribh
denounces Patrick"? Or do they signify a multiplicity and division that
extends even beyond death, as the bone sings of in "Three Things"?

The ascription of the ballad to the Abbé also seems a simple detail aimed
at creating medieval atmosphere, but contains provocative ambiguities. Yeats
subtly sets up an antinomy by conjoining "Abbé" (the sacred and consecrated)
with "bordel" (the profane and lustful),[2] an antinomy which reappears more
obviously in the "sacred" and "leching" song that the audience demands from
the poet-lover and the suggestion of both bedmate and virgin in the title
"chambermaid."[3]

In a series of letters between Yeats and Dorothy Wellesley in 1936, where
they exchange versions of ballads based on this plot situation,[4] Yeats, who

was much more fascinated by these ballads than Wellesley, takes pains over the designation of the source of the incident. In September, he comments, "When we meet we will decide upon the name of the fourteenth or fifteenth [century] fabulist who made the original story" (LP 104). Although she showed no interest in this "fabulist" in her response,[5] Yeats informed her in November, "I am describing *The Three Bushes* as 'founded upon an incident from the *Historia mei Temporis* of the Abbé Michel de Bourdelie [sic]' " (LP 114). He carefully chooses a Priest who records his own history and, as I will discuss more fully in connection with the last two stanzas, functions in the plot as well.

Yeats's choice of a name for the Priest suggests another ambiguity, since it contains a pun on the French *bourde*, meaning "fib."[6] Yeats's comment that he was searching for a "fabulist" underlines this pun. The juxtaposition of "historia" and "bourde" gives the first hint of the duplicity on which the whole situation is predicated. That the Abbé is named Michel[7] may also be significant, given Yeats's fondness for this name for his fictional adepts, such as Michael Robartes and the would-be adept Michael in his early unpublished novel, *The Speckled Bird*.

The tension between truth and deception becomes much more explicit in the first four stanzas, culminating in the pun on "lie" in the fourth stanza. The overly intellectual Lady lies by means of truth, setting up syllogisms that seem to provide a justification for her actions. However, she either starts from false premises or refuses to include herself in her universal statements. In the first stanza, she constructs her first (faulty) syllogism: love needs physical food; songs need love; therefore, the poet-lover needs physical love. She euphemizes the sexual act, equating it with communion imagery and carrying on the sacred-profane tension of the Abbé's name. She concludes that she, his muse, would be culpable if he stopped singing. Her tendency to address the Lover as "young man" suggests the tone of a schoolmarm as well as a coquette as she finishes her logical construct.

In the second stanza, she implies that she sees this sacrament as a black mass in connection with herself. She wants "no lit candles" and uses a snake image (echoed in her third song), suggesting that to "creep" into his bed at midnight would constitute her fall into the realm of mortality. The Lady's dilemma flows from her conviction that her chastity is essential to her existence. To requite his love would thus bring her death. To lose his love, however, would also cause her to "drop down dead." The "proper food" for his love would be poison to her, whereas her chastity would leave him starving. The Lady decides that they both must "rely upon" someone else to maintain their love—the Chambermaid.

The Lady is obviously deceiving the Lover, yet Yeats seems sincere when he refers to her as a "lovely lady." Although he is half mocking toward her, he is also basically sympathetic toward what he accepts as a real dilemma between her need for both love and chastity. In fact, his need to explore the Lady's motivation and her mental resolution of the extreme dichotomy she perceives between spiritual and physical love is one of the major reasons for his fascination with this ballad and also underlies the six songs, since the first two stanzas of the first song he wrote, "The Lady's Second Song," were originally spoken by her in the ballad.[8] Yeats was disposed, both by his unending attraction to Maud Gonne and by his occult studies and wish to be an adept, to take the Lady's key focus—her virginity—seriously.

The Lady's premise—that sexual love will destroy spiritual love—will prove false in its sterile disjunction from the concrete world, but she builds what she considers a logical truth from that premise. The complexity of her mental resolution of her dilemma is not delineated until the songs, but her repetition of "drop down dead," although semicomic in its melodramatic overtones, does emphasize her agony. She is repeatedly blind to her own inconsistencies: how can she be "all the same" with the Chambermaid if she refuses to "strip the body bare"? And why does she "heave a sigh" when the Chambermaid shows the effect of her passionate night? Yet, the Lady convinces herself that she has found the only viable solution to her dilemma.

The stanzas describing the Lover suggest that the Lady's plot achieves the desired result for him. The relationship between his nights, with a woman whom he still thinks is the Lady a year later, and his artistic ability is ambiguous, however. The Lady set up this whole scheme so that he could continue singing his songs of love; yet in the sixth stanza he refuses to sing another song because he must join her in bed. When he relents and sings a laughing-crying, sacred-leching song, the contrasts suggest that the Chambermaid is more crucial to his inspiration than the Lady. In general, the Lover is unaware: he never realizes who his bedmate is; he unwittingly foreshadows his own death by describing himself laid out in his shroud at midnight; his unpremeditated rush precipitates his death. In terms of typical medieval symbolism, he is blinded by his overwhelming physical desires, as is underlined by the sexual symbolism surrounding his death. His horse (masculine) puts its hoof into a rabbit hole, which carries both the traditional association of the rabbit with lust and the feminine imagery of the womb. The semicomic pun in his dropping on his head (made explicit in the phallic substitution in "The Chambermaid's Second Song") clinches the picture of his lustful blindness.

Yet the Lover's actions could also suggest that he is as passionately immersed in life as the Lady is chastely distanced from it. The narrator, although he ambiguously states the affirmative through two negatives, implies that the Lover did sing the highly antinomial song before he left his audience. Yet the same stanza technically undercuts the Lover's poetic ability, since it is the choppiest stanza in the ballad. Yeats starts two lines with the strong monosyllable, "no," followed by a comma; the slant rhymes are harsh. The earliest extant draft shows perfect rhymes and smoother meter in lines two, four, and six:

> A letching song' said they
> . . . .
> No not before that day
> . . . .
> Not till he rode away.[9]

Since Yeats firmly believed that "regular rhyme is needed in this kind of work" and that the "fundamental sing-song" (LP 90) of the meter must not distract the reader, his revision toward unevenness in describing the poet-lover must be significant.

Is Yeats suggesting that even the seeming completeness of a traditional form is a delusion, just as the Lover is still deluded about the source of his inspiration? Or is Yeats implying that the Lover is a more complex poet than the "fundamental sing-song" can convey? Or perhaps the Lover is simply so blinded by lust that his choppy verse reflects his poetic ability? The ambiguity that surrounds his poetic ability redounds onto his lustfulness as well. If he possesses fine creative ability, he cannot be dismissed as a mere beast who craves his proper food, not caring where he gets it. Yeats clearly leaves the Lover deceived and connects the Lover's death to his physical desires, but the effect of this deception and death on his poetic ability remains ambivalent.

The Lady's reaction to the Lover's death is surprising. If she has guarded against her death by preserving her chastity, why does Yeats say that when the Lover dies the Lady "dropped and died thereon, for she / Loved him with her soul." The logical connectives are highly significant, especially the unobtrusive "for." She dies *because* she loves with her soul. Ironically, she has preserved her physical virginity in order that she could love him with her soul, but the relationship between chastity and her soul is not so simple as she presumed. The contrast between the Lady's fate and the Chambermaid's is emphasized in the first line of the next stanza, where Yeats says that the Chambermaid "lived long." The implication is that the Chambermaid must not have loved with her soul if she could survive his death.

Yet Yeats does not suggest that the Chambermaid nourishes her own (and the Lover's) body at the expense of her soul. Not only does she demonstrate that her love was more than physical by tenderly caring for their graves, but she also confesses and is forgiven on her deathbed, then rewarded by the planting of the third bush. The last two stanzas are present from the first extant draft; moreover, Yeats wrote this part with such conviction that he made very few revisions in the last two stanzas.[10]

Like the ascription to the Abbé and the Lady's chastity, the confession adds to the general medieval coloring of the ballad, but it leaves many unanswered questions. What does the Chambermaid confess? Earlier she seemed a mere pawn in the Lady's scheme to deceive the Lover. Is Yeats implying that her passionate involvement in physical love—hinted at in the Lover's "gay" looks and the Chambermaid's "half asleep" look the next day— is the sin she must confess? If so, why does the Priest forgive her, since there is no indication that she regretted her actions? Instead, she immortalized the deception by planting two bushes on the Lady's and Lover's graves.

The Priest's reaction is equally puzzling. Is this "good man" merely generally sympathetic to the human condition or does he understand "her case" because he, too, has experienced both spiritual and physical love? Since it seems logical to conflate this Priest who hears the whole story from the Chambermaid with the Abbé who wrote the incident in his *Historia mei Temporis*, the conjunction of the sacred and profane in his name is further developed here. This is only hinted at in "The Three Bushes," but a statement Yeats made in his first version of *A Vision* shows how fascinated he was by the potentiality for this double role of spiritual judge and physical lover: "Three Roman Courtesans who have one after another got their favourite lovers chosen Pope have, it pleases one's mockery to think, confessed their sins, with full belief in the supernatural efficacy of the act, to ears that have heard their cries of love" (V, 1925, 195). The parallel is not exact, since it would be impossible for the Priest and the dead Lover to be the same person; nonetheless, the punning suggestion that he is the Abbé of brothels adds provocative overtones to the reason he "understood her case."

The pun on "fib" in his name also relates to his attitude toward the Chambermaid. By commanding that she be buried on the other side of the Lover and that the third bush be added, the Priest is consecrating and immortalizing the triangle of deception that the Lady created and the Chambermaid carried out. Even death does not destroy the deception and division on which their love was based.[11] Death does not bring a simple union of body (Lover) and soul (Lady), imaged by their two merged bushes. The Priest reintroduces the third member of the triangle, symbolically guaranteeing that the tensions between body and soul will extend beyond death and that only deceptive oneness will be achieved. Thus, the confessional interchange between the Priest and the Chambermaid leads to the re-creation of the triangle of deception and incompleteness.

Both the ascription at the beginning of the ballad and the emphasis on the bushes at the end suggest that the interchange between the Priest and the Chambermaid leads to the creation of a work of art. The Chambermaid and the Priest cultivate the image of beauty on the lovers' graves and the Abbé turns the Chambermaid's story into part of his *Historia*. Since the whole ballad is a record of the story that the Chambermaid confesses to the Priest, it can be interpreted as a re-enactment of that verbal interchange with the Priest as listener interjecting the refrain. [12] The different inflections with which the exclamation "O my dear" could be spoken allow a progression from shock to tender sympathy in the hearer. Is Yeats implying that poetry is not only a verbal art (his pronouncements on the oral nature of poetry are numerous) but also more specifically a confession and forgiveness of sin?

If so, what is the forgiveness of sins in Yeats's view? Does forgiveness obliterate all tension and division? How does the image of the three bushes resolve the ambiguity of the title? Is Yeats suggesting that art achieves the unity that lovers fail to find even after death? In that case, in the artistic imagination, as in the Godhead, three are really one. Equally plausibly, however, Yeats could be implying that the three bushes come together to form a work of art that is far from immortal: like all bushes, they will eventually wither. In the midst of his many letters that refer to "The Three Bushes," Yeats mentions to Wellesley that he has just finished "Lapis Lazuli" (LP 91). Perhaps the three bushes are meant to reflect the aesthetic theory that "all things fall and are built again" (P 295). If so, the emphasis is on the last line—knowing where "its roots began." Since the roots of the three bushes are in the three separate graves of the lovers, the work of art is predicated on the same incompleteness, division, and deception as the love act. The three bushes create an illusion of oneness that transcends the onlooker's fragmented view of life, but the onlooker's very act of plucking a rose from the bushes hastens the withering process.

The attendant songs continue to probe the questions left at the end of the ballad: what is the relationship between the Lady's refusal of physical love and her death because she loved with her soul; conversely, what is the connection between the Chambermaid's bodily love and her ability to survive the Lover's death; is the Lover a superficial lover and poet; and what sin is confessed by the Chambermaid, resulting in what kind of forgiveness by the Priest?

None of these questions relates only to this poem, however. They reflect Yeats's concerns about human love and art throughout his career. When he tries again to answer them by retelling the story in the six songs, Yeats is doing what he has done continually in his lyric poetry. After rereading all of his lyric poetry in 1932, he commented, "what man is this who in the course of two or three weeks—the improvisation suggests the tune—says the same thing in so many different ways" (L 798). At the same time, the fragmentary nature of the songs reverses the technical impression of completeness achieved at the end of the ballad, even though they repeat the same themes. Nonetheless, the "improvisation suggests the tune." The aesthetic impression of the ballad, especially the last stanza, is clarified by what seems to be the opposite aesthetic conclusion in the songs.

This pattern of building to seeming wholeness and then fragmenting that completeness reflects the direction that Yeats traveled in arriving at the vision of love and art that he embodied in this late sequence. He starts with a view of both love and forgiveness that shuns the temporal and looks forward to a transformation to perfection at death. Gradually, his view shifts to an acceptance of the inevitability of incompleteness, although he insists on a near approach to completeness. The four figures in this sequence also each relate to a group of personae that Yeats used repeatedly to dramatize and probe his evolving convictions about the relationship between lovers and between the poet and his art. These four figures, as I have already hinted at in connection with the Lady, recall autobiographical experiences that were essential to the shift in Yeats's viewpoint. Most significantly, as the songs will demonstrate, the actions, attitudes, and poetic techniques of these figures portray the development of two of Yeats's deepest convictions about love and art: that "the tragedy of sexual intercourse is the perpetual virginity of the soul"[13] and that "literature is the forgiveness of sins."[14]

"The Tragedy of Sexual Intercourse Is the Perpetual Virginity of the Soul"

In the six attendant songs, Yeats separates the roots of the three bushes, retelling the same story from each lover's viewpoint and thus exposing the inner motivations and emotional reactions of each. This fragmented version delineates which of the lovers, who speak in the same order in which they are given prominence in the ballad, think that completeness can be achieved and which accept ultimate incompleteness in their love and by analogy in their art. There is a significant thematic progression from the Lady's views to the Chambermaid's, dramatizing Yeats's own major shift in perspective in his lifelong exploration of the degree of unity that can be achieved in love. This shift was affected by his experiences, particularly those relating to Maud Gonne, between 1890 and 1910. His shift in belief about love, moreover, was paralleled by a change in aesthetic theory—a change that he also mirrors in the contrasting aesthetic effects that each lover creates.

The Lady's protection of her chastity and her equation of herself with her soul imply that she perceives herself as the embodiment of Yeats's conviction that "the tragedy of sexual intercourse is the perpetual virginity of the soul," a statement Yeats made in a conversation with John Sparrow at Oxford in 1931. The record of this conversation presents a summary of Yeats's deepest beliefs toward the end of his life. In its fuller context, Yeats's striking statement relates to his view of the original and irreconcilable antinomy between the one and the many:

The finest description of sexual intercourse ever written was in Dryden's translation of Lucretius, and it was justified; it was introduced to illustrate the difficulty of two becoming a unity: "The tragedy of sexual intercourse is the perpetual virginity of the soul." Sexual intercourse is an attempt to solve the eternal antinomy, doomed to failure because it takes place only on one side of the gulf. The gulf is that which separates the one and the many, or if you like, God and man.[15]

Yeats is dramatizing the implications of this statement in this sequence; however, the Lady fails to embody the tension involved in Yeats's dictum. Her songs reveal that she lives and dies by an inverse pattern: virginal body and violated soul. By so doing, she does not overcome the tragedy involved in human love, but creates an illusive resolution of the irreconcilable antinomy. Her songs, constituting half of the attendant songs, also reflect attitudes that Yeats held in the first half of his career—attitudes that always attracted him, as the power of the Lady's songs attests.

"The Lady's First Song" uncovers her underlying physical desires and indicates that this threat to her physical virginity attacks her identity. She perceives no middle link between the spiritual and the bestial. If she is attracted to the physical, she is no better than a beast:

> I turn round
> Like a dumb beast in a show,
> Neither know what I am
> Nor where I go,
> My language beaten
> Into one name;
> I am in love
> And that is my shame.
> What hurts the soul
> My soul adores,
> No better than a beast
> Upon all fours. (P 299)

Her song throws a different light on the first stanza of the ballad: the Lady instigates the whole situation. She has not been propositioned by the Lover; rather, she needs to satisfy her own cravings, even if only through a surrogate. Both the Lover and the Chambermaid are her pawns. By denying the possibility of the human middle ground, the Lady forces herself to choose either divinity or animality. Yeats uses the biblical overtones of the ineffable "I am" to start the Lady's self-apotheosis. As will become even clearer in her second song, she sees herself as a godhead in her own self-referential world.

Significantly, she also feels that her creative ability is threatened. Love makes her a "dumb beast" and her "language is beaten / Into one name." Her ability to manipulate words is dependent on her unassailed, solipsistic virginity. In the ballad, she worries about providing inspiration for the Lover;

here, she is a poet herself who is in danger of losing her own source of song. Seven times in this short song she repeats "I" or "my," implying that, in terms of Yeats's system in *A Vision*, she is an antithetical (subjective) artist. If so, she must meet her Daimon or antiself through interplay with another. Yet, as the ballad has already shown and the subsequent songs will reinforce, she refuses any real interchange with others. Instead, she manipulates them for her own purposes.

She summarizes her whole problem in the two short lines: "What hurts the soul / My soul adores." She embodies the opposite of the tragedy of sexual intercourse that Yeats called the "virginity of the soul." Her body is virginal, but her soul is utterly violated by her longings. In the ballad, she dies because she loved the Lover with her soul. Ironically, she thinks that she must eliminate her physical longings to preserve her soul, but Yeats's statement suggests that the soul's virginity can only be experienced during intercourse.

The Lady's refusal to engage in physical love with the poet-lover aligns her with the many figures based on Maud Gonne in Yeats's poetry. In the First Draft of his *Autobiography*, Yeats recounts how Maud Gonne told him in the late 1890s that she had a "horror and terror of physical love" (M 134). As Bradford reports, this was the time that Maud Gonne and Yeats entered into their first period of spiritual marriage, since Maud refused a regular marriage.[16] Nevertheless, Yeats says that Maud "was now always very emotional and would kiss me tenderly." She wanted the poet's love, but as Yeats recalls through his depiction of the Lady, Maud forced him either to live in "unctuous celibacy," as he did through much of his youth, or to find his "proper food" elsewhere.

The tension between the Lady's fear of losing her chastity and her strong physical urges as revealed in her first song also relates her to Yeats's own conflicting desires, especially in the 1890s. His occult reading in sources such as Blavatsky, Boehme, and alchemy, as well as his membership in the Order of the Golden Dawn, a Rosicrucian society, had convinced Yeats of the power of the adept.[17] He longed to become an adept in his art, transforming all to perfection in the alembic of his imagination. The magus, as all these sources point out, must be celibate. If he works with a woman, they are united only spiritually as *artifex* and *soror mystica*.[18] Anything that drags him down into the bestial, as the Lady fears, delays his achievement of his ultimate goal.

Sexual love robs the adept of his power and the artist-adept of his creative ability. Repeatedly, in early poems such as "The Man who dreamed of Faeryland" and, most especially, in *The Shadowy Waters*, Yeats wrestles with his fear that human love will dissipate his creative power. Fighting against that fear are his physical desires since, as he says in his First Draft, he could never "escape from the disturbance of my senses" (M 33). The Lady's dilemma recalls, most poignantly, Yeats's own ongoing attraction toward being the celibate, aloof adept and his simultaneous desire for passionate love. In fact, the Lady's decision to use her Chambermaid as a surrogate in bed is almost a parody of Yeats's youthful identification with the adept Axel, whose declaration, "As for living, our servants will do that for us,"[19] Yeats had treated as sacred.

Consistently equating the sexual act and death, the Lady describes the tryst in her second song in terms that suggest the washing of the corpse and strewing of the bier with flowers as strongly as the marriage bed:

> What sort of man is coming
> To lie between your feet?
> What matter we are but women.
> Wash; make your body sweet;
> I have cupboards of dried fragrance
> I can strew the sheet.
> *The Lord have mercy upon us.*

But she will not sacrifice herself; rather, she as Creator will manipulate her puppet creatures to atone the original sin, which Yeats, following the Platonic tradition, sees as the fall into division—both in the separation of the sexes and the disjunction of body and soul.

She gives her commandments in the second stanza, declaring that body and soul must be kept simplistically separate if the inner struggle she described in her first song is to be avoided:

> He shall love my soul as though
> Body were not at all,
> He shall love your body
> Untroubled by the soul,
> Love cram love's two divisions
> Yet keep his substance whole.
> *The Lord have mercy upon us.*

Having rejected the individuation of matter (the "sort of man" he really is), because she knows that would cloud her untroubled solution, the Lady creates an idealized, ritualized pattern. She accepts the division of the human condition, but not the tension between the two parts of the antinomy. She wants to restore the harmony of Eden without personally experiencing the fall. If she ignores her own body while the Chambermaid ignores her soul, then each of them will feel whole. The Lover, meanwhile, will love one spiritually and the other bodily; he too will attain a feeling of sated wholeness by eliminating tension. The verb "cram" suggests both the active role of the Lover in fulfilling the opposing needs of each of the women and the "proper food" that he will be glutted with as a result. This mental construct is much more harmonious than the emotional anguish she was trying to escape in her first song. She has eliminated the antinomy between the one and the many by denying the need to join them.

Yeats, however, simultaneously undercuts her vision of unity by his choice of "cram," which sinks to a much lower level of diction. The same "soul"-"whole" puns (with the opposite spelling of "soul") are used here as in Crazy Jane's proclamation to the Bishop that "nothing can be sole or whole / That has not been rent" (P 259). The change of "sole" to "soul" is significant, since to the Lady the soul is all that matters. She is not willing to be rent, but plans to find her own unity by allowing someone else to experience the physical rending that Crazy Jane chooses. Crazy Jane expresses paradox; the Lady's plan to "cram" the divisions of love is sophistry. In the final stanza of this song, she unwittingly reveals how divided the substance of the Lover must be if he is to fulfill her plan. His "soul" and his "limbs" will end up so separate that the blessedness that he achieves will have to be divided between them:

> Soul must learn a love that is
> Proper to my breast,
> Limbs a love in common
> With every noble beast.
> If soul may look and body touch
> Which is the more blest?
> *The Lord Have Mercy upon us.*

Her final question could suggest that each is equally blest in her untroubled system, but it could also hint that she wonders if touch may yield more consolation.

Her underlying obsession with the body surfaces once more at the beginning of her third song:

> When you and my true lover meet
> And he plays tunes between your feet,
> Speak no evil of the soul,
> Nor think that body is the whole
> For I that am his daylight lady
> Know worse evil of the body. (P 301)

She has ritualized the sexual act even further, making it a musical performance—but also unintentionally making clear where the poet-lover's source of inspiration is. She contradicts what she set up as the untroubled approach to love in her second song when she said that he would be oblivious of the soul when he engaged in bodily love. Now she fears they may malign the "daylight lady" when they play in the dark. She tries to assert and justify her divine power, sounding like a Solomon who thinks he can split the child without killing it: "But in honor split his love / Till either neither have enough."

Her diction and imagery become increasingly dense as she builds her final verbal expression of the harmony and wholeness she hopes to achieve by dividing body and soul:

> That I may hear if we should kiss
> A contrapuntal serpent hiss,
> You, should hand explore a thigh,
> All the labouring heavens sigh.

She has handed down her own Smaragdine Tablet: what is above corresponds to what is below and vice versa. However, only if the Lady can love as if "body were not at all" will the serpent's hiss be truly contrapuntal; whereas only if the Chambermaid is "untroubled by the soul" when she loves will she hear "the labouring heavens." If the two kinds of love are mixed, the pattern of the correspondence cannot be achieved so neatly. The Lady sees her insistence on separation of spiritual and physical love as the only way to restore the harmony of perfect correspondence. If they are kept separate, human love is not a tragedy, but a comedy that can be manipulated to a satisfactory resolution.

The parallel between the circumstances in Yeats's second period of spiritual marriage with Maud Gonne, from June 1908 to December 1909,[20] and the Lady's viewpoint is even closer than the correspondence between the ballad and the events in the 1890s. In one of the few available extant letters from Maud Gonne to Yeats, written early in this second period of spiritual marriage, Maud used images that the Lady echoes in her second and third songs. Like the Lady, Maud is arguing for a strictly spiritual love between herself and Yeats:

We went some where in space I dont know where—I was conscious of starlight & of hearing the sea below us. You had taken the form I think of a great serpent, but I am not quite sure. I only saw your face distinctly & as I looked into your eyes (as I did the day in Paris you asked me what I was thinking of) & your lips touched mine. We melted into one another till we formed only *one being, a being greater than ourselves* who felt all & knew all with double intensity—the clock striking 11 broke the spell & as we separated it felt as if life was being drawn away from me through my chest with almost physical pain. . . . Then I went upstairs to bed & I dreamed of you confused dreams of ordinary life. We were in Italy together. . . . We were quite happy, & talked of this wonderful vision I have described—you said it would tend to increase physical desire—This troubles me a little—for there was nothing physical in that union—Material union is but a pale shadow compared to it.[21]

Maud's connection of the serpent and a kiss, her realization that Yeats's desires are physical, her own desire to join him in soul as if the body did not exist, her denigration of "material union" in comparison to spiritual union, and even the detail of the clock striking, all foreshadow the images and beliefs that Yeats uses much later to portray the Lady.

In a diary entry written later in this period of spiritual marriage, Yeats describes both Maud and himself in terms that, like Maud's letter, strongly parallel the Lady and the Lover in "The Three Bushes":

> PIAL [the Golden Dawn initials for Maud] told me that we must be apart. . . . Since she said this she has not been further from me but is always very near. She too seems to love more than of old. In addition to this the dread of physical love has awakened in her. This dread has probably spoiled her life, checking natural and instinctive selection and leaving fantastic duties free to take its place. . . . I was never more deeply in love, but my desires, always strong, must go elsewhere, if I would escape their poison.[22]

The Lady's sincere love for the poet, thwarted from physical expression by her fear of physical love, closely corresponds to Yeats's description of Maud here. His mention of "fantastic duties" also parallels the Lady's tone, which suggests that she is doing all for the good of the Lover. Yeats, like the Lover, feeds his physical desires elsewhere. In fact, during this second period of spiritual marriage, Yeats was simultaneously engaged in an affair with Mabel Dickinson.[23] Most significantly, Yeats no longer believed that there was a remedy for this dichotomy between spiritual and physical love.[24] In all, the events of their second period of spiritual marriage constituted a climax and turning point in Yeats's view of the possibility of overcoming this dichotomy; however, unlike the Lady, he refused to limit his experience to one or the other. Thus, Yeats recreates part of himself in both the Lady, who sees the division between body and soul, and the Lover, who needs physical as well as spiritual love.

Halfway through the songs, the Lady, who reflects Yeats's earlier hope that he, as celibate adept, would be able to build a perfect harmony in imagination, creates the intensest poetry of the sequence in the last four lines of her third song. Apparently, by guarding her virginity she has perfected her creative power; thus, the triangle of their love is a material illusion of incompleteness that really constitutes an imaginative harmony.[25] Her complete images, however, are the kind that Yeats accused himself of having created in his youth in "The Circus Animals' Desertion": "Those masterful images because complete / Grew in pure mind" (P 347). The Lady's whole world is intellectual. She has worked out a logical mental construct by keeping herself aloof from bodily contact, but by so doing she has tried to restore Eden without ever admitting and, most importantly, enacting her own part in the fallen human condition. Such a withdrawal from human intercourse can, as Yeats well knew, yield masterful images. Those images, nonetheless, can desert the poet at any moment because they are not rooted in the concrete. She is the most articulate artist among the three lovers; yet Yeats implies that her verbal salvation is an illusion that cannot be sustained in the context of concrete reality.

The Lady imagines herself on the side of the one, but, as Yeats's comments to Sparrow indicate, she, like all humans, is still caught in multiplicity. Because she refuses to take part in physical love, her solution is not even based on the most powerful human attempt to unite the many into the one. Ironically, she faintly echoes Dryden's translation of Lucretius's description of physical love in her reference to the Chambermaid's thighs, but the distance between the Lady's view of love and Lucretius's—which Yeats twice designates as the best description of sexual love[26]—is immense. Lucretius very graphically depicts two lovers who passionately, but vainly, seek a union of hearts.[27] The Lady's merely intellectual attempt to create oneness will not teach her the vanity of her delusion.

The Lady does not see body and soul as two interpenetrating gyres, but as abstractions that can easily be separated. Such an abstraction, as Yeats says in *A Vision*, can "consume itself away" (V, 1925, 134), as the Lady so readily does when the Lover dies. Her self-appointed divinity is not the uncomposite, self-begotten oneness that Yeats embodied in such figures as the dancer at the end of "Among School Children." Indeed, such self-begotten simplicity is impossible for an antithetical artist, such as the Lady (and Yeats), as I will discuss in connection with *A Vision* and the poetry most strongly affected by it. The figure who consciously experiences the tragedy of sexual love and by so doing finds a lasting source of power for the antithetical artist is the Chambermaid. Thus, to emphasize the contrast between the Lady and the Chambermaid, I will discuss the Chambermaid's songs next, returning to "The Lover's Song" in the context of "The Chambermaid's Second Song."

The Chambermaid embodies the tension that Yeats calls "the tragedy of sexual intercourse" because she discovers the perpetual virginity of her soul during intercourse. "The Chambermaid's First Song," originally entitled "The Chambermaid's Prayer before Dawn" (LP 113), demonstrates her detached otherness, even while she cradles the Lover on her breast:

> How came this ranger
> Now sunk in rest,
> Stranger with stranger,
> On my cold breast.
> What's left to sigh for,
> Strange night has come;
> God's love has hidden him

> Out of all harm,
> Pleasure has made him
> Weak as a worm. (P 300-301)

Her second question indicates that she anticipated this union passionately and sought satisfaction in it; whereas the Lover's deep rest suggests that he found consolation in her physical embrace. "Ranger," meaning hunter or adventurer, reinforces the image of the Lover galloping headlong to her arms. Yet their wholehearted attempt at union leaves them "stranger with stranger"; her breast is "cold." Her body submitted, but she remained virginal. Her virginity is psychological, not physical. In fact, Yeats implies that the only way she can discover the virginity of her soul is to lose the virginity of her body. Her soul, no longer violated by physical longings, as the Lady's is, is independent of the Lover and she can view their union objectively, even as she experiences it passionately. She evidences that virginity of soul is "perpetual" by surviving her Lover; Yeats implies that the Chambermaid can do so because she does not love with either her soul or her body alone.

Her assertion that

> Strange night has come;
> God's love has hidden him
> Out of all harm,

not only begins to suggest that the Lover has died, but also connects the Chambermaid to a pattern of imagery that Yeats encountered in his occult studies and used to portray some of his most powerful female figures, such as Sheba, Leda, A Woman Young and Old, and Crazy Jane. The conjunction of intercourse, strange night, and God's love implies that Yeats is employing imagery common in Frazer's *Golden Bough*, the Cabbala, and other hermetic sources, to designate the *hieros gamos*, or sacred marriage, between God and a human. Such a union, typically involving intercourse within the temple precincts between a young woman and a stranger or priest as a surrogate for the god, made the woman an independent or psychological virgin: she could never be owned by a man or be consumed by love because she had experienced the virginity of her soul.

The perspective on love in this song reflects the influence of another crucial experience, which climaxed the shift in Yeats's viewpoint during the first decade of the twentieth century. The diary entry that I quoted above in connection with the Lady suggests that Yeats and Maud Gonne did consummate their love physically during their second period of spiritual marriage,[28] an inference that Mrs. Yeats confirmed.[29] Yet the diary entry, written after the brief affair, when once again "the dread of physical love had awakened in her" demonstrates that even that union with his ideal beloved did not fully satisfy his desires: much is still "left to sigh for." Thus, the events of his second period of spiritual marriage with Maud Gonne are doubly significant to the view of human love that Yeats later embodied in "The Three Bushes." Not only the Lady's mental construct of completeness, but the Chambermaid's concrete view of incompleteness were influenced by Yeats's experiences at that time.

The Chambermaid seems to reduce her realistic view of the inability of human lovers to find perfect union of body and soul within themselves or between them to stark, almost brutal, terms in her thudding repetition of "as a worm" at the end of her first song and throughout her second song. When Wellesley objected to the worm image (LP 116), Yeats defended it, replying: "The worm is right, its repulsiveness is right...all suggested by the naked body of the man, & taken with the worm by that body abject and helpless. All suggest her detachment, her 'cold breast,' her motherlike prayer" (LP 118).

The naked Lover lies dead on the bier that the Lady prepared for him and the Chambermaid shared with him; as in the ballad, his death is connected with sexual love:

> From pleasure of the bed,
> Dull as a worm,
> His rod and its butting head
> Limp as a worm,
> His spirit that has fled
> Blind as a worm. (P 301)

The Chambermaid reduces the Lover to phallic and spiritual helplessness: he is alien and repulsive to her. Yet, Yeats also designated this as her "motherlike prayer" over the Lover. Her formulaic repetition of "as a worm" suggests an incantation as she sings to the worm-man cradled in her arms. Her three repetitions of "worm" convey all the overtones of death and cyclic regeneration traditionally connected with worms.[30] He comes from worms, returns to the worms, and from those worms life will grow again. Yeats originally had four similes and eight lines in this final song,[31] but his revision to three embodies cyclic incompleteness and the need to start again better than an even number would.

Both repulsiveness and redemptive love are suggested by the Chambermaid's prayer. The Lady tries to play God, but creates a merely intellectual correspondence that dies with her. The Chambermaid, who refers to a God outside herself—a God whose love reaches the Lover through her—sees the Lover's death as part of a cyclic process that is characterized by imperfection and deception, but, since it is ongoing, is not hopeless. The Lover's body is described in abject terms because Yeats shares the neo-Platonic attitude that reincarnation represents a failure to achieve release from the multiplicity of matter to the oneness of spirit; however, the tenderness of the Chambermaid's prayer also indicates Yeats's ability to bless and celebrate the need to return to this world.

By cutting "The Chambermaid's Second Song" down to six lines, Yeats made it match "The Lover's Song" in length. The interchange of technique and content between these two songs is crucial to the Chambermaid's (and Yeats's) final vision in this sequence. The ambiguity toward the Lover's poetic ability in the ballad seems to be decided in his favor when we hear his song, one of Yeats's most exquisite short lyrics, built on a delicate pattern of short and long "i," "s," and "n" sounds:

> Bird sighs for the air,
> Thought for I know not where,
> For the womb the seed sighs.
> Now sinks the same rest
> On mind, on nest,
> On straining thighs. (P 300)

The rhyme scheme—a a b c c b—conveys both his expansion of passion and his final feeling of rest.[32] He is playing the tunes that the Lady imagined in her third song, an implication reinforced by the fact that he takes the last two rhymes in her third song ("thigh" and "sigh") and uses them for his middle and final rhymes. Yet his song lacks the metaphysical intensity of "The Lady's Third Song." His poetry is not mindless: he unobtrusively brings the "bird," "thought," and "seed" of the first three lines to the matching rest of "nest," "mind," and "thighs."[33] However, he has none of the frantic need to construct a logical resolution of the antinomy between body and soul that the Lady exhibits. His song flows effortlessly from his abandonment to his physical pleasure.

Yeats seems, in fact, to have created this lyric almost effortlessly. He wrote to Dorothy Wellesley on November 9, 1936, "This morning, this came" (LP 112) and then quoted a version of "The Lover's Song." That version differs from the final version in only two places (the addition of the word "now" in the fourth line and a change from "intellect" to "mind" in the fifth line). Stallworthy mentions one possibly earlier version in which "mind" and "now" were present,[34] which suggests that Yeats changed them and then changed back to his original version. Thus, this beautiful lyric may have "come" to Yeats in its finished form.

As is well known, Yeats generally labored painfully over his revisions, reworking each word and line through numerous drafts before publication and revising heavily for each edition; in addition, Yeats often warned against the temptation to create without toil, which he thought was detrimental to the artist. Given the Lover's death because of his lust, in picking up the final rhymes of "The Lady's Third Song," this song may imply that the Lover's sleep on the Chambermaid's breast is an escapism that can ultimately destroy the source of his art in spite of the exquisite songs such poets sing for a while. Like all the other figures in this sequence, the Lover relates to Yeats's past; in his youth he often depicted masculine figures cradled passively on a woman's breast; and he wove exquisite verbal tapestries before he learned to get down on the "marrow bones" (P 80) during the crucial first decade of the twentieth century when his style changed as radically as his views on love.

The utter simplicity of "The Lover's Song" ultimately militates against such an interpretation, however, especially if his song is viewed in juxtaposition to "The Chambermaid's Second Song." His change from the singular to the plural in repeating the Lady's final rhymes is not incidental: he accepts his continuing connection to the multiplicity of this world. He does not resolve the antinomy in the union of the sexual act; he opens himself to further experiences of incompleteness.[35] Yeats subtly conveys this in the word "sinks" which gathers up all the most recurrent sounds into a word that jars against the diction of the rest of the lyric. "Sinks" perfectly suggests the heaviness of his descent into matter, his fall into the world of sexual division, and the postcoital languor with which he falls asleep on the Chambermaid's breast. This word links his song to the image of himself as the worm in "The Chambermaid's Second Song." He is open to the "dull," "limp," and "blind" condition of the worm.

This interpretation may seem to put too much weight on a simple lyric; however, Yeats clearly connected the sleep the Lover falls into with the failure of sexual intercourse to solve the antinomy and with death in *A Vision*, the proof sheets of which he was editing at the same time he was writing this sequence (L 866). He states: "The marriage bed is the symbol of the solved antinomy, and were more than symbol could a man there lose and keep his identity, but he falls asleep. That sleep is the sleep of death" (V, 1938, 52). But this is not a final death. Right before this, he says: "Death cannot solve the antinomy: death and life are its expression. We come at birth into a multitude and after death would perish into the One did not a witch of Endor call us back." The Chambermaid's chant over his body calls him back to the cycle of birth, pleasure, death, birth, etc. Likewise, the intermingling of the third bush from the Chambermaid's grave suggests that the multiplicity they suffered from in this life is not resolved into a simple union of two into one after death. Unlike the Lady, whose chastity implies preparation for cataclysmic transformation followed by union after death—a transformation that the artist-adept achieves in his imaginative power in life—the Lover and the Chambermaid embody their cyclic view of death and rebirth each time they engage in sexual intercourse.

At other points in *A Vision*, Yeats indicates that the individual may eventually be released from the cycle of reincarnation, finally becoming one with his permanent self. This permanent self is also the primal innocence that the individual had before descending into the realm of multiplicity. The Lady refuses to accept her fall into matter and tries to create Eden by mental gymnastics, but betrays her underlying physical desires in all of her songs. The Lover and Chambermaid see themselves as fallen and try to restore oneness through bodily union. The virginity of each of their souls keeps them from losing their individuality and merging into one, but their wholehearted attempt brings them closer to ultimate release even as it paradoxically sharpens their experience of their failure to transcend.

Poetically, their songs also reflect their recognition of their connection to the imperfect, concrete world. Yeats builds to the poetic climax of "The Lady's Third Song," then starts his poetic deflation in "The Lover's Song." By "The Chambermaid's Second Song," he seems to have reached a nadir of poetic inspiration. The metaphoric intensity of "contrapuntal serpent" has become the simplistic analogy "as a worm." Half of the rhymes are mere repetitions of this formula. The Chambermaid's language has been literally beaten into one word, as the Lady feared would happen to herself because of her lustful desires. But this, too, promises regeneration, since the Chambermaid and the Lover can "lie down where all the ladders start / In the foul rag and bone shop of the heart" (P 348). The Chambermaid, connected to the concrete, but not consumed by it because of the virginity of her soul, will sing on and call the Lover back to another incarnation in which he, in turn, can rebuild his sacred-leching songs of love.

"Literature Is the Forgiveness of Sins"

In calling the Lover back to the tensions of another life, the Chambermaid parallels the Priest, who re-creates the love triangle by rejoining the Chambermaid to the Lover and Lady in their graves. Unlike the Lady, neither the Chambermaid nor the Priest expects that death will obliterate the original sin. As in connection with his views on "the tragedy of sexual intercourse," Yeats is recapitulating the evolution of his own views on the forgiveness of sins through the juxtaposition of the Chambermaid's views and the Lady's.

This contrast is especially evident in "The Lady's Second Song." The Lady gives lip service to the sin of division, but sees it as easily overcome. As long as she, the adept, keeps celibately aloof, she can eliminate the tensions of the interpenetrating gyres of body and soul, or lover and lover, from her consciousness. Like figures in Yeats's early work, such as Aherne in "The Tables of the Law," she sees herself as outside the realm of sin because she, a god in her own mind, has seen into the mystery of things. In her intellectual solution, she obliterates any need for ongoing mercy: she has restored harmony in her imagination. Her speeches to the Chambermaid in both the ballad and her second and third songs sound somewhat like confessions, but they are really justifications of herself to herself. There is no real dialogue or interchange involved. She is too securely locked in her own mental world for even verbal interchange.

Just as her virginal body, but violated soul, reflects Yeats's early views on human love, so her refusal to accept her participation in original sin and her belief that she can restore the golden age in her imagination recall Yeats's early views on imperfection and the power of the imagination. His view that "literature is the forgiveness of sins" goes back to the 1890s. Lady Gregory records this statement in her *Seventy Years* as a saying of Yeats's around the turn of the century.[36] Before that, Yeats had connected Blake's view of Christ with the forgiveness of sins. In this early period, Yeats consistently linked the forgiveness of sins with the power of the imagination to create a oneness where all imperfection is obliterated, all matter transformed to spirit.

Since the Lady is clearly speaking to the Chambermaid, the Chambermaid most likely speaks the refrain, "The Lord have mercy on us" (P 299). The Chambermaid feels the need for forgiveness from sin and does not look to her own divinity as a source of mercy. This refrain foreshadows her eventual confession to the Priest. However, the Chambermaid does not merely express an orthodox view of her guilt. This refrain, coupled with her interest in the concrete man who is coming to her bed, indicates her acceptance of her participation in original sin and ties in with her view of the necessity of reincarnation in her songs. In "An Indian Monk" (1932), Yeats comments on the significance of her prayer: "The devotee must say continually, even though his thought be elsewhere, 'Lord Jesus Christ, have mercy upon us'; a modern Russian pilgrim of their school repeated these words . . . until they had grown automatic and were repeated in his sleep; he became, as he said, not speaker, but listener" (EI 429-30). Yeats contrasts the Russian's prayer to an Indian mystic's, connecting the Russian's to original sin: "The prayers, however, are unlike, for the Russian's prayer implies original sin, that of the Indian asks for an inspired intellect." The Chambermaid's repetition of this prayer shows her awareness of her fallen state and implies her ability to be both speaker and listener in a sincere confession of sin and plea for forgiveness in contrast to the Lady, whose prayer resembles the mystic's.

The Chambermaid, too attuned to the concrete for logical abstraction, has no delusion that she can resolve the antinomy between body and soul by focusing on one side and experiencing the other contrapuntally. She fully experiences both bodily intercourse and the virginity of her soul. She and the Lover re-enact the original sin of division each time they engage in sexual love.

The Lover indicates this when he says, "For the womb the seed sighs" (P 300). He not only longs to be united with his beloved, but also seeks to relive his own conception, to beget himself again and by so doing to re-create the androgynous whole, the self-begotten one, that is his permanent self. But the Chambermaid knows that they have many incarnations to live before they find that oneness and are no longer strangers on each other's breast. The virginity of her soul is the sin that perpetuates their division, but it is also the self-preserving force that enables her to call him back to try again to find unity, rather than being consumed by his death as the Lady's violated soul is.

The Chambermaid and Priest demonstrate that, although Yeats continued to believe in the poet-lover's essential relationship to the forgiveness of sins, he no longer saw that forgiveness as the transformation of matter to spirit. Forgiveness in "The Three Bushes" involves the ability to bless the repeated failure to transcend, to accept the inevitable return to the worm. A passage from Yeats's commentary on Blake, written in the early 1890s, illustrates how "The Chambermaid's Second Song" reiterates an early belief but shows a radical change in his expectations in connection with that belief.

Commenting on the symbolism of the worm in Blake, the young Yeats says: "The worm is the dragon in embryo. It is the Devourer, of a fury so secret as to pass for helplessness. To love the Worm is to perform the most God-like act possible. He who does this cannot be other than its opposite, safe in His own impenetrable immortality. So far as we love the Worm pityingly, God is in us" (YE-B 1: 413). The Chambermaid's attitude toward the helpless lover, whom she sees as both hidden by "God's love" and "weak as a worm" in her first song, seems to parallel what Yeats said of Blake's worm so many years earlier. The worm with its phallic connotations in her second song is still the "dragon in embryo." The Lady's initial food image coupled with the Lover's obvious satiation make the "Devourer" a fitting designation as well. Nevertheless, the Chambermaid's songs evidence a major shift in Yeats's perspective. When the Chambermaid loves the worm, she is not "safe in His own impenetrable immortality." Only by being rent does she discover the perpetual virginity of her soul; this virginity of soul, moreover, is not a security but a tragedy that she continually tries to overcome. The Chambermaid forgives and is forgiven through her ability to recognize and participate in the stark reality of the human condition while simultaneously blessing the continuance of this imperfection.

The combination of passion and detachment within her that this forgiveness demands relates to the confession scene at the end of the ballad. Bodily intercourse and virginity of soul parallel the roles of sinner and priest, participant and witness or judge, in the confession. The Chambermaid's songs over the Lover imply that love is the forgiveness of sins: her confession to the

Priest suggests that in like manner literature is the forgiveness of sins. Just as she re-enacts the original sin of division in sexual intercourse, so she relives her sin by recounting it to the Priest with such force that he understands her case. In the midst of physical love, she maintains the objectivity of the virginity of her soul, viewing the Lover as alien; the narrator's comment that the Priest had her buried beside "her lady's man" implies that she maintained the same detachment toward the Lover in verbalizing her experience. The Priest acts primarily as a detached witness and judge, but Yeats hints that the Priest's understanding is based on his own experience of "her case." Their roles are interchangeable, but both passion and detachment must be present at all times. The Lady's speeches fail to reflect how literature is the forgiveness of sins because she refuses to dialogue, even with her own underlying desires.

Throughout his career, Yeats found this verbal interchange, which is analogous to sexual intercourse, essential to his creative process. From his earliest letters to Katharine Tynan to his late letters to Dorothy Wellesley, Yeats repeatedly tells his female correspondents how crucial his verbal interchange with them is to his poetry. Moreover, he makes the analogy to both sexual intercourse and confession. An example of each is found in letters relating to "The Three Bushes." In November 1936, he wrote to Ethel Mannin, "We poets would die of loneliness but for women" (L 867). In the next paragraph, he quotes "The Lover's Song" to her. The refrain from "The Three Bushes"—"O my dear"—echoes through his letters to Dorothy Wellesley during the months he was working on the sequence.[37] In January 1937, he wrote to her, "I wonder if my letters bore you—I seem to have made you my confessor" (LP 132).

From his earliest work to this late ballad, Yeats struggles to delineate the relationship between the poet and the priest. Often, he pits an orthodox priest, who is a stern judge of sinners, against the poet-sinner—a pattern he followed from Oisin and Patrick to Crazy Jane and the Bishop. In contrast to this priest, he tries to build an image of the adept, the priest or magus who transforms the material to the spiritual. Both of these priest figures are too detached, however. Gradually, he develops an image of the priest, such as the one in "The Three Bushes," who experiences, judges, and blesses simultaneously.

In A Vision, both the 1925 and 1937 versions, Yeats comments frequently on expiation and atonement, demonstrating the importance of the forgiveness of sins both to the relationship between lovers and to the creative process. His comments imply that the deceit and darkness that surround the passion of the Lover and the Chambermaid indicate both their need for reincarnation and their hope for final deliverance. Expiation, which he describes as occurring between death and rebirth, fits into his use of the analogy of Purgatory.[38] Since he often symbolizes Purgatory as the time between dusk and dawn, there are purgatorial implications to the interplay between the Lover and the Chambermaid. As the images of death and rebirth associated with the Lover imply, each act of love takes place between two lives. Their relationship is part of a purgatorial process, which although still incomplete, is purifying and ultimately redemptive.

The following chapters will trace the roots and growth of "The Three Bushes"—from the first luxuriant, but false, blossoms that foreshadow the Lady's views, to the starker, more fragmented, but ultimately more sustaining fruits that the Lover's, the Chambermaid's, and the Priest's attitudes toward love and art embody. Concentrating primarily on his poems and using material from his other works to illuminate them, I will delineate the evolution of Yeats's convictions about the virginity of the soul during intercourse and the ongoing process of the forgiveness of sins that this tragedy demands, and, paradoxically, redeems.

2

Celibate and Adept

Lover and Priest in the Earliest Works

The concerns that will evolve into Yeats's mature conviction that "the tragedy of sexual intercourse is the perpetual virginity of the soul" are already present in his work before the turn of the century. Although his relationship with Maud Gonne was a major influence in shaping his vision of the poet-lover, his earliest works, written before he met her in 1889, demonstrate that he already perceived a conflict between his desires to be both lover and artist. At this point, the Lady's fearful rejection of love develops most strongly, but there are some early hints of the Chambermaid's experience of the virginity of her soul in the midst of human love. Yeats also begins his explorations of the relationship between the artist and the priest, creating two contrasting types of priest figures: the orthodox Christian priest and the hermetic adept. From the beginning, he includes the confessional pattern and emphasizes the desire for forgiveness.

The highly derivative and overblown verse as well as the romantic dramatic situations in Yeats's earliest closet dramas leave the impression that he is depicting the melodrama rather than the tragedy of love; yet, in retrospect, these juvenilia contain comments on unrequited love that are the beginnings of some major image patterns and themes in Yeats's poetry. In *Mosada*, 1884, the title character experiences the absence of physical love in this life with a resultant longing for perfect union after death—a pattern that characterized Yeats's lovers throughout his early period. Mosada, a young Moorish enchantress, is condemned to death by her former lover, who is now a monk. Knowing she will not be united to her lover before death she asks that "when death comes / My soul shall touch with his, and the two flames / Be one" (P 499). She is the first of Yeats's personae to long for the Swedenborgian conflagration of two into one light after death.[1] In later comments on this total union of spirits, Yeats stressed that the oneness must be accomplished without the loss of identity by either lover. His depiction of Mosada already foreshadows the Lady's violated soul. Mosada is so convinced that love will only be requited after death that she kills herself just before her lover recognizes her.

Yeats portrays another Enchantress whose soul is violated by her desire for love in *The Island of Statues*, also written in 1884. An early analogue for the Lady who would "drop down dead" if she lost her chastity, the Circe-like Enchantress turns all the young men who visit her island into stone. She admits to Naschina, a mortal maiden, that she (the Enchantress) freezes the men to maintain her peace. The Enchantress's soul is awakened and totally violated, however, by one kiss from Naschina, who is disguised as a young man. The Enchantress laughs, symbolically forsaking marmorean peace for transient happiness.[2] She dies, leaving only a frog in her place. Like the later Lady, she tries to protect herself, but is easily consumed by her desires.

Naschina is Yeats's earliest embodiment of a woman who experiences the virginity of the soul, not only in spite of, but because of, sexual involvement. Naschina plucks a scarlet bloom, thereby gaining power over the Enchantress. The plucking of the red flower simultaneously suggests initiation into the occult and sexual initiation, since Naschina not only conquers the Enchantress, but also soon turns her lover, Almintor, back to flesh.

Before she dies, the Enchantress predicts the consequences of Naschina's act, stressing the high price that Naschina must pay and suggesting that Yeats was already developing a theory of the perpetual virginity of the soul:

> Hear thou, daughter of the days.
> Behold the loving loveless flower of lone ways,
> Well-nigh immortal in this charmèd clime,
> Thou shalt outlive thine amorous happy time,
> And dead as are the lovers of old rhyme
> Shall be the hunter-lover of thy youth.
> Yet ever more, through all thy days of ruth,
> Shall grow thy beauty and thy dreamless truth,
> As a hurt leopard fills with ceaseless moan
> And aimless wanderings the woodland lone,
> Thy soul shall be, though pitiless and bright.   (P 478-79)

The "loving loveless...nigh immortal" flower that brings her lover to her guarantees that she will outlive her pleasure with him. Her soul, which will wander alone, is essentially and perpetually inviolate. The detached self-possession that enabled her to pluck the flower ensures that she can never be reduced to the carnality of a frog. Yet there are significant differences between Naschina and Yeats's later psychological virgins, such as the Chambermaid. Most importantly, Naschina stands "shadowless" at the end of the play. Her body will grow more beautiful in her unnatural longevity, but since she is no longer one of the flawed, her soul will be "pitiless." She lacks the sympathy and tenderness that Yeats's later Chambermaid will show toward human frailty.

In all, Naschina is a provocative early expression of Yeats's dilemma as poet-lover. She portrays his own simultaneous attraction to and repulsion from both the carnal and the spiritual realms. She must acquire supernatural power before she can approach her lover, but that power ultimately separates her from her lover by making her "shadowless." She is atypical of Yeats's early figures in that she acts to gain her lover, rather than languishing in frustrated longing: however, the supernatural implications of her act overshadow and outlast its physical reality. Naschina embodies the confused wishes of the young poet who believes that his art must flow from supernatural realms (Yeats joined the Dublin Hermetic Society in 1885), but who also wants human love; who, as Yeats says in his First Draft, was filled with curiosity by women, but "dread[ed] the subject of sex" (M 32).

As in *The Island of Statues*, Yeats creates two women who parallel the Lady and the Chambermaid in his autobiographical novel, *John Sherman*, completed in 1888, but not published until 1891.[3] These women, who function as contrasting kinds of muses to John Sherman, also parallel two kinds of mythological virgins with whom Yeats was familiar from his reading.

The final picture shows Mary Carton cradling John Sherman, closely resembling the Chambermaid chanting her "motherlike prayer" over the Lover: "She looked upon him whom she loved as full of a helplessness that needed protection, a reverberation of the feeling of the mother for the child at the breast" (JS 111). Mary Carton has longed for John's love; her voice is trembling as she speaks to him at the end. Yet her motherlike gaze at him implies that she has not lost herself in his embrace. She retains an objective, albeit tender, consciousness at the height of their love, offering an early hint of the psychological virginity of the Chambermaid.

When Sherman goes out to purge himself on the mountain, the narrator mentions that the cairn that he chooses was "considered by antiquarians to mark the place where certain prisoners were executed in legendary times as sacrifices to the moon" (JS 110). Yeats is drawing upon the symbolism of the moon as *magna mater* in works of comparative mythology, such as Blavatsky's *Secret Doctrine*, which he read in 1888.[4] Blavatsky stresses the connection of the Virgin Mary with the moon, pointing out that this virgin-mother is the consort of her own son.[5] Even Mary Carton's name[6] aligns her with the *magna mater*. To be engulfed in this bosom can be as threatening as life-giving, however. Yeats says rather ominously of Sherman: "He threw himself down upon the cairn. The sun sank under the sea" (JS 110).

The resurrection supposedly follows for Sherman; yet Mary's final attitude toward him as an infant is ambivalent. Since Yeats had begun work on his Blake edition, Blake's Christ may be hinted at, as Sherman is reborn as creative artist. On the other hand, given Sherman's desire to return to the security of Ballah (Beulah in Blakean terms),[7] the risk of losing his creative urge is equally strong. Sherman supposedly finds fulfillment, but Mary Carton's protective arms offer more of an escape for Sherman than the Chambermaid's will for the later Lover.

Margaret Leland represents a very different kind of virgin muse to Sherman. She is not the nurturing (although engulfing) *magna mater*, but the cruel consuming virgin who exploits her lovers. Although she is English, Margaret is reminiscent of Yeats's definition of the Gaelic muse, the Leanhaun Sidhe, in his *Fairy and Folk Tales of the Irish Peasantry*, published in 1888: "The Leanhaun Shee (fairy mistress) seeks the love of mortals. If they refuse, she must be their slave; if they consent, they are hers, and can only escape by finding another to take their place."[8] Margaret is human, but like the later Lady, she manipulates others as if she were a goddess. Sherman escapes her only by getting Howard to take his place, as is required by this sidhe. This escape, too, may be dangerous to his creativity, since Yeats says that this sidhe "gives inspiration to those she persecutes."

The Lady will be a much less threatening version of this sidhe, since by the time he wrote "The Three Bushes," Yeats saw this figure as more controlled than controlling, but in his early works, such women gain increasing power. After Yeats had met Maud Gonne, such controlling muses would be depicted in a more idealized manner, but his satiric portrayal of Margaret's self-centered use of others shows his earlier, and perhaps more objective, assessment of such figures.

In these early works, Yeats not only explores the poet-lover's dilemma in connection with human love, but also emphasizes the relationship of the artist to the priest and the theme of forgiveness. Generally speaking, the numerous priest figures in Yeats's earliest work fall into two categories, both of which Yeats judges in terms of their ability to forgive. The orthodox, institutional priest functions as an unbending judge who condemns the lover. In *Mosada*, Yeats simultaneously combines and separates the priest and lover by representing them as one split personality, Ebremar-Gomez, clearly reflecting the opposing tensions within Yeats himself. Ebremar, in his monkish personality, is the first appearance of the hierarchical, argumentative cleric who will reach his dramatic high point in Crazy Jane's Bishop. William Howard and John Sherman reflect this split as well. In addition to the many oppositions in Yeats's personality that Finneran summarizes in connection with the introverted Sherman and the extroverted Howard,[9] these two offer a contrast between the unbending priest and the sinning and forgiving lover. Howard, the pompous clergyman, foreshadows Crazy Jane's Bishop even in textual details. Howard, who likes vestments and popery, is called a "clerical coxcomb" (JS 88) as the Bishop will be in the refrain to "Crazy Jane and the Bishop." Howard's sermon to Sherman about what he can take into the grave suggests, in much less direct language, the Bishop's exhortations in "Crazy Jane Talks with the Bishop." Sherman's prediction that Howard "might hope to die a bishop" (JS 96) seems prophetic. That the argument that begins in the inner dialogue in Ebremar-Gomez is still fought with such intensity between Crazy Jane and her Bishop shows how difficult Yeats found the exorcism of this unforgiving figure.

The reason Yeats cannot rid himself of this figure in his early works is demonstrated in the most significant early embodiment of this dialogue—the debate between Oisin and Patrick. Their debate never becomes a creative dialogue in which the opposing viewpoints interpenetrate. Instead, they exhibit the Lady's tendency toward separation and abstraction. Patrick judges Oisin's love to be mere lust. In turn, Patrick's Christian world is incomprehensible to Oisin. All is black or white in Parts I and III of *Oisin*: the God of joy or hellfire, forever young or in extreme old age, Christian subjection or pagan pride. Patrick and Oisin each accept one side and totally reject the other: neither lover nor priest recognizes the antinomial tensions within him.

That their dialogue never becomes a healing confession is attributable to Oisin as much as to the unbending Patrick. Later figures will affirm and forgive their own past in the intensity of debate with figures such as Patrick. Oisin, however, lacks the high degree of self-possession that this requires. He is afraid of his own sexuality and confused in his longings. What he chooses at the end is impossible: he cannot turn his back on the changed reality he finds in Ireland upon his return. He has deliberately re-entered the world of change by leaving Niamh's isle, yet he finds no inspiration from suffering. His choice to join the Fenians in hell is not an affirmation of his past in the reality of the present—as Crazy Jane's will be—but a desire to escape to a former way of life.

The escape Oisin longs for is offered by a contrasting priest figure: the adept. While on Niamh's island, Oisin is brought to see her father, Aengus, the god of youth and love. Yeats depicts Aengus as a Druid magus with his "sceptre flashing out / Wild flames of red and gold and blue" (P 362), aligning this Druid with his own desire to be a poet-adept on Innisfree by placing Aengus in "a house of wattles, clay, and skin" (P 362).[10] Those who kiss Aengus's sceptre engage in a wild dance while he falls into a swoon, evidencing that his changeless art is ultimately escapist. Their dance leads them to a thicket full of "damask roses" where these contented lovers murmur words that become especially poignant when looked back upon from the perspective of "The Three Bushes":

"Upon the dead
Fall the leaves of other roses,
On the dead dim earth encloses:
But never, never on our graves,
Heaped beside the glimmering waves,
Shall fall the leaves of damask roses.
For neither Death nor Change come near us...." (P 363)

Yeats's rereading of *Oisin* in 1932 may well have affected the adornment of the graves of the mortal lovers in "The Three Bushes."

Yeats has Oisin make a confused choice for humanity over the Druid's power, but he was attracted to the image of the poet as sharing in the secret power of the adept. He told Katharine Tynan: "In the second part of 'Oisin' under the disguise of symbolism I have said several things to which I only have the key. The romance is for my readers. They must not even know there is a symbol anywhere. They will not find out. If they did, it would spoil the art" (L 88). The artist, like the adept, hermetically conceals his secrets.

At the same time, as this passage from a letter to Katharine Tynan attests, Yeats was using his letters to a woman in a confessional manner, starting to engage in the creative dialogue reflected much later in his letters to Dorothy Wellesley and in "The Three Bushes." In these letters, Yeats continually criticizes his poetry, revealing his fears and convictions about himself as a writer. In one letter, he says, "Please do not mind my writing these opinions to you. I like to write to you as if talking to myself" (L 83). Speaking of the same time in *Four Years 1887-1891*, Yeats commented: "I had various women friends on whom I could call towards five o'clock mainly to discuss my thoughts that I could not bring to a man without meeting some competing thought" (A 93). This attitude may be merely sexist, or he may mean that each sex needs contact with a mind of the opposite sex to beget its own thought. Yeats was probably primarily unburdening himself in these early letters and visits, yet there are some hints of the self-begetting, self-judging mind that he would eventually see as the source of creativity.

Indeed, the most healing confession scene in these early works occurs between John Sherman and Mary Carton, with whom John has corresponded regularly since childhood. Before they forgive each other, they go through a purgatorial process.[11] John confesses that he manipulated Howard to marry Margaret. Mary is at first unforgiving and burns his letters as a sign that their relationship is over. After John spends the night on the mountain purging himself, he returns to Mary at dawn. At this point she confesses that she too was wrong in her ambitions for him and then cradles him on her bosom in reconciliation.

This final reconciliation involves a symbolic restoration of Eden. When Yeats says of Sherman on the last page, "He re-entered Ballah by the southern side," Sherman seems to have regained paradise. The infant image involved in Mary cradling him suggests that his past has been wiped away. As I have indicated, there is a hint of the Chambermaid's virginity of soul in the objective otherness of Mary as she looks at John, but the Chambermaid and the Lover will experience a very different kind of dawn as they return to the concrete world. In these early works forgiveness is often thwarted, but the end of *John Sherman* suggests that Yeats hoped that if forgiveness did occur, it would transport the lovers to paradisal oneness.

In all, Yeats's earliest works indicate that the following statement in his *Autobiography* is correct: "I am persuaded that our intellects at twenty contain all the truths we shall ever find, but as yet we do not know truths that belong to us from opinions caught up in casual irritation or momentary fantasy. As life goes on we discover that certain thoughts sustain us in defeat, or give us victory, whether over ourselves or others, and it is these thoughts, tested by passions, that we call convictions" (A 116). Hints of his ultimate convictions about the tragedy of love and the forgiveness of sins as embodied in "The Three Bushes" are present in the confused, unconscious manner that his comment suggests. These early truths were soon literally "tested by passion" in his long, frustrating relationship with Maud Gonne.

Disembodied Rose and Celibate Adept

A much more symbolic woman, reflecting Yeats's growing devotion to Maud Gonne, dominates the group of poems first published in *The Countess Kathleen and Various Legends and Lyrics* (1892) and later gathered under the subtitle "The Rose" in *Poems* (1895). This Rose occupies a middle sphere: she can suffer but is above the angels, who must bow down before her in "The Rose of the World." The poet-lover also tries to put himself in an in-between zone. As priest, he mediates between God and mankind, maintaining a neutral tone—neither willing to be totally mysterious nor to speak the common tongue.

This priest figure resembles the Druid in *Oisin* more closely than Patrick. In conjunction with his occult reading and initiation into the Rosicrucian society of the Hermetic Order of the Golden Dawn in 1889-90, Yeats increasingly tended to equate the artist with the adept. The later Priest in "The Three Bushes" is a "good man" who understands the fallen human condition. At this early stage, the priest figure develops in the opposite direction. He wants to be more than human and holds himself aloof from other humans, afraid that his art will be weighed down by the dross of matter.

Yet Yeats is not sure he wants to accept this role completely either; thus, the poet-lover imagines a neutral shore onto which he can drift from one direction while his disembodied Rose wanders there from the opposite direction. In earlier works, such as *Oisin*, he had separated the two sides of the gulf too completely, allowing no interplay. Now, he focuses on the middle zone as if trying to deny that the two sides exist. In this neutral, asexual zone, both virginity and intercourse are meaningless terms. Likewise, there is no sin to forgive, since the poet-lover and the Rose do not recognize their participation in the original sin of division. The viewpoint Yeats will recapitulate through the Lady—in both her evasion of physical love and her tendency to be an adept with words—is evolving in these Rose poems.

Although its title is based on the Rosicrucian symbol of the intersection of time (cross) and eternity (rose), "To the Rose upon the Rood of Time" actually epitomizes the absence of interpenetration. The moment of blossoming is missing: the Rose merely "is" on the cross; the poet does not delight in the violent moment of conjunction. He begs her to "come near" but to "leave me / A little space for the rose-breath to fill" (P 31). He is content to have her breathe her inspiration into him, but he seems afraid that she will embrace him. Such an embrace would bring a mysterious passivity. The poet would cease to hear the cravings of ordinary things; instead, he would "learn to chaunt a tongue men do not know." Transcendence would be only too easy if she got too close. Thus, they will be near each other in a middle zone where he can still hear "mortal hopes." In this manner he will find "eternal beauty wandering on her way." Because she is always wandering,[12] there is no moment of encounter, just an edgeless state where they come near, but do not touch, each other.

When Yeats looked back on these poems in 1925, he was struck by the suffering quality of the Rose (VP 842), but this "sad Rose" suffers only in the sense of passion, not tragedy. Yeats himself was slow to see suffering as her essential quality. In 1895, he noted that these poems are "the only pathway whereon he can hope to see with his own eyes the Eternal Rose of Beauty and of Peace" (VP 846).

In "The Rose of the World," he describes that pathway, but it leads nowhere. Making a distinction between "passing" and "wandering," he repeats a form of "pass" four times in the first two stanzas to stress the transient nature of the world. Yet this ephemeral world is called a "fresh grassy world / Before her wandering feet" (P 36) in the last stanza. For her, the world will always be a grassy road because she who "lingered" by God's seat coevally with him[13] was never begotten and born and therefore cannot die. The Rose is associated with Helen at the end of the first stanza; here, however, Helen is not the incarnate result of a violent annunciation: she was present and transfigured before the world began.

In 1903, looking back on his earlier desire for disembodied beauty, Yeats recalled his emphasis on transfiguration and demonstrated a confusion about the order of incarnation and transfiguration that affected the Rose poems:

"The close of the last century was full of a strange desire to get out of form, to get to some kind of disembodied beauty, and now it seems to me the contrary impulse has come. . . . Long ago I used to define to myself these two influences as the Transfiguration on the Mountain and the Incarnation, only the Transfiguration comes before [?after] the Incarnation in the natural order" (L 402). Wade's query when editing the letter underlines Yeats's confusion about the time sequence. In "The Rose of the World," Yeats sees the transfiguration as preceding the incarnation. The luminous Rose, in spite of her "red lips," has been on the mountain for all eternity with the world as a plaything below her. Yeats has the order backwards; the Rose must be incarnated before she can be transfigured. Otherwise, she is merely transcendent. Throughout these Rose poems, however, Yeats, like his later Lady, avoids the moment of begetting that incarnation requires, while simultaneously asserting that the Rose is not distantly transcendent.

Yeats may have been influenced by Boehme's views on the union of the celestial and earthly virgin in Mary in this seeming confusion of transcendence and immanence, since Yeats names Mary as one of the symbolic equivalents of the Rose (VP 811) and he was fascinated with Boehme.[14] In describing how the earthly virgin became united with the celestial, Boehme says: "The pure and immaculate virgin in whom God was born is before God and an eternal virgin. She was pure and without blemish even before heaven and earth were created; and this pure virgin became incorporated in Mary, so that it rendered her a new being within the holy element of God."[15] Yeats's order parallels Boehme's: the already transfigured virgin is incarnated in Mary who is in turn transfigured. Boehme puts Mary in an ambiguous middle state, stressing that she is not deified, but proclaiming that "no other woman since the time of Adam became clothed with the celestial virgin except Mary,"[16] just as Yeats maintains that the Rose is not transcendent, but the angels must bow before her. As in the Rose poems, Boehme requires no moment of intercourse for incarnation. Following the Christian tradition, he emphasizes that Christ was incarnated in Mary "without any carnal commingling."[17]

This virginal Rose represents Maud Gonne, who told Jeffares that the Rose poems were addressed to her.[18] Yeats is intent on imagining Maud Gonne in highly stylized, symbolic terms. His comments on her suggest that she appealed to his imagination as a symbol from his first encounter with her in 1889: "I had never thought to see a living woman of so great beauty . . . and a stature so great she seemed of a divine race" (M 40). She wanders on her way, a little distant from men, because no man, including the poet himself, is worthy of her. Yeats keeps her in a neutral state in relation to the poet-lover so that his inadequacies will not end their relationship.

Other comments imply that he also kept Maud Gonne in this indeterminate state in his imagination for fear that the individual, incarnate woman would not correspond perfectly to ideal beauty. For example, after her initial overwhelming impact on him, he "grew master of myself again" and thought "What wife could she make?" (M 42-43). Even at this time, Yeats seems to sense that the Rose is a mental construct through which he keeps his beloved distant enough to protect his ideal image of her. Like the Lady who tells the Chambermaid that it does not matter what sort of individual the Lover is, the early poet-lover does not focus on the physical reality of his beloved. His Rose must remain an aloof daytime beloved, who is seen, not touched.

Yeats did not think that his concept of Intellectual Beauty was self-invented, however. Rather it is a spiritual reality apprehended through a physical reality. In "The Moods" (1895), Yeats explains his view of the artist's relationship to tangible things in the 1890s:

> Everything that can be seen, touched, measured, explained, understood, argued over, is to the imaginative artist nothing more than a means, for he belongs to the invisible life, and delivers its new and ever ancient revelation. We hear much of his need for the restraints of reason, but the only restraint he can obey is the mysterious instinct that has made him an artist, and that teaches him to discover immortal moods in mortal desires, an undecaying hope in our trivial ambitions, a divine love in sexual passion. (EI 195)

Maud Gonne, in her person, is a medium through which eternal beauty is revealed, just as Boehme described the unfolding of the celestial virgin in the earthly virgin. Attunement to this revelation demands passivity in the artist. He chants to his Rose and when he has achieved the rhythm that attends the state between waking and sleeping, then the Rose that has always been present is recognized. Openness is demanded, but no intercourse in any tactile sense.

In "The White Birds," Yeats wants to share this asexual life with his beloved. He wishes they were both white (virginal) birds, far from the rose (the feminine) and the lily (the masculine). As usual, he describes this state as "on the wandering foam." The biographical details connected with this poem indicate that Maud Gonne forced this neutral state on him, to some extent. On a trip to Howth she told him that she would rather be a seagull than any other bird, and he wrote this poem to her soon after. The night before the trip he had asked her to marry him for the first time, but she told him "she could not marry—there were reasons—she would never marry; but in words that had no conventional ring she asked for my friendship" (M 46). The parallel between Maud and the Lady is becoming more exact. Like the Lady, Maud wants to keep his love, but refuses to join him in the marriage bed.

Their dilemma, moreover, is caused by their attunement to higher things, as the Lady's will be. Shortly before Yeats proposed to Maud, she dreamed that she and Yeats were brother and sister in a former incarnation. The alchemical symbolism of meteor, blue flame, rose, and lily that fills this poem is connected with this brother-sister relationship. Yeats recalls, "I began to form plans of our lives devoted to mystic truth, and spoke to her of Nicholas Flamel and his wife, Pernella" (M 49). Flamel and his wife, whom Yeats had read about in *Lives of Alchemystical Philosophers* (1888),[19] typified the relationship of *artifex* and *soror mystica* in alchemy. They worked to find the philosopher's gold in complete spiritual unison but without any physical relationship.[20]

Not only Maud's but Yeats's own ambivalence toward a physical relationship is reflected in the symbolism of "The White Birds." His vision of himself as artist, as these Rose poems attest, was increasingly affected by his occult reading and experience. Throughout these poems, his consistent image of the poet is as Druid, wizard, or alchemical adept. The young Yeats liked to image himself as a magician, as his *Autobiography* and *The Speckled Bird* evidence. Others saw him in that role as well. When he was in Sligo in the 1890s he found that he "had the reputation of a magician" (M 76). If the artist is to be an adept, however, he must be solitary and celibate. Looking back on this period in 1915, Yeats rather sarcastically designates the state he kept himself in as "unctuous celibacy" (M 72), but in the early 1890s this view of himself as the anointed, pure adept was important to him, both in his attempt to be worthy of Maud Gonne and in his view of himself as an artist.

Although he tries to envision a sexless unity of two adepts in "The White Birds," Yeats creates the more typical contrast between requited lovers and the solitary adept in "The Man who dreamed of Faeryland." The visions in stanzas one and three depict fulfilled lovers; in contrast, stanzas two and four present a vision of a single dancer, who is clearly marked as an adept by the mention of the "sun and moon...in a single fruit" (P 44). Neither kind of vision offers comfort, however, because of the man's ambivalence toward involvement or noninvolvement.

When he is attracted toward involvement with other humans, as he is in stanzas one and three, his imagined picture of the perfect union of lovers in the other world intervenes. When he tries to reach wisdom by holding himself aloof, in the alternate stanzas, he dreams of the Druid dancer achieving the alchemical perfection of the marriage of Sol and Luna. Even if he dies alone, the worms will trigger his imagination to dream again. His lack of comfort in the grave is suggestive of the "perpetual virginity of the soul," but Yeats will come to see this as experienced most fully in the attempt at physical union. The Man Who Dreamed of Faeryland sees his noninvolvement as the source both of his perpetual alienation from others and of his art.

Unsettled questions underlie his dilemma. Is transient human love the means to lasting love or is the "silken dress" a web that will keep him from apprehending reality? If he focuses on the mortal beloved will he find the immortal Rose or settle for a little human tenderness? And can he take the chance of immersing himself in human experience when he might lose his poetic impetus by so doing? The poet-lover's agonized confusion breaks through the historical façade of the poem in the final question:

> Why should those lovers that no lovers miss
> Dream, until God burn nature with a kiss?
> The man has found no comfort in the grave.[21]

Perhaps the real problem of this man is that his love, reflecting Yeats's for Maud Gonne, is unrequited. However, "lovers that no lovers miss" could also suggest that the man is content to dance alone. Perhaps he will never be ready for the flaming union at the end of the world because he has not learned to love the worm and sacrifice himself to the cycle of death and life. If he did, he would know not only death, but also human tenderness. The effect on the artist of his evasion of full initiation into experience is left a painful dilemma, as is typical in this group of poems. If he continues dreaming, the fish, worm, and knotgrass will continue singing to him—even after death he will be inspired to song. That song, however, will be divorced from reality and bring neither comfort nor wisdom to the dreamer.

In contrast to his incantations of the disembodied Rose and aloof self-analysis, Yeats addresses the beloved directly in "The Two Trees." The poem contains Cabbalistic, Platonic, Scandinavian, Blakean, and biblical symbolism, much of which has been documented.[22] In addition, a passage in Yeats's commentary on Blake suggests an interpretation that applies directly to the fear of sexual involvement implied in so many of these Rose poems. This poem is unique in that it advocates sexual involvement over chastity. In his section on the "great wound" of division into the sexes in Blake, Yeats says:

> The sexes—even the mortal sexes—are the gates of Paradise if we go inward through them into that infinite of our own bosoms where is the seat of the identity with the bosom of God. But if we go outward through them to mere love of child, family, personal glory, and patriarchal pride, we go to the "false centre." We reach Satan's seat, which is Nature, whose pillars are the literal meaning of Scripture...whose attribute is opacity, and whose function is reason. Chastity reaches this outer gate no less than patriarchality. Both are individual and "selfish." The holiness, or life of chastity deserves eternal death.... The holiness of chastity is therefore cruel.   (YE-B 1: 398)

Read with this passage in mind, "The Two Trees" warns the beloved that if the journey inward is to be life-giving, it must be sexual.

The imagery is not explicitly sexual, but the holy tree itself is implicitly so, since "The surety of its hidden root / Has planted quiet in the night" and around it "the Loves a circle go" (P 48). The "flaming circle" reached by this inward gaze images the beloved as having reached into the Blakean God within and, significantly, Yeats includes himself in that circle. By contrast, the "glass of outer weariness" exhibits all the cruelty, reasoning, cold selfishness, and Satanic associations that Yeats attributes to evil chastity[23] in his Blake commentary.

This interpretation is also supported by the similarity between the attributes of the two trees and two visions that Maud Gonne had about her future[24] during the time that Yeats says he "was still full of William Blake" (M 61). Her first vision involved an angelic form who "showed her three circles: a garden, 'the circle of almost fulfilled desire'; a place in [a] wood with a fallen tree, 'the place of peace eternal, which is very brief for every human soul'; a mountain with a winding road and a cross, 'the circle of labour from divine love' " (M 62). This circular, peaceful garden with its winding road matches the depiction of the first tree with its flowers and its winding circle of love. In the second vision, the angel showed her "the hells she had fallen in: a great sea with hands as of drowning men rising out of it—a memory of a drawing by Blake perhaps—the circle of unfulfilled desire; a great precipice with dragons trying in vain to climb it—a continual climbing and falling, the circle of unfulfilled aspirations; and then a vast emptiness and the falling petals of a torn rose, the circle of revenge" (M 62). The demons, futility, barrenness, and cruelty of the second tree parallel the feelings of this vision. Yeats interprets the visions as indicating Maud Gonne's fulfilled and unfulfilled desires. In the context of his repeated marriage proposals he must have hoped that she would turn from the barren tree of unfulfilled chastity to the fertile tree where the wizard awaits, murmuring a song of invitation to her.

Yet, as usual in this period, Yeats's own desires were not so clearcut as this, either. Soon after describing these visions, he says, "I explained the fact that marriage had slipped away by my own immaturity and lack of achievement" (M 63). Perhaps he was inviting himself to take the journey inward through the gate of the sexes as well. In his note about the suffering quality of the Rose, he cites a comment by a mystic who designates the soul as "your beloved" (VP 842). "The Two Trees," although obviously addressed to Maud Gonne, may also address his own soul as "beloved." His song may require the inward, fruitful journey, rather than the solitary celibate life he so often envisioned for the artist at this point.

The two trees contrast too completely. Eventually, Yeats will see that no system of positive and negative mirror images can embody the complex reality of love. Some of the "broken boughs" of the second tree must grow on the holy tree of joy: the Rose must really blossom on the rood of time. But that will require the moment of interpenetration that the poet-lover is evading at present. Although Yeats revered Blake, he still seemed much less convinced of the need for sensual involvement than Blake was. Both Maud Gonne's continued refusal to requite his love and his own urge to be the pure adept kept him ambivalent toward physical love. More typically in the early 1890s Yeats worked at becoming the adept—recognizing the danger of aloofness that entailed—while he waited for his eternally virginal Rose to wander toward him.

Perfect Love and Perfect Forgiveness

The Rose becomes even more unattainable in the poems from the middle and late 1890s, gathered in *The Wind among the Reeds* (1899). Although Yeats had seen her as suffering in the earlier poems, now she is "incorruptible," "far-off most secret, and inviolate" and "Immortal." She no longer joins the poet-lover on the neutral shore; she is irrevocably on the other side of the gulf. To join her, the poet-lover must pass through the gates of death. In fact, Yeats, like many occultists at the turn of the century, felt that the materialistic age was in its autumn and the spiritual age was about to dawn. Then the two embodied souls would lie breast to breast in endless fulfillment. Yeats emphasizes forgiveness in this period, but he consistently connects it with the restoration of the golden age. Both love and forgiveness are ultimate, irrevocable actions accomplished by the cataclysm of all to spirit.

To attain this final embrace, the poet-lover must deprive himself of earthly attempts at fulfillment. In that waiting period, his soul is utterly violated by the image of his ideal beloved, while he fights to keep his body uninvolved with human attachments. Yet he does not perceive this battle as perpetual. The Man Who Dreamed of Faeryland lamented that he found no comfort even in the grave; the lover of *The Wind among the Reeds* expects to find his only, and eternal, comfort in the grave.

In general, the Rose, analogous to the Lady, dominates the poet-lover even more strongly than in the previous group of poems, but his need for physical love is becoming harder to ignore. A flesh and blood woman, willing to share an earthly embrace, appears in some of the poems. One of Yeats's major symbols in *The Wind among the Reeds*, through which he contrasts the unattainable beloved and the more willing woman, is the hair of the beloved. The fast-bound or cascading nature of the beloved's hair functions as a yardstick of her virginity. Through his symbolic use of hair and through allusions to the sources of this symbol, Yeats starts to contrast physical and psychological virginity. As in all these early works, the woman who prefigures the psychological virginity of later figures such as the Chambermaid is not delineated fully, since the ideal beloved, the inviolate daytime Lady, still controls the poet-lover's imagination; nevertheless, the nighttime alternative is starting to war against his dominant desires in a more complex fashion.

In some ways the poet-lover parallels the Lady even more closely than does the Rose. He tries to build a golden world in imagination, as the Lady will create perfect verbal harmony in her third song. He is troubled by physical desires, although he agrees with the Lady that they hurt the soul. Yeats originally published these poems under titles designating Irish personae as the mouthpieces of each poem. In those titles, the contrasting viewpoints that parallel those of the Lady and the Lover are consistently connected to certain personae. Aedh, a celibate adept who foreshadows the Lady most strongly, is assigned more poems than any other mouthpiece.[25] The two other most common personae, Michael Robartes[26] and Red Hanrahan,[27] reach out for physical love in a manner that prepares for the Lover; however, they are ultimately subordinated to Aedh in this volume. Ironically, Robartes and Hanrahan will live on in Yeats's imagination, whereas he will soon find Aedh's views, which now predominate, impossible and inadequate.

Distinguishing these three personae from each other and from the characters who bear the same names in *The Secret Rose* (1897), Yeats defines them alchemically and artistically:

> I have used them in this book more as principles of the mind than as actual personages. It is probable that only students of the magical tradition will understand me when I say that "Michael Robartes" is fire reflected in water, and that Hanrahan is fire blown by the wind, and that Aedh . . . fire burning by itself. To put it a different way, Hanrahan is the simplicity of the imagination too changeable to gather permanent possessions, or the adoration of the shepherds; and Michael Robartes is the pride of the imagination brooding upon the greatness of its possessions, or the adoration of the Magi; while Aedh is the myrrh and frankincense that the imagination offers continually before all it loves. (VP 803)

His comment that they are principles of the mind helps explain why he eventually deleted their names from the titles; ultimately, they all embody parts of Yeats's own reaction as adept, poet, and lover to his situation. Nonetheless, the distinctions he makes among them help distinguish the conflicting urges and beliefs in Yeats's own viewpoint at the time.

The poems spoken by the most frequent persona, Aedh, provide a focal point from which the major concerns of Yeats as lover and artist at this time can be viewed. If Aedh's poems are considered in the chronological order in which they first appeared in periodicals, Yeats's increasing struggle with his conflicting desires as poet and lover is dramatized. The first two were published late in 1892. In both poems, the Rose is mentioned and the poet-lover tries to lock her in his imagination. She has been plucked from Eden by the ineffable powers in "The Poet pleads with the Elemental Powers," so he, as adept, invokes the elements that have names to "encircle her I love and sing her into peace" (P 72). The Rose no longer even wanders toward incarnation. Incarnation is now seen by the poet-lover as an act of desecration: her inviolateness must be preserved by his imagination.

He accomplishes this even more completely in "The Lover tells of the Rose in his Heart," a poem that embodies much of Yeats's aesthetic theory in the 1890s. The Rose no longer suffers with humans. The "cry of a child by the roadway" and "all things uncomely and broken" (P 56) are in opposition to her, or at least to his image of her. That image is barricaded in his heart—three times removed from material things, since he started with the image, built a "casket of gold" to keep it in, and now dreams of that image. He is no longer experiencing the Rose's blossoming; he is re-creating it in dreams.

Aedh wants to withdraw to a "green knoll apart" to build all things anew in his imagination, thus creating an Eden of love where the Rose can blossom unthreatened by "unshapely things." If he is successful, he will truly create a "casket of gold," since all material things, including himself, will have to be destroyed so that they can be remade. He, as adept and artist, is the vessel through which this happens. As Yeats says in "The Autumn of the Body," "The arts are, I believe, about to take on their shoulders the burdens that have fallen from the shoulders of the priests...and certain of us are looking everywhere for the perfect alembic that no golden or silver drop may escape" (EI 193). Aedh as priest is at the opposite extreme from the Priest in "The Three Bushes," who understands and blesses the Chambermaid's starkly realistic viewpoint. Earlier in "The Autumn of the Body," Yeats mentions "Homer's preoccupation with things" (EI 192). Although Yeats does not put it in the same terms at this point, Aedh's art, which rejects "all things uncomely," removes him from the world of original sin that Yeats will eventually associate with Homer in "Vacillation." Aedh, by contrast, works to fulfill "the saying of William Blake that art is a labour to bring again the golden age" (UnP 2: 92).

In his essays written in the 1890s, Yeats repeatedly insists that the imagination must be enlarged by sympathy with all things. However, this sympathy is a transforming power, not a shared brokenness. His most extended discussion of this transforming imaginative sympathy is in "William Blake and His Illustrations to the *Divine Comedy*," where Yeats's description of how the artist employs sympathy parallels Aedh's process in this poem: "Mere sympathy for living things is not enough, because we must learn to separate their 'infected' from their eternal, their satanic from their divine part; and this can only be done by desiring always beauty, the one mask through which can be seen the unveiled eyes of eternity" (EI 139). Thus, Aedh rejects and imaginatively remakes their "infected" parts in the casket of gold where eternal beauty blossoms.

If Aedh's imagination is to be a fitting alembic, he must withdraw from multiplicity: "The more a poet rids his verses of heterogeneous knowledge and irrelevant analysis, and purifies his mind with elaborate art the more does the little ritual of his verse resemble the great ritual of Nature and become mysterious and inscrutable. He becomes, as all the great mystics have believed, a vessel for the creative power of God" (EI 201-2). As in the earlier Rose poems, no sexual conjunction is involved. Working as the solitary, mysterious adept, Aedh wishes to be ready for spiritual union with the Rose.

Aedh, as magus, has great power, as Boehme's definition of imagination (quoted by Yeats in 1896) emphasizes: "And imagination, which we are apt erroneously to consider an airy, idle, and impotent faculty of the human mind, dealing in fiction and roving in phantasy or idea without any [sic] powerful and permanent, is the magia or power of raising and forming such images or substances, and the greatest power in nature" (UnP 1: 400). His power should be used as a medium through which the Divine Moods are revealed; yet, Aedh's celibate dedication to creating pure poems, focusing on the image in his own heart, could easily become narcissistic.

Aedh connects narcissism, virginity, and the difficulty of creating pure poems in his next poem, "He gives his Beloved certain Rhymes," first published in January 1896. Here, the beloved, named Dectora in the story "The Binding of the Hair" (in which this poem first appeared), is symbolically aligned with the inaccessible virginal muse because of her bound hair, in contrast to the *magna mater* who bathes young men in her flowing hair.

In recalling the mid-1890s in his *Autobiography*, Yeats quotes Mallarmé's description of a similar figure:

> The horror of my virginity
> Delights me, and I would envelope me
> In the terror of my tresses, that, by night,
> Inviolate reptile, I might feel the white
> And glimmering radiance of thy frozen fire,
> Thou that art chaste and diest of desire
> White night of ice and of the cruel snow. (A 214)

Dectora is a much less openly threatening and cruel muse than Mallarmé's Hérodiade (in the poem itself at least), but the image of her lifting her pale hands and winding her hair around her head is reminiscent of Hérodiade enveloping herself in her inviolate virginity. Frazer's *Golden Bough*, which Yeats read about this time,[28] also suggests a connection of hair and virginity. In describing ancient rites in which the virgin was required to have intercourse with a stranger within the temple precincts, Frazer stresses that a common substitute for this intercourse was the cutting off of the virgin's hair which was offered to the goddess.[29] Hérodiade and Dectora refuse to sacrifice even their hair. By so doing, they cut themselves off from fertility, demanding instead that all mirror them.

The end of the passage Yeats quotes from Mallarmé creates this narcissistic mirror:

> And all about me lives but in mine own
> Image, the idolatrous mirror of my pride
> Mirroring this Herodiade diamond-eyed.

The universe responds similarly to Yeats's virgin in the second stanza of his poem:

> You need but lift a pearl-pale hand,
> And bind up your long hair and sigh;
> And all men's hearts must burn and beat;
> And candle-like foam on the dim sand,
> And stars climbing the dew-dropping sky
> Live but to light your passing feet. (P 64)

All is instantly refocused around her bound hair.

Biographically, this inaccessible virgin relates to Maud Gonne,[30] but a comment Yeats makes on the passage from Mallarmé suggests that she embodies some of Yeats's own urges as well: "Yet I am certain there was something in myself compelling me to attempt creation of an art as separate from everything heterogeneous and casual...as some Herodiade in our theatre, dancing seemingly alone in her narrow moving luminous circle" (A 215). Yeats mirrors his own virginal, aloof art in the second stanza of "He gives his Beloved certain Rhymes." In the first stanza, he is rather self-pityingly in touch with the labor involved in his craft. The second stanza functions as a poem within the poem. When he shifts his concentration onto her virginal effortless gesture, the Rose finally blossoms in his heart and in the poem. Aedh once again evidences the sacrificial labor to which he must be faithful, but this labor is separate from his beloved. Each dances, "seemingly alone." Yet the second stanza is a highly wrought artifice of effortlessness. Strongly alliterative phrases—"pearl-pale," "burn and beat," and "dew-dropping"—speed up the odd-numbered lines, alternating with the slower long "i" sounds in the even-numbered lines. The art of engagement in life through toil seems to be the underpinning of even this stanza inspired by the effortless gesture of the chaste muse.

Aedh's celibate devotion to his Rose is temporarily supplanted by a sensual relationship in a series of poems originally assigned to Robartes and Hanrahan and reflecting Yeats's affair in 1896 with Olivia Shakespear (called Diana Vernon in his First Draft).[31] Two companion poems, published in the same issue of the Savoy, January 1896, were originally assigned to Robartes. "He bids his Beloved be at Peace" shows that Robartes is an adept like Aedh, but he uses his occult powers very differently. He knows all the hermetic formulae and describes in elaborate symbolism the coming of the apocalyptic horses, but rather than longing for the transforming cataclysm, he finds momentary escape in the embrace of a woman. Brooding over the possessions of his own imagination, as Yeats's note explains, Robartes delights in his well-versed recitation of the horses' relationship to the cardinal points. The metrically even quatrains with their circular rhymes (a b b a, etc.) mimic the trancelike state in which he invites his beloved to join him. The violent images of the first eight lines dull the senses rather than heightening them. At the end, the horses are still stamping their feet and tossing their manes, but their power over him is deadened, momentarily at least.

Instead, Robartes wants his beloved's hair to "fall over my breast / Drowning love's lonely hour in deep twilight of rest" (P 62). Yeats alludes primarily to Sara's offer to veil Axel with her hair,[32] a passage Yeats quoted in his review of *Axel* in 1894 (UnP 1: 324). Axel, of course, refuses. Robartes, by using the verb "drowns," hints that he, too, should deny himself this sensual embrace. If Robartes, designated as "fire reflected in water," broods on his own possessions, the water will merely reflect his brilliance, but if his fire is submerged, it will be extinguished. Robartes may be jeopardizing his creative powers by asking for this sensual escape.

In "The Travail of Passion," Robartes's beloved responds to his bidding. As the consistent use of the plural throughout the poem indicates, this lyric is more than an autobiographical record of Yeats's affair. He portrays the moment when the "angelic doors are opened wide" and the Divine Moods are revealed through the artist's "mortal clay" (P 70). At this moment, as the extended analogy to Calvary makes clear, the poet-lover must suffer. As is typical of Yeats's early work, this suffering is a passive purification. Then, the imagination, equated as in Blake with Christ, is bathed in the perfume of symbols—"lilies of death-pale hope, roses of passionate dream." This incarnation is different from that in the earlier Rose poems. Here, sexual conjunction, although still less explicit than in later works, is the source of the union of the spiritual and the sensual. The rose and lily that the lovers wished to fly away from in "The White Birds" are together at the end of the poem: the Rose is really blossoming on the rood of time.

Yet Robartes seems to fear that his passion can enslave him as well as ennoble him. In his catalogue of the analogy with Calvary, he builds up to right before the moment of death, mentioning "the vinegar-heavy sponge," then skips over the moment of death to "the flowers by Kedron's stream." His lack of an image of the actual moment of death hints that even at the height of his passion, he fears that full submission to sexual involvement may chain him to untransformed clay.

Robartes's inability to commit himself to either celibate adeptship or sexual love continues in "He remembers forgotten Beauty," first published in July 1896. Robartes, no longer speaking with the immediacy and agony of "The Travail of Passion," quite consciously uses his fancy to see his human beloved's likeness to eternal beauty. In words that would certainly appeal to the Lady in "The Three Bushes," Robartes describes the correspondence of their physical love to spiritual love: "And when you sigh from kiss to kiss / I hear white Beauty sighing, too" (P 63). The logical "too" tacked on to his

description shows how distanced he is; it is an analogy, not a imaginative reality. When he recites his ritual formula in the last four lines, he is truly brooding over the possessions of his own mind. Although he is obviously involved in a sensual relationship with a woman, Robartes holds back from fully experiencing that involvement. He fears the abandonment to the moment on a woman's breast into which the later Lover sinks. Instead, Robartes uses physical love, rather solipsistically, to feed the "high lonely mysteries" of his imagination.

Hanrahan, to whom two other poems published in 1896 are assigned, also experiences the embrace of a woman, but he feels that embrace is sinful. The wind to which Yeats's note connects Hanrahan's fire is associated with the wind of lust in the second circle of Dante's hell in "The Lover speaks to the Hearers of his Songs in Coming Days." Yeats's lovers can be delivered from the "penitential throng" (P 71), however, since Hanrahan wove their sin into song. Even at this early stage, Yeats hints that the simple directness of Hanrahan's physical inspiration will eventually save him, not his devotion to "Cleena of the waves"—the ideal beloved he pursues between lapses in *The Secret Rose.*

Although Hanrahan feels that his sin will be consecrated only after death and in the 1890s Yeats generally looked for the obliteration of sin in the apocalypse, Yeats does insist on the redemptive power of sin in his commentary on Blake's system:

> Further, there is sin and its Joys. There is not only an evil chastity but a good immorality. This, the most perilous of all truths, was taught by Blake as unflinchingly as the rest. . . . To take the evil side merely continues the sin and may lead to his receiving, by learning to offer, forgiveness; while to choose the error that is not sin is to choose ultimate destruction through holy egotism that cannot help believing itself above forgiveness, and so hardens itself in the solitude that is death eternal. (YE-B 1: 398-99)

This pattern of continuing in sin as a means of achieving and giving forgiveness will prove crucial to Yeats's own later system in *A Vision,* although in these early works he tends to choose the potentially evil chastity and individualism of the adept. Through Aherne, in the story "The Tables of the Law," Yeats explores the danger of the magus hardening into death eternal. Aherne, a cold antithesis to Hanrahan, laments: "I am not among those for whom Christ died . . . I have lost my soul because I have looked out of the eyes of angels" (My 305-6). Because, like the Lady, he does not admit his participation in original sin, he cannot find forgiveness. Hanrahan, by contrast, has not lost his soul irrevocably because he falls under what Aherne calls "a simple and an arbitrary law that we may sin and repent" (My 305). He is an early analogue to the Lover and Chambermaid whose ability to partake fully in original sin assures their eventual redemption.

Since Hanrahan has also woven that sin into song, he has looked at it with the heightened sympathy that Yeats connected with the imagination and forgiveness in "William Blake and the Imagination": "The sympathy with all living things, sinful and righteous alike, which the imaginative arts awaken, is that forgiveness of sins commanded by Christ" (EI 112). Hanrahan shows this sympathy in "He reproves the Curlew" where the cry of the bird pierces him, reminding him painfully of the moment on his beloved's breast. His love corresponds to nature, not to "white beauty" as Robartes's does, nor to the Rose as does Aedh's. In "He gives his Beloved certain Rhymes" (which has the same rhyme scheme as "He reproves the Curlew") Aedh imagines the universe molding itself to his beloved's gesture; Hanrahan sees his love as fitting into the natural order.

Nevertheless, Hanrahan feels his attraction to physical love is a degradation of his search for the ideal. His pain at the curlew's cry is not a tragic admission of the alienation that attends his desire for physical union, but a plea that he can rededicate himself to the pursuit of that ideal. Hanrahan cannot settle for ritual formulae as Robartes does. As "Maid Quiet" (originally entitled "Hanrahan laments because of his Wanderings") indicates, Hanrahan must wander as long as "the winds that awakened the stars / Are blowing through my blood" (P 70). His imagination is hurtled on too vehemently by his passions to brood over its own possessions.

Although his headlong submersion in life—despite his lamentations that he would prefer the ideal—will eventually earmark Hanrahan for blessing much later in "The Tower," Hanrahan is not Yeats's ideal for the artist in the 1890s, since his overwhelming physical desires ban him from being an adept. Neither Robartes's nor Hanrahan's approach represents a lasting source of inspiration for their art. Through them, Yeats indicates how short-lived he saw this physical kind of relationship as a source of art in the 1890s. He describes how his affair with Diana Vernon ended after about a year because she sensed that he was still devoted to Maud Gonne. After this, he says, he remained celibate for seven years. Since Maud Gonne still refused to have any physical relationship with him, she remained a vehicle of the ideal beloved, the inviolate Rose, with whom, he now felt, he could be united only after death. Thus, Aedh returns as the most recurrent persona of the later poems in *The Wind among the Reeds*. Aedh has not remained unaffected by physical desires, but he does not find a comforting solution to his wish to remain an artist as does Robartes, nor is he uncontrollably driven as is Hanrahan.

A series of poems published in 1898 dramatizes Aedh's vision of the ultimate union beyond death, his conflicting urge for physical union in this life, and his acceptance of the lonely course he must adhere to until he and his lover are united in the final embrace. In the first of these, "He wishes his Beloved were Dead," Aedh imagines himself and Dectora in an eternal embrace. Fittingly, he uses her hair, so tightly bound up in chaste noninvolvement in "He gives his Beloved certain Rhymes," to explain why she would then loosen up and lie next to him. Through a feminization of the beard of Macroprosopus (the giant in whose image the world was founded),[33] Aedh tells her that she will realize that her "hair was bound and wound / About the stars and moon and sun" (P 73). The beloved is the primal *magna mater* and he will nurse from her and be her consort simultaneously. Their love has been ordained since before the world began, but her human consciousness has lost touch with this primal sympathy.

Their return to primal oneness is what Yeats designated as forgiveness at this point:

> You would come hither, and bend your head,
> And I would lay my head on your breast;
> And you would murmur tender words,
> Forgiving me, because you were dead.

To Yeats, this is the imaginative unity that is Blake's "forgiveness of sins commanded by Christ." Such forgiveness involves a return through art to perfection. In "William Blake and His Illustrations to the *Divine Comedy*," Yeats says that "only those whose sympathies had been enlarged and instructed by an art and poetry could obey the Christian command of unlimited forgiveness" (EI 129-30). He explains that this is "not the forgiveness of the theologian, who has received a command from afar off, but of the poet and artist, who believes . . . that he has discovered in the practice of his art that without a perfect sympathy, there is no perfect imagination, and therefore no perfect life" (EI 131). Only a perfect sympathy, such as the beloved's, can be real forgiveness; the separation of sin is obliterated in this total union. Male and female, the first separation, are forever bound in a forgiving embrace. In Blakean terms, literature has restored the golden age. Although Hanrahan offers some hints of Yeats's later interpretation of sin, the image of forgiveness in "He wishes his Beloved were Dead" is what Yeats meant when he told Lady Gregory, at the turn of the century, that "literature is the forgiveness of sins." Aedh does not mention his own death, suggesting that he has already transmuted himself psychically so that he is ready for the final embrace. If only she would make the same imaginative leap to union with him—however, the human identity of the beloved is more apt to "rise and hasten away."

Three companion poems, published as "Aedh to Dectora: Three Songs" in May 1898, explore Aedh's difficulties in waiting for the eternal embrace. In "He hears the Cry of the Sedge," the lover is wandering on the shore, but he no longer desires this neutral state. Earlier, the asexual blossoming of the Rose in his imagination was sufficient for Aedh, but now he longs for the sensual

Swedenborgian conflagration of their souls after death. He does not delight in the destruction that must precede that apocalyptic union, but this starkly beautiful lyric attests that he is resigned to it. With calm desolation, he declares that they will never be united before death.

In "The Lover mourns for the Loss of Love," Aedh describes how, like the Lover in "The Three Bushes," he found his "proper food" elsewhere by substituting love with his "beautiful friend," but could not rid his heart of Dectora's image. Since his soul remains violated by his desire for the ideal, his own image is not there. He does not possess himself and thus has nothing to offer his "beautiful friend."

She, by contrast, does seem to possess herself. In fact, she shows some of the characteristics of a very different kind of virgin from Dectora. The "beautiful friend," as a closely parallel incident in the First Draft indicates, is Diana Vernon, who broke off her affair with Yeats when she sensed, "There is someone else in your heart" (M 89), after Yeats had been to dine with Maud Gonne. "Diana Vernon" is the name of the heroine of Scott's *Rob Roy*,[34] but perhaps Yeats also found "Diana" appropriate because of his reading of *The Golden Bough*. Frazer, reacting to the "popular modern notion of Diana or Artemis as the pattern of a straight-laced maiden lady," shows how far this is from the ancient idea. The designation "virgin" clearly did not involve physical virginity in the ancient mythologies summarized by Frazer: "The truth is, that the word *parthenos* applied to Artemis, which we commonly translate virgin, means no more than an unmarried woman, and in early days the two things were by no means the same."[35]

Instead, what distinguishes the virgin is her self-possession. She is not married and therefore not the property of a man. As I have already indicated in connection with the use of hair as a substitute, Frazer describes the rituals in which virgins were required to sacrifice their virginity by having relations with a stranger within the temple precincts.[36] Sometimes this was done in preparation for marriage, but the permanent temple virgins also performed the rite, ensuring their virginity by sacrificing it to a virgin goddess, e.g., Diana. In the *hieros gamos*, or sacred marriage, the stranger was a substitute for a god. This pattern will become more important in Yeats's later work, but there is already a parallel in "The Lover mourns for the Loss of Love." The Lover is using the human woman as a surrogate for the immortal ideal that controls him; whereas the woman experiences her alienation from him even though she desires physical union. Her ability to view their involvement objectively, although it causes her pain, does indicate that she possesses herself in a way that he does not.

Yeats's commentary on Blake also describes Oothoon as virginal, in spite of her experience of physical intercourse: "Thus Thel and Hela, the virgins, find their sister in Oothoon, that third virgin who was a violated wife—for her wifehood and violation belonged to her own exterior regions, her virginity to her inward life" (YE-B 1:412). Yeats does not emphasize psychological virginity in *The Wind among the Reeds*, yet the self-possessed friend is an early suggestion of the psychological virgin who will be so important in embodying his later view of the virginity of the soul during intercourse. Significantly, virginity of soul does not make the beautiful friend "shadowless" as it had Naschina. She is very human in her sorrow.

Still dominated by the ideal image of Dectora, but increasingly unable to ignore his physical desires, Aedh tries to substitute poetry for sexual involvement in the third of these songs, "He thinks of Those who have spoken Evil of his Beloved." He will vindicate her and himself by the image he creates in this "mouthful of air" (P 68). He invites her to "half close your eyelids, loosen your hair" as if both entered into sexual union through the dream of the poem. Yeats undercuts this use of poetry as a surrogate for sexual union even as he expounds it, however. The fourth line, where Aedh pits his song against the world, is curiously clumsy in its repetition of "the great and their pride." Earlier, Aedh came much closer to building "a perfect beauty in rhyme" (P 67) in "He tells of the Perfect Beauty." Perhaps Aedh's loss of power over words reflects the dichotomy that has come into his heart. He can accept neither the absence of physical love nor its presence. He tries to turn to art as an outlet for his frustration, but, in spite of the technical adeptness he has already shown, he finds that something is lacking there, too.

Aedh's final poem, "He wishes for the Cloths of Heaven," is an exquisitely ambivalent mirror, reflecting both his power with words and his threatened impotence. Like Aedh's early poem, "The Lover tells of the Rose in his Heart," this poem consists of eight lines and has a regular rhyme scheme. In one sense, the identical rhymes tie it together into a perfect poem, mirroring the perfection of Aedh's imagination. Yet, the poet-lover denies this in the poem: he does not have the cloths "enrought with golden and silver light" (P 73). As lover, Aedh is clearly still awaiting the perfect marriage of Sol and Luna. As artist, moreover, inspiration no longer comes so easily to him from this lack of physical involvement. The repeated rhyme words, especially in the second half, could reflect his frustrated impotence as artist and lover. In the first and third lines the imaginative "if" still controls; he compensates for the repetitive rhyme words by alliteration and internal rhyme. In the last four lines, however, he stammers out the reality of his impotence, repeating "dreams" three times and "tread" twice.

In "He gives his Beloved certain Rhymes," Aedh belabored his "poor rhymes" in the first stanza, then his imagination took over in the second. In "He wishes for the Cloths of Heaven," he loses his imaginative power as the poem progresses. Yeats, as craftsman of this whole exquisitely wrought volume, knew that he was already an adept with language; many of the poems in this volume, including this one, received little revision in later years. Yet, Yeats uses his skill to hint at the dangers of technical prowess. It can become a "casket of gold" cut off from reality and holding only dreams. Aedh comes to a technical conclusion similar to that the Chambermaid will reach many years later in her repetition of "worm" at the end of "The Three Bushes" sequence. Nonetheless, Aedh's viewpoint is the opposite of hers. Far from insisting on (and blessing) carnality and decay as the Chambermaid will, Aedh tries to remain in the protective shell of his own dreams. But his need to repeat "dreams" impotently hints that words, as well as dreams, may eventually fail him. Aedh epitomizes the dilemma of the artist adept: to be successful he must cut himself off from involvement in the material world, but by so doing, he may lose the source of his poetry.

The ambivalence that Aedh's final poem conveys suggests that aesthetically Yeats is reluctantly leaving those who build caskets of gold and joining those who share in the brokenness of this world. As lover, he is still trying, rather desperately, to believe that the divine comedy of the hour of ultimate union with the eternal Rose will come, but as poet, he is beginning to sense, and take inspiration from, the irrevocable tragedy of his own imperfection.

Yeats's ambivalence toward his own predominant vision of love at the turn of the century is captured in the contrast between two portrayals of the poet-lover finally enjoying the embrace of the Rose in *The Secret Rose* (1897). On the cover Yeats put an illustration by Althea Gyles depicting the buried skeleton of an Aedh-like knight who sacrificed human love in his quest of the ideal beloved. A four-petalled rose blossoms on the cross just below the middle of the tree, symbolizing the eternal embrace of the man and woman who hold hands and kiss right above it. Since the tree grows from the genital area of the corpse, this illustration summarizes iconographically the denial demanded of the poet-adept and the reward that awaits him. It would be a fitting illustration for "The Three Bushes" as well, if Yeats had stopped the ballad after the Chambermaid planted the two roses, thus suggesting that the Lady and Lover had achieved the union in death that they had never experienced in life.

The uneasiness with this ideal resolution, which will eventually lead Yeats to have the Priest plant the third bush, is already apparent in this early volume, however. "Rosa Alchemica" depicts the danger that union with the ideal represents for the artist. Yeats portrays an adept in a nightmarish dance with the Rose: "Suddenly I remembered that her eyelids had never quivered, and that her lilies had not dropped a black petal, nor shaken from their places, and understood with a great horror that I danced with one who was more or less than human, and who was drinking up my soul as an ox drinks up a wayside pool; and I fell and darkness passed over me" (My 290). Yeats is beginning to hint at the irony he will later dramatize by having the Lady drop down dead even though she has guarded her physical virginity while allowing her soul to be violated. This passage suggests that Yeats senses that his own frustratedly celibate longing may be thwarting his development by cutting him off from creative interaction with others. In the letter to Russell where he speaks of transfiguration and incarnation, Yeats says that the "contrary impulse" (L 402) toward incarnation overtook him near the turn of the century. Accordingly, the poet-lover will reverse his direction in the next fifteen years, focusing on this world, developing his own self-possession, and emphasizing dialogue in a manner suggestive of ongoing sin and forgiveness.

3

The Contrary Impulse

"Our Deceit Will Give Us Style"

One element essential to "The Three Bushes," but not stressed in Yeats's work before the turn of the century, is the deception practiced by both the Lady and the Chambermaid upon the Lover. The theme of deceit begins to take on prominence in Yeats's work in the first fifteen years of the twentieth century. At first, Yeats refers to a deceit over which the individual has no control, an inevitable failure to meet expectations, but, by 1905-6, he is advocating a consciously chosen deceit which saves the poet-lover's soul from being swallowed, as he had envisioned in his dance with the Rose in "Rosa Alchemica." This deliberate deceit is quite different from the escapist and ultimately self-consuming trickery that the Lady perpetrates in "The Three Bushes." Rather, this is a self-preserving deceit related to Yeats's increased emphasis on self-possession during this period. From this conscious deceit comes a freedom that affects his poetic style, as well. The inevitable betrayal and alienation connected with the human condition remain in the background, however, and surface in a complex relationship to deliberate deceit in *Responsibilities*.

In 1900 Yeats published his first version of *The Shadowy Waters*,[1] reiterating the same concerns as those of *The Wind among the Reeds*. Forgael dedicates himself to the quest of immortal beauty and shuns mortal love in preparation for the eternal embrace. Like Aedh, moreover, his heart becomes divided when his attraction to earthly love awakens. Forgael's dilemma is more complicated, however, in that Dectora, the woman who represents ideal love to him, simultaneously offers him earthly love. He cannot lose the earth-centered, passionate woman, as Aedh did in "The Lover mourns for the Loss of Love," as he continues to pursue the unattainable beloved who corresponds to the Rose. Dectora, on the other hand, cannot deny her physical love for Forgael in her wish to join him on the immortal quest. Their cross-purposes are never brought to a convincing resolution in this 1900 version. In fact, their final speeches hint that they are deceiving themselves and perforce each other in their motivation as they set out on the immortal quest together.

There is also a slight textual emphasis on deceit in *The Shadowy Waters*. Three times earthly love is described as "brief longing and deceiving hope / And bodily tenderness."[2] Two elements in this formulaic summary are familiar from Yeats's other early work. The brevity of earthly love is lamented repeatedly; whereas bodily tenderness is mentioned specifically, although rejected, in "The Man who dreamed of Faeryland." The third element, "deceiving hope," represents a slightly different emphasis, since it implies that the lover feels betrayed in his wish for earthly love to last. This tripartite formula for human love is one of the few actual phrasings that Yeats retained between the 1900 and 1906 versions of *The Shadowy Waters*;[3] however, as the differences between the two endings show, his attitude toward the relationship between love and deceit as well as that between art and deceit had changed radically by 1906.

The ending of the 1900 version is inconclusive. Dectora cuts the rope that links their ship to the other ship and chooses to go with Forgael into the endless waters, but the motivation and consequences for each of them are left ambiguous. Dectora's final speech is packed with occult symbolism, suggesting that she has rejected human love in expectation of the eternal consummation.[4] Her offer to cover him with her hair is an obvious parallel to Sara in *Axel*,[5] where the lovers recognize only the immortal embrace. Dectora, however, uses the occult symbolism in a strikingly concrete way, especially in the image of the "silver fish that my two hands have taken / Out of a running stream" (VP 769). Throughout this closet drama, Dectora, unlike Aedh's image of her in *The Wind among the Reeds*, perceives love as a physical act.[6] She tells Forgael:

> The love I know is hidden in these hands
> That I would mix with yours, and in this hair
> That I would shed like twilight over you. (VP 765)

At the same time, she is attracted to the unattainable and shares Forgael's vision of Edain and Aengus in the earlier scene where Forgael lures her to the immortal quest. Her vision is short-lived, however, and she soon returns to a desire for human love. Her decision to go with Forgael at the end seems motivated more by the force of her love for him than by devotion to the immortal. If she must serve as a chaste *soror mystica* to be near the *artifex* Forgael,[7] she will do so, but her final invitation, "Bend lower, that I may cover you with my hair" (VP 769), implies that her hope for a physical union remains.

Forgael, whose physical urges have just surfaced, making him cry out,

"Master of our dreams, / Why have you cloven me with a mortal love" (VP 768), can only stammer in response to her, "The harp-strings have begun to cry out to the eagles" (VP 769). Earlier, Forgael thought that Eden was out of time and space, but Dectora's presence has undermined his undivided dedication. Her physical embrace at the end may well inspire the murmuring of the harp, although he would like to think that the eagles do so. Each of them cherishes a "deceiving hope."

Their cross-purposes reflect Yeats's own divided heart.[8] Forgael's quest relates to Yeats's view of himself as artist; moreover, the situation between Forgael and Dectora parallels the spiritual marriage that Yeats and Maud Gonne entered into in 1898.[9] Yet Dectora's desire for physical love does not parallel the "horror and terror of physical love" that Maud Gonne expressed. Yeats may merely be indulging in wish fulfillment in giving Dectora these physical urges; however, a comparison between Dectora in the 1900 version and Yeats's comments about his own physical desires suggests that, although she has obvious affinities with Maud Gonne, Dectora even more profoundly embodies Yeats's own feelings.

Dectora is capable of visionary experience, but it soon fades and she returns to mortal cares, just as Yeats could not rest in the confidence of a continual vision. At times, he looked "out of the eyes of the great stone Minerva" (M 134), much like Dectora allowing Edain to see Aengus through her. More typically, however, Yeats indicates that he wanted to love Maud Gonne as a woman, not a goddess, just as Dectora loved the man Forgael, not the god Aengus. Dectora, especially in the 1900 version, is a rather vague, ambivalent figure, but, as such, she comes closest to Yeats's own agonized indecision in the late 1890s. For all the impersonality that Yeats tried to cloak his early work in by projecting his ideas through figures such as Forgael, Dectora, Aedh, Robartes, and Hanrahan, the dilemma he considers in *The Shadowy Waters* is so personal and emotionally rending that he is incapable of imagining even a literary resolution.

The ending of the 1906 version is, by contrast, clear-cut. Dectora's last speech retains many of the same images as in the 1900 version, but Forgael's final speech unambiguously proclaims that she has become his mystical partner and that their quest for the immortal inspires his art. Forgael has finally achieved what Yeats longed for in poems such as "The White Birds." He and his beloved are united in the immortal quest; his art flows from that union; images beget images without any physical intercourse. Ironically, however, Yeats can finally depict this totally spiritual love unambiguously because he no longer believes it is a real possibility for himself. A comment he attached to *The Shadowy Waters* in 1906 strikes a coolly detached note: "I hope I have set it to rights now, and that if it finds an audience familiar with the longings of a lover for impossible things . . . it will hold the attention" (VP

815). Yeats is still intrigued by the symbolism of this poem, but he knows that the situation between Forgael and Dectora is "impossible." Dectora is more individualized in the later version; neither she nor Forgael is as painfully connected to Yeats's own desires as lover and artist. The later version is more a literary artifice than a self-revelation.

Yeats's essays, shorter poems, and letters between 1900 and 1906 suggest that his overwhelming longing for total union with the ideal beloved is being tempered by his growing desire for self-possession, which he starts to connect with a conscious deceit. When he repeats the phrase "deceiving hope" in the 1906 version, it has taken on new resonances in the context of his other writings. In 1906, he also wrote his collection of short essays called "Discoveries," where he associates a deliberate deceit with his art:

> We are only permitted to desire life, and all the rest should be our complaints and our praise of that exacting mistress who can awake our lips into song with her kisses. But we must not give her all, we must deceive her a little at times, for, as LeSage says in *Le Diable boiteux*, the false lovers who do not become melancholy or jealous with honest passion have the happiest mistresses and are rewarded the soonest and by the most beautiful. Our deceit will give us style, mastery, that dignity, that lofty and severe quality Verlaine spoke of. (E1 272)[10]

This comment demonstrates how radically the axis of Yeats's perspective shifted in the years between 1899 and 1906. Life, not death, has become the poet's impetus. Moreover, he has learned to dance with his muse without being consumed. Deliberate deceit allows him to imagine a clear ending to *The Shadowy Waters* without identifying himself with that ending. His soul cannot be totally violated by his desire for the beloved as it was in *The Wind among the Reeds*; he is beginning to possess himself too inviolately to be consumed by a longing like that of the Lady in "The Three Bushes."

As a letter he sent to Mrs. Patrick Campbell in 1901 clarifies, Yeats wished to conjoin inviolateness and passion in his work. Commending her acting, he adds: "This is exactly what I am trying to do in writing, to express myself without waste, without emphasis. To be impassioned and yet to have a perfect self-possession" (L 360). His cold passion, because self-conscious, could never bring the cataclysmic transformation he both longed for and dreaded in the 1890s, yet it freed him to depict transcendence with much more ease.

His changed attitude accounts for not only the revised ending of *The Shadowy Waters*, but also his method of depicting the Swedenborgian union of two lovers after death in "Baile and Aillinn," written shortly after the turn of the century. When the narrator tells of the lovers being transformed into two swans linked by a golden chain, he asks, "What shall I call them?" (P 401) and proceeds to list analogy after analogy of two things apparently becoming one. Stressing that it is a literary deceit, not a cry of the heart such as Aedh gave in "He hears the Cry of the Sedge," in the narrative frame of this poem Yeats adopts an almost playful tone which he never used in the 1890s when referring to this kind of love. The rhymed couplets give the impression that the poet is enchanted with an old story, not longing for the same experience himself. Yeats still feels some attraction to this ultimate embrace, which surfaces at the end of the poem, but even there his playful tone negates his own overinvolvement.

An almost cynically playful tone also starts to appear in some of his short lyrics. This changed tone is a self-preserving deceit in this transitional period.[11] The only two short lyrics he published in periodicals between 1904 and 1908 are characterized by this self-mocking tone that functions as an emotional defense as well. He mocks his own former approach to love in "Never Give All the Heart," cynically proclaiming that women see love as a play which leaves the lover who is "deaf and dumb and blind with love" (P 79) at a disadvantage. Some of his self-pity remains, but he is able to use an urbane mask of wit to show that he has survived. He warns women to do likewise in "O do not Love too Long."

These poems, written in 1905, represent fairly early poetic responses to Maud Gonne's marriage in 1903. Yeats's biographers agree that her marriage was a complete shock to him. Bradford points out that, as far as Yeats was concerned, he and Maud were still pledged to each other in their spiritual marriage[12]—a point he would make poetically much later in "A Deep-sworn Vow" (1917). Several of his most powerful poems in this middle period—most notably "Reconciliation" and "The Cold Heaven"—refer to the effect of her marriage on him; one of his early poetical reactions, however, is a self-mocking mask. The mask, at this early stage, is a defensive armor.[13] His lyrics are couched in a cool wit that keeps his soul inviolate.

As his theory of the mask continues to develop, he connects it explicitly to love and a self-preserving deceit in "The Mask" in *The Green Helmet and Other Poems* (1910). By this point, Yeats sees love and deceit as inseparable, not because of the inevitable loss of the loved one, as in the phrase "deceiving hope" in *The Shadowy Waters*, but as a result of a deliberate choice. The dialogue in "The Mask" playfully dramatizes love as a game in which the image that the lover projects of himself is what attracts the beloved. She senses that he is not giving all, that his soul is somehow protected by the cold, jeweled glitter of the mask, but he knows that to remove the mask would be to lose the happiness Yeats referred to in his comments on deceit in "Discoveries." His approach is pragmatic, obviously affected by his experience in the theater: players can communicate only through their words and appearances.

Since the deceit involved in love will eventually be essential to the situation in "The Three Bushes," the slight hint of the actual wording of the refrain of the later ballad in the twice repeated "my dear" (P 95) of "The Mask" is provocative. In fact, he connects this phrase to love and deceit in two other poems in this middle period, both of which pave the way for "The Three Bushes."

The closest parallel to "The Three Bushes" is an untitled poem, the first three stanzas of which Yeats included in an appendix to his *Collected Works* in 1908 (as a possible song for the pupils in *The Hour Glass*). Yeats notes that this poem is an English version of a Gaelic ballad, which aligns it with the ballad tradition he later imitated in "The Three Bushes." Since it is an important early parallel, I quote it in full:

> I was going the road one day
> (O the brown and the yellow beer),
> And I met with a man that was no right man
> (O my dear, O my dear).
>
> "Give me your wife," said he,
> (O the brown and the yellow beer),
> "Till the sun goes down and an hour of the clock"
> (O my dear, O my dear).
>
> "Good-bye, good-bye, my husband,"
> (O the brown and the yellow beer),
> "For a year and a day by the clock of the sun"
> (O my dear, O my dear).
>
> "I know of a girl" said I
> (O the brown and the yellow beer),
> "Who can shorten the time by the clock and the sun"
> (O my dear, O my dear).
>
> "And one's as good as another"
> (O the brown and the yellow beer),
> "So get you away with your no right man"
> (O my dear, O my dear). (P 548-49)

The first three stanzas parallel "The Three Bushes" in the arrangement for a surrogate in the marriage bed, although here two men make the arrangement that affects a woman. The wife, rather like the Lady in her alienation from the human condition, will spend "a year and a day"— matching the first anniversary in "The Three Bushes"— with a "man who is no right man," presumably a man from faery. Although there is no unwitting partner as in "The Three Bushes," there is an element of betrayal in the 1908 ballad in the husband's giving his wife over to the supernatural figure. This betrayal involves more inevitability than the later ballad, since the wishes of a supernatural suitor would be harder to deny; however, the husband's decision in the last two stanzas to find his proper food from another girl implies a self-preserving duplicity. He refuses to be robbed of the opportunity for human love while his chosen mate consorts with an ideal lover. His comment that "one's as good as another" foreshadows the Lady's suspicion that "maybe we are all the same / That strip the body bare."

This ballad is lightheartedly bawdy in these assertions, yet Yeats's choice of this Gaelic ballad, with the surrogate lovers and the refrain "O my dear, O my dear," suggests that a pattern similar to that of "The Three Bushes" already appealed to his imagination. In fact, this ballad was in his mind intermittently right up to the time he wrote "The Three Bushes," since he included stanzas one to three in his notes to *Plays in Prose and Verse* in 1922 and, most significantly for my purposes, added the last two stanzas (which he must have known since Lady Gregory printed the whole ballad in 1901) for an unpublished edition in 1937.[14] Moreover, *The Hour Glass,* in which he originally inserted this ballad, is a play based on the story of a priest's need for forgiveness, which also prefigures "The Three Bushes."

The refrain in the 1908 ballad not only uses the same exclamation,[15] but also functions in a similarly complex manner to that in the later ballad. In both ballads, the refrain could be spoken by a totally separate choric voice; this effect is strengthened by the parentheses in the 1908 ballad and the italics in "The Three Bushes." At the same time, the refrain could easily be spoken by either the husband or wife in each stanza; just as the refrain in "The Three Bushes" can be variously assigned to the four characters. The refrain interpenetrates the verses, yet remains virginally aloof, a technique Yeats used throughout his career.

As I pointed out while analyzing "The Three Bushes," biographical data suggests that this use of a surrogate lover matched Yeats's life experiences at this time as well. His letters and journal entries between 1908 and 1910 contain many references that would provide much of the raw material that he later transformed to art in "A Man Young and Old" and "The Three Bushes." His realization of the irrevocable dichotomy between spiritual and carnal love[16] culminates in his admission, in a crucial entry in 1909, that Maud Gonne was his "deceiving hope," an echo of his formula for human love in *The Shadowy Waters.*

Although I have already quoted part of this diary entry in chapter 1 to suggest the close parallel between the events in Yeats's second period of spiritual marriage to Maud Gonne and the situation in "The Three Bushes," I quote a fuller version so that his reference to Maud Gonne as his "deceiving hope" can be seen in the context of his conclusions about love at this time:

PIAL [the Golden Dawn initials for Maud] told me that we must be apart—we are divided by her religious ideas, a Catholicism which has grown on her—and she will not divorce her husband and marry because of her church. Since she said this she has not been further from me but is always very near. She too seems to love more than of old. In addition to this the dread of physical love has awakened in her. This dread has probably spoiled her life, checking natural and instinctive selection and leaving fantastic duties free to take its place.... I was never more deeply in love, but my desires, always strong, must go elsewhere if I would escape their poison. I am in continual terror of some entanglement parting us, and all the while I know that she made me and I her. She is my innocence and I her wisdom. Of old she was a phoenix and I feared her, but now she is my child more than my sweetheart.... Always since I was a boy I have questioned dreams for her sake—and she herself always a dream and a deceiving hope... the phoenix nesting [?] when she is reborn in all her power to torture and delight, to waste and to ennoble. She would be cruel if she were not a child who can always say "You will not suffer because I will pray." [17]

On the simplest biographical level, she has been his deceiving hope because she has continuously tantalized him while refusing to give herself to him. More significantly, he realizes that he created that deceit himself—she has always been a dream to him, an admission that the Rose poems support. This kind of deceiving hope was a soul-consuming fiction, but one that no longer has power over him. A complete role reversal has occurred from his early works where he longed to be cradled on the bosom of the virgin-mother. Now, he envisions himself as protecting her through his own increased self-possession.

In the process of freeing himself from the soul-consuming deceit of his earlier idealization of Maud Gonne, Yeats deliberately develops a self-preserving deceit, such as he advocated in "Discoveries." He accepts the split between carnal and spiritual love that she still imposes, but he refuses to "give her all" as he said in "Discoveries" and finds his physical satisfaction elsewhere, with Mabel Dickinson. Much like the husband in the Gaelic ballad, he chooses not to deny himself physical love while his chosen partner is controlled by spiritual love. Yeats sensed that the triangle involved not giving all to either woman, since he included "The Mask" in a letter to Mabel Dickinson, telling her that she gave him the idea for the poem. [18]

Thus, although many artistic transformations will still take place before the creation of the later ballad, the kernel of the situation in "The Three Bushes" is present in Yeats's experiences in 1909. Maud Gonne's fear of physical love prefigures the Lady's; Mabel Dickinson, like the Chambermaid, provides the desired physical relationship; Yeats, like the Lover, has a divided relationship with the two women. As Yeats's complex attitude in the diary entry demonstrates, he sees these women as answering needs within himself. He is becoming more aware of himself as sharing in all the roles that he will eventually dramatize in the love triangle in "The Three Bushes."

A few years later in *Responsibilities*, he again connects love, deceit, and the phrase, "my dear," in "The Dolls," another poem that foreshadows some of the concerns of "The Three Bushes." On one level, as Yeats's note indicates, the whole poem is a satire against artists who are "frozen into 'something other than human life'" (VP 820). In this satirical interpretation, the doll-maker's wife uses conscious deceit to trick the doll-maker into producing a living thing. The whole poem is a sophisticated joke culminating in the wife's commonplace lie at the end.

The wife's deception functions on a more serious level, as well. Her lie presupposes an earlier duplicity at the time of intercourse. Like the later Chambermaid, she is inviolately detached even as she is passionately involved with her husband. The last two lines, where the lyric intensity of the second-to-last line contrasts so effectively with her final equivocation,[19] mirror the inextricable intertwining of love and deceit in her relationship with the doll-maker. Her crouching and murmuring in his ear also prefigures the Chambermaid's confession to the Priest, a parallel reinforced by her use of "My dear, my dear, O dear" (P 127). In her dual detached awareness and passionate involvement she evidences the virginity of soul that Yeats would later call "the tragedy of sexual intercourse." There is no blessing at the end of her confession as there will be in "The Three Bushes." Yeats is still wrestling to accept the implications of this tragedy, although as I will discuss in connection with "The Cold Heaven," he has begun to find a healing power in himself.

How the child relates to the doll-maker is ambivalent. Under the ironic façade, Yeats's attitude is almost frighteningly equivocal. Is the "noisy and filthy thing" what the artist wants to produce or are the dolls who are copied in nonbestial, patterned fashion to be preferred? The child can in turn reproduce its kind, but the artist loses control over the living thing and it will eventually die; whereas the dolls are fixed, controlled and more permanent: they will outlast the child. The doll's accusation that "the man and the woman" (P 126) have brought the child there implies that the doll-maker is the father of the child, which is also implied in his sexually suggestive "groan and stretch."[20] Yet he seems repulsed by his own offspring. Previous to this, he has made only dolls, but now, by a deceit he cannot comprehend, the doll-maker has produced a child.

The problem of unity versus multiplicity is now less clearcut to Yeats than in the 1890s. If the embrace of the ideal beloved is deferred until after death, as he had advocated earlier, their union produces only the androgynous whole—their perfect, irrevocable union. From temporal unions, by contrast, imperfect, corruptible offspring result. By the inevitable deceit of birth, each of us, as Yeats says in "The Two Kings" (1913), is "betrayed into a cradle" (P 439). In this world, the lover tries to regain his perfect integrity through total union with another, but produces multiplicity instead because he maintains a self-preserving deceit, as does the wife. Likewise, the artist aims for the stasis of formal perfection, but simultaneously resists it through the deceit of his ever-changing style. The "noisy and filthy thing" that results signifies the poet-lover himself, who is indeed an "accident" rather than an eternal essence.

Although his attitude toward this "noisy and filthy thing" remains ambivalent in "The Dolls," Yeats has evolved to a perspective much closer to that of the reduction and regeneration of the worm-man at the end of "The Three Bushes"; moreover, he is beginning to connect this process to a confessional interchange, such as that between the doll-maker and his wife. "The Dolls," written at the end of this transitional period, evidences that his attitude not only toward deceit, but also toward incarnation and forgiveness, shifted to a contrary direction during the first years of this century.

"It Is Myself That I Remake"

Yeats repeatedly connects deceit with incarnation in this transitional period. His attitude toward this embodiment, as "The Dolls" demonstrates, is complex, especially in its relationship to the artist. Yeats's comments on deceit in "Discoveries" mention "that severe quality that Verlaine spoke of" (EI 272) as one of the consequences of that deceit. Earlier in the same section of "Discoveries," Yeats quotes Verlaine on this quality: " 'The poet should hide nothing of himself,' though he must speak it all with 'a care of that dignity which should manifest itself if not in the perfection of all form, at all events with an invisible, insensible, but effectual endeavour after this lofty and severe quality.' " This passage evokes a complex relationship between deceit and incarnation: the poet hides nothing of himself, yet crafts his revelation into a dignified artifice. The incarnation of the poet, like his deceit, is both inevitable and deliberate, involving both the "uncontrollable mystery" (P 126) of his inner passion and the carefully cut agate into which he forms himself.

In this section of "Discoveries," Yeats criticizes his earlier poetry for its failure to incarnate his true self because of its lack of involvement in this world. He distinguishes the kind of embodiment he connects with Verlaine from the impersonality of his own earlier work:

> I had not learned what sweetness, what rhythmic movement, there is in those who have become the joy that is themselves. Without knowing it, I had come to care for nothing but impersonal beauty. I had set out on life with the thought of putting my very self into poetry, and had understood this as a representation of my own visions.... Then one day I understood quite suddenly, as the way is, that I was seeking something unchanging and unmixed and always outside myself, a Stone or an Elixir that was always out of reach, and that I myself was the fleeting thing that held out its hand. (EI 271)

In his earlier work, Yeats lacked the serene dignity and self-possession that he connects to Verlaine; his soul was too personally violated in his search for impersonal beauty. He could not put his "very self" into his poetry because he was looking for that self in an ideal outside himself. This life was not important; only in an eternal state could he be fully incarnated.

By 1906, however, Yeats insists that the artist, in particular, must focus on temporal things: "If it be true that God is a circle whose centre is everywhere, the saint goes to the centre, the poet and artist to the ring where everything comes round again. The poet must not seek for what is still and fixed, for that has no life for him; and if he did, his style would become cold and monotonous ... but be content to find his pleasure in all that is for ever passing away that it may come again" (EI 287). The possibility of reincarnation does not diminish the uniqueness of each incarnation; he continues, "... for those things return, but not wholly, for no two faces are alike." Yeats never became materialistic in viewpoint, as poems such as "September 1913" and "Paudeen" affirm in this period; in "His Friend's Illness," he still contends that the whole material world weighs less than one soul. Nevertheless, he is now emphasizing the individual incarnate soul in its struggle in this world.

In the context of his focus on each person's incarnation in the temporal world, Yeats's view of love gradually shifts until he unequivocally affirms the artist's need for human love, rather than the mystical embrace after death. He repeatedly stresses the perfect union of lovers after death, especially in his narrative poems in this period, but he has radically changed his attitude toward the poet-lover's involvement in this embrace and his exclusion from human love in preparation for this mystical union. In both "The Old Age of Queen Maeve" and "Baile and Aillinn," the poet is distinctly separate from such lovers. At the end of "Baile and Aillinn," the narrator suggests that the poet must not long for a union "like them that are no more alive" (P 402), although his interjections to his beloved in "The Old Age of Queen Maeve" show that his own unrequited love remains part of his motivation as a poet.

Yeats's affirmation of human love increases in this period until in "King and No King," written in December 1909, toward the end of his second period of spiritual marriage, he questions whether the "blinding light" of the eternal embrace will be "so good a thing as that we have lost" (P 92). He is no longer satisfied with the brother-sister relationship between the *artifex* and his *soror mystica*.[21] Alluding to Beaumont and Fletcher's play *King and No King*, in which the king is undone by the words "brother and sister" when he falls in love with the Queen and then finds out that she is his sister,[22] Yeats points out that "old Romance" is kind since the king turns out to be adopted (and therefore "no king") and then becomes king again by marrying the queen. Yeats's resigned, but rueful, tone implies that he, too, feels that he is "king" and "no king" in his spiritual marriage with Maud and longs for the resolution that Beaumont and Fletcher's king achieved. Bradford points to this poem as Yeats's "most explicit comment on Maud Gonne's refusal to let their love take a normal pattern."[23] Perhaps Yeats laments their cross-purposes: he could not be content with spiritual love; she found carnal love repulsive.

A few years after Yeats's acceptance of the necessity of physical love, he created a heroic female personality, Edain in "The Two Kings" (1913), who is not patterned after Maud Gonne.[24] Instead, Edain prefigures the later Chambermaid in her unequivocal choice of earthly love—a love all the sweeter for its brevity. Edain proclaims:

> "Never will I believe there is any change
> Can blot out of my memory this life
> Sweetened by death, but if I could believe,
> That were a double hunger in my lips
> For what is doubly brief." (P 440)

Forgael had rejected human love because it was but "brief longing, deceiving hope, and bodily tenderness"; Edain chooses it for precisely those characteristics. This poem, included in the first edition of *Responsibilities*, suggests that Yeats has passed a watershed in his attitude toward human love.

Edain is offered and refuses everything that the poet-lover of the 1890s longed for and sacrificed to attain. Her primal lover, Midhir—her immortal husband from before her birth—tries to woo her back to his lasting embrace, but she chooses the embrace of Eochaid, her husband in this life. She recognizes the inevitable imperfection, weakness, and transience attached to human love. Midhir tells her she has been "betrayed into a cradle," connecting the act of human intercourse with the alienation inherent in temporality and incarnation. Edain is not blind to the fall involved in her incarnate state, nor does she deny that someday, as Midhir claims, she will return to his arms. She celebrates and lives in the present, nonetheless. Her human husband, Eochaid, is more precious to her because of his weakness:

> ... "How should I love," I answered,
> "Were it not that when the dawn has lit my bed
> And shown my husband sleeping there, I have sighed,
> 'Your strength and nobleness will pass away.'
> Or how should love be worth its pains were it not
> That when he has fallen asleep within my arms,
> Being wearied out, I love in man the child?" (P 440)

Edain, in heroic pentameters befitting a queen, faces and tenderly cherishes the same "worm" of weakness and mortality that the Chambermaid will sing of in simpler lyrics.

Edain also prefigures the Chambermaid in her reluctant acceptance of duplicity because of the betrayal into flesh. Having been sent by her husband to nurse her brother-in-law, Ardan, she brings him food every day until he tells her that the only thing that can cure him is intercourse with her. After nine days, during which others bring him food, she reluctantly consents. Like the Chambermaid, Edain is willing to provide the food without which the man would supposedly die. Her willingness is never carried into action, since Ardan's whole illness turns out to be a ruse arranged by Midhir to bring Edain into contact with Midhir; yet her willingness to be used as surrogate lover foreshadows the Chambermaid's role.

Although Edain is willing to participate in bodily betrayal of her husband's rights, she refuses to betray him in order to achieve instant immortality in Midhir's arms; or perhaps more accurately, she refuses the violation of her own self-possession that the immortal embrace would entail. Midhir offers her unmixed happiness if she will allow him to claim her as his wife again, but she insists on the poignant realization of love's brevity as a condition of love. Her objective awareness of her husband's weakness as she envisions herself gazing at him in bed suggests the virginity of her soul during intercourse: she is self-possessed even during their tender embrace. Her passion does not carry her into a consuming ecstasy. To her, love is not an escape, but rather a reminder of our ultimate separateness from each other:

> What can they know of love that do not know
> She builds her nest upon a narrow ledge
> Above a windy precipice. (P 440)

Her self-possession allows her to overcome Midhir's attempt to embrace her. She thrusts him away declaring that nothing can "blot out of my memory this life." Paradoxically, her incarnate self-possession allows her to remain in Eochaid's mortal embrace instead, yet this perpetual self-awareness guarantees that she will remain inviolate in his arms as well.

Yeats's portrayal of Edain is a definitive step in his evolution to his depiction of his later psychological virgins, such as Crazy Jane and the Chambermaid. Like the virgins Frazer describes, Edain can never be owned by any husband; she freely submits to Eochaid and freely refuses Midhir. Yeats dramatizes Eochaid's recognition of her inner sovereignty in describing his reaction to her story:

> ... King Eochaid bowed his head
> And thanked her for her kindness to his brother,
> For that she promised, and for that refused. (P 440)

Like the ancient virgins, Edain attained this self-awareness through intercourse. Yeats's view of the virginity of the soul was no doubt influenced not only by Frazer, but by his friend, G. R. S. Mead, whose *Thrice-Greatest Hermes* was published in 1906.[25] Mead includes a section entitled "Concerning the Sacred Marriage," which must have interested Yeats, given his own spiritual marriage. Mead, quoting Philo, says: "For the congress of men for the procreation of children makes virgins women. But when God begins to associate with the soul, He brings it to pass that she who was formerly woman becomes virgin again."[26] As Philo indicates, only women, such as Edain, who have known "congress with men" can experience their perpetual virginity of soul. Yeats had given hints of such a psychological virgin in Naschina and the "beautiful friend" in "The Lover mourns for the Loss of Love." In 1913, he clearly affirms Edain's viewpoint. She need not become "shadowless" like Naschina, nor go "weeping away" like the "beautiful friend."

Edain does not speak of bearing Eochaid's children. Yeats focuses on her own betrayal into a cradle and its consequences for her. Likewise in connection with his work, Yeats's focus is on incarnating himself in the process of making and remaking his work. As with deceit, this involves both a deliberate making and a mysterious experience of being made. He still recognizes the mysterious element in inspiration; significantly, he now images it through the analogy of intercourse. In 1909, he wrote in his journal, "Man is a woman to his work and it begets his thoughts" (M 232). This comment, as well as Yeats's growing ability to create female characters, such as Dectora and Edain, who are individual women, yet personae for Yeats himself, suggests that Yeats is evolving toward an androgynous model for the self-begetting of the artistic imagination.

There is a certain passivity implied in the image of the man allowing his work to beget his thoughts. However, the final product is formed from him and by him. The implication of the labor entailed in the begetting of himself is also strong. In a preliminary poem to the second volume of his *Collected Works* in 1908, Yeats proclaims that he is actively involved in incarnating himself through his work:

> The friends that have it I do wrong
> When ever I remake a song,
> Should know what issue is at stake:
> It is myself that I remake. (P 548)

His recognition of the inviolate virginity of his soul, coupled with his conviction that he must have intercourse with the temporal world for true creativity, allow him to see himself and his work more objectively and to delight in the imperfection that he finds there since it incites him to remake himself.

In his journal for 1909, he repeatedly stresses that the poet must first make his own soul and then he will be able to create tragedy from that soul. Yeats is no longer advocating contemplation of a perfect Rose that would be corrupted if it were thrust from its casket of gold into the world. At this point, when he was deeply immersed in the theater, he seems to fear the opposite extreme: a directionless activity with no true self-identity behind it. He wants a balance of inner and outer realization: a poet "should combine the greatest possible personal realization with the greatest possible knowledge of the speech and circumstance of the world" (M 152). Like Edain's self-possession in love, the poet's attempt to realize himself in the world is simultaneously the condition for success and ever-receding failure: "The artist grows more and more distinct, more and more a being in his own right, as it were, but more and more loses grasp of the always more complex world" (M 152). The harder he tries to realize himself, the more he recognizes his inadequacy, just as figures like Edain (and the later Chambermaid) enter passionately into the sexual act, yet are simultaneously made aware of the failure of their love to eliminate imperfection. Increasingly, Yeats is experiencing the virginity of his soul in his ever stronger attempts to remake himself.

"Words," in *The Green Helmet and Other Poems* (1910), dramatizes the same process in poetic creation. The artist aims at perfect expression but is doomed to failure by the very raw material that gives him power. In this poem, he dwells first on the failure, then takes that failure as an impetus to renewed effort. His somewhat bitter, reflective mood in the first two stanzas gives way to a more explosive immediacy in the third stanza where he rekindles his repeated feeling that his creative power with words is strong enough to unite him with his "darling" in perfect understanding:

> That every year I have cried, "At length
> My darling understands it all,
> Because I have come into my strength,
> And words obey my call." (P 90)

His attempt to bridge the gulf between them with words is passionately intense, even as he reaffirms his choice of a medium that ensures failure:

> That she had done so who can say
> What would have shaken from the sieve?
> I might have thrown poor words away
> And been content to live.

This poem is one of a group that was originally entitled "Raymond Lully and his wife Pernella" (Lully being, as Yeats notes in an errata slip, an error for Nicholas Flamel). In the 1890s Yeats had longed to share a relationship with Maud Gonne like that of Flamel and Pernella,[27] which allowed them to produce the philosopher's gold;[28] now he rejoices that he cannot shake gold from his sieve of words. Since his words cannot bring about the perfect union, he must continue sifting those words. He has chosen to incarnate himself in a *prima materia* that isolates and objectifies the flow of consciousness, one that necessarily reduces, even as it paradoxically enhances, his passionate desire to make her understand all that he has become. The plural form of "words" is significant; this raw material connects him to the multiplicity of the material world, not the casket of gold where oneness reigns.

By the end of *Responsibilities,* when he again writes about his own crafting of poetry in "A Coat," Yeats's voice is so self-assured and he possesses himself with such ease that he is willing to walk naked. In his earlier, heavily draped poetry, his body was covered "from heel to throat" (P 127), but his soul was so transparent that he was easily stripped by others. Now, he resents their pretense that they had "wrought" his song: he is the maker. He reveals what he has been making—his naked self, a lighthearted prefiguration of the worm as naked, unaccommodated man in "The Three Bushes." The "enterprise" that he finds in "walking naked" suggests that his soul is no longer so easily read. In that naked body, he maintains the virginal, self-preserving deceit of his soul.

His style now conveys the simultaneous self-revelation and self-crafting that he connected to Verlaine in "Discoveries." The poem has been stripped to short lines, direct statement, and simple diction. The only polysyllabic words refer to his former technique. Yet his enterprise in this new style shows through in the semicomic double rhymes that culminate in the final "naked." The poet hides nothing of himself, yet incarnates himself in a carefully cut agate. The process by which he begets his newer self is still mysterious to the poet, as "The Dolls" conveys. However, this self-incarnation is no longer an escapist or narcissistic approach like the poet-lover's in the 1890s and the later Lady's; his rebirth involves incarnate intercourse with others and the world.

"Life Confesses to the Priest... But We Confess to Life"

Yeats's self-reflective viewpoint in "A Coat" shows him assuming a judgmental role, both toward himself and toward the poets who imitated him. Gradually during this transitional period, his attitude evolves from the often melancholy, self-pitying attitude in his early work to a more objective, often self-mocking, stance. The role of judge of his own work puts him in a rather detached, witnessing role in relation to the self he incarnates in that work, while he retains the passionate intensity of his struggle to embody himself in his work.

He is beginning to project himself into both roles in the confession at the end of "The Three Bushes." Like the Chambermaid, he experiences and confesses his part in the fallen world. Like the Priest, he witnesses, judges, and forgives the weaknesses and wrongs of others because he shares their brokenness. The artist is both sinned against and sinning, both detached and passionately involved.[29] In a journal entry in 1909, he explicitly connects the artist to confession: "Life confesses to the priest and honours him, but we confess to life and tell it all that we would do" (M 158). The artist, involved in life, must "confess to the priest," as the Chambermaid will, but he simultaneously has the freedom that comes from the artifice of imagination and style, which can create what he "would do."

Earlier in this entry, Yeats stresses the witnessing role of artists: "We are, as seen from life, an artifice, an emphasis, an uncompleted arc perhaps. Those whom it is our business to cherish and celebrate are complete arcs.... We are compelled to think and express and not to do." Accordingly, unlike the earlier poet-lover-adept who projected himself as the would-be main participant in the mystical embrace of his ideal Rose, the narrator of Yeats's poems after the turn of the century often functions as a witness and recorder of the "completed arc" of the eternal embrace. In "Baile and Aillinn," for example, poets are described as carving the record of other lovers into the wood of the yew and apple trees that grow on the graves of Baile and Aillinn. A story in "Swedenborg, Mediums, and Desolate Places" (1914) tells of a priest in a Noh play who prayed to unite two lovers who were denied love even after death. He knows they have been united when the cave they are in lights up. The Noh priest, like the narrator in "Baile and Aillinn," and, later, the Priest in "The Three Bushes," is not experiencing the love union himself, but shows pity and tenderness towards the lovers and records their story.

Yeats subtly connects himself as poet-lover to the role of recorder in a wonderfully poignant pun[30] on Maud Gonne's name in "Fallen Majesty," first published in 1912:

> ...this hand alone,
> Like some last courtier at a gypsy camping-place
> Babbling of fallen majesty, records what's gone. (P 123)

He is describing the woman to whom he has been passionately attracted for over twenty years, but he detaches himself to do so. The "hand alone" that babbles hints at the utter detachment of automatic writing. His synecdoche for himself in these lines also recalls a comment he made in his journal about the artist's difficulty in shunning contemplation for the sake of action. He writes, "It is hard to become a mere hand and ear" (M 175)—a comment that underlines the listening and recording function of the artist, and hints at the listening and blessing role of the priest in the confessional.

His judgmental stance involves forgiveness, but he no longer expects an obliterating forgiveness that restores a golden Eden of primal unity. He gradually demythologizes the Rose, seeing her as an individual human being capable of weakness and wrongdoing. Although he still attaches no blame to her in "Old Memory," in *In the Seven Woods*, he reluctantly admits that she has aged in "The Folly of Being Comforted." He reverts to heroic extravagance in excusing her of blame in the last line of "No Second Troy," but the rest of the poem accuses her of causing his misery, teaching violence to the ignorant, and being "high and solitary and most stern" (P 91). "Friends," in *Responsibilities*, matter-of-factly depicts her hardness which "took / All till my youth was gone / With scarce a pitying look" (P 124). Significantly, however, this more realistic picture of her elicits forgiveness as "up from my heart's root / So great a sweetness flows."

His judgment of himself as needing pardon also intensifies in this period. He begins *Responsibilities* in a confessional mode by begging pardon from his "old fathers" that "for a barren passion's sake" he has produced "nothing but a book" (P 101). Toward the end of this volume, in "The Cold Heaven," he relives this passion, ridding it of its barrenness. He begins this poem with an immediacy and force that emphasizes that he is a passionate participant, not a detached witness:

> Suddenly I saw the cold and rook-delighting heaven
> That seemed as though ice burned and was but the more ice,
> And thereupon imagination and heart were driven
> So wild that every casual thought of that and this
> Vanished, and left but memories, that should be out of season
> With the hot blood of youth, of love crossed long ago. (P 125)

The burning ice of the sky—a perfect image for his returned but unrequited love—revives passion. The poem refers to Yeats's reaction to Maud Gonne's marriage,[31] but it is not a recounting of his immediate reaction. The redeeming nature of the poem depends upon the fact that the sky drives all "but memories" from his mind; then he can relive time past in time present. By taking "all the blame" on himself, he makes the reliving an expiatory and renewing experience.

The imagery depicts him as raped by his own guilt:

> And I took all the blame out of all sense and reason,
> Until I cried and trembled and rocked to and fro,
> Riddled with light.

His rocking while being riddled with light simultaneously images rape and the labor of birth. In the ecstasy that accompanies this intercourse and bringing forth, his soul comes to life like a naked, new-born child:

> ... Ah! when the ghost begins to quicken,
> Confusion of the death-bed over, is it sent
> Out naked on the roads, as the books say, and stricken
> By the injustice of the skies for punishment?

The image of the soul as alien and alone suggests that his sense of responsibility forces him to give birth to the virginity of his own soul through this violent intercourse. It is not a pleasant experience: the pain and rending are stressed. Yet, it is purgatorial and powerfully self-begetting. In his *Autobiography*, Yeats says that "No mind can engender until divided in two" (A 208) and here he images that rending and engendering of himself. The prevalent religious overtones of heaven, the analogy to a scapegoat, and the purgatorial image of the soul at the end are not incorporated as an analogy for earthly passion as were the religious elements in "The Travail of Passion"; rather, his relived passion is a religious experience. Certain passages he wrote in defense of his Golden Dawn order suggest that this experience of being riddled with light from above identifies him as an adept, but his vision of the adept has changed from the 1890s. Yeats wrote to his fellow adepts:

> We receive power from those who are above us by permitting the Lightning of the Supreme to descend through our souls and our bodies. The power is forever seeking the world, and it comes to a soul and consumes its mortality because the soul has arisen into the path of Lightning among the sacred leaves. The soul that separates itself from others, that says, "I will seek power and knowledge for its own sake and not for the world's sake," separates itself from that path and becomes dark and empty.[32]

By allowing the lightning to follow the movement downwards to incarnation in and for the world, he permits the power to consume the mortality of his soul and experience the perpetual inviolateness of that soul.

A passage in his postscript to his essay to the Golden Dawn members cautions against seeing this role as that of a scapegoat whose burden cannot be relieved: "Certain Frates and Sorores think that the senior takes upon himself the sins of the Order, as the legendary Sin Eater takes a dead man's sins upon himself. This is an error . . . He lays the sins of the Frates and Sorores, and his own sins among them, in the hands of the Third Order, and instead of laying a burden upon himself, lightens his own burden and the burden of others."[33] The "I" of "The Cold Heaven" fully experiences the pain of his own guilt and feels punished by the "injustice of the skies," but by so doing he takes the blame "out"—this word can complete the verb or start the prepositional phrase in line seven—of his barren passion and lightens his burden and that of others by forgiveness and renewal.

Yeats's insistence that the adept must be connected to the world, not to knowledge for its own sake, demonstrates how his image of the adept is changing. He no longer envisions the adept as being isolated from sin or from others—locked in his imagination as he was in "The Lover tells of the Rose in his Heart." His sacrifice is now for the sake of others. His view that "literature is the forgiveness of sins" has changed in accordance with his view of the artist as adept. His poetry allows him to relive his sin, imaged in terms of intercourse and birth, in all its immediacy—remaking himself in the process, but not perfecting himself. At the end of the poem, he is once again exposed to the struggle of the human condition. As he says in "Discoveries" and dramatizes in "The Cold Heaven," "It may happen that poets will be made more often by their sins than by their virtues" (EI 278).

The process of remaking himself demands the dialogue inherent in the confessional interchange between the participant and judge. Both the introductory and closing poems in *Responsibilities*, where Yeats asks and gives pardon, are printed in italics as if he is stressing that they are spoken aloud to the listening reader. Not only in narrative poems, but also in lyrics, such as "Adam's Curse" and "The Mask," he shows a fondness for dialogue that was less prevalent in his earlier lyric verse. In addition, Yeats's work with Florence Farr on speaking to the psaltery was carried on during the first decade of the twentieth century. Repeatedly, he insists that poetry is intended for the ear. This dialogue is ultimately with the artist who is both participant and recorder of an experience. The inner dialogue must be uttered aloud, nevertheless. He writes to Florence Farr, in words reminiscent of an earlier comment to Katharine Tynan, that he misses her in London since there is no one "to whom I can talk as if to myself" (L 508).

In "Words" he sets off his own thoughts in quotation marks as if he speaks them to himself. This sets up a slight tension, lifting the sections in quotation marks out of the remembered flow of his thoughts. He recommends just such a technique in drama in "J. M. Synge and the Ireland of His Time" (1909): "In all drama which would give direct expression to reverie, to the speech of the soul with itself, there is some device that checks the rapidity of the dialogue. When Oedipus speaks out of the most vehement passions, he is conscious of the presence of the Chorus" (EI 333). Yeats achieves this check to the flow of the poem in his narrative poems by interjecting sections in italics where the narrator functions as a chorus. [34] These italicized sections tend to be repetitive and function like refrains. He uses a similar technique in the italicized refrains of his lyric poems. [35] These create a mysterious sense of dialogue between the poet and the poem, the poet and the reader, and the reader and the poem.

This repetition of sections in italics is one more way Yeats embodies the tension between passion and detachment, between immediate experience of the artist as sinner and the detached sympathy of the artist as priest. These two roles are not kept separate. He no longer cries out against the passion that mars his aloof dedication to the immortal quest as he did at the end of *The Wind among the Reeds* and in *The Shadowy Waters*; nor does he think he can lose himself in passionate immediacy. His poetry now reflects the interpenetration of what he called "turbulent energy" and "marmorean stillness" (EI 255). The opposite movements of "The Cold Heaven" and "The Magi," both based on the poet's reaction to the blue sky, demonstrate that even extremes of involvement and detachment are intertwined with their opposites.

"The Cold Heaven," for all its immediacy, passion, and irrationality in the first nine and one-half lines, shifts, after the ecstatic "Ah," to the slight mental aloofness inherent in a question. The image of burning ice unites passion and detachment[36] from the beginning in a consuming struggle that passion at first seems to win in the peak moment of being riddled with light; detachment, however, is born at that moment. By the end, the individual experience of the first part has fanned out to the universality of the image of any ghost—an image garnered from books, not from the direct impact of the sky. "The Magi," conversely, starts in impersonal, universal detachment: he repeats "all" four times in the first six lines. His "mind's eye" (P 126) seems as stiff and patterned as the magi's eyes and clothes. But the impetus and object of their search—"Calvary's turbulence" and "the uncontrollable mystery on the bestial floor"—break into the fixity of the poem in the last two lines. The final image is brutally passionate and irrational. Fittingly, the image at the end of "The Magi" prefigures the beast at the end of "The Second Coming," since "The Magi" and "The Cold Heaven" stand in a relation to each other that Yeats will soon envision as interpenetrating gyres: the beginning of each matches the end of the other and each moves toward its opposite pole. Neither passionate involvement nor virginal aloofness is compartmentalized, as the Lady in "The Three Bushes" would like to keep each; the artist must keep up the interchange between the two.

In "The Dolls," Yeats dramatizes this inner dialogue as an interchange between a man and a woman. The man-woman dialogue within the divided mind is endless because the struggle of these opposing principles is never finished. Thus, the artist must continuously remake himself through his simultaneous passionate involvement and virginal detachment of soul. At the end of this period, however, Yeats still seems slightly repulsed by the "noisy and filthy thing" that he incarnates himself as by means of this interchange. He has not yet fully accepted that "Love has pitched his mansion in / The place of excrement" (P 259-60), even though he now senses that he is irrevocably connected to the ever-recurring accidents of this world.

By the publication of *Responsibilities*, Yeats had begun to project himself into roles that prepare for all the figures who come together in "The Three Bushes." Like the Lady, he sees duplicity as inherent in the human condition and perforce in love, but like the Lover he no longer lets an approach like the Lady's keep him from passionate involvement in life. He is also creating figures, such as Edain, who embody the simultaneous experience of passion and virginity within them, as the Chambermaid will do. In addition, he has started to develop a judgmental, choric stance that allows him as artist, like the later Priest, to witness and record the experience of himself and others through a confessional interchange where he alternately functions as sinner and judge. By 1914, he has already gathered most of the *prima materia* for the vision of "The Three Bushes," which he will continue to shake from his sieve in words of increased power.

4

"O! Solomon! Let Us Try Again"

In his great outpouring of lyric poetry and philosophic prose between 1915 and 1928, Yeats develops the philosophic underpinnings of the vision that is already suggested in *Responsibilities*. He laments, in his introduction to his first version of *A Vision* (1925), that he has said "little on sexual love" (xii), yet the sections he does include—most especially "The Cones of Sexual Love" and "The Daimon, The Sexes, Unity of Being, Natural and Supernatural Unity"—offer provocative parallels and glosses to his views on love as presented in his lyric poetry. His tone is much more authoritative in the second version of *A Vision* (1937), but this earlier, more personal,[1] and, at times, more groping version shows his deepening awareness of the need for human love, the endless conflict love involves, and the virginity of the soul within each of the partners in that relationship.

The imagery in his poetry, particularly in parallels to the *hieros gamos*, also continues to suggest mythological and occult allusions which stress the virginity of the soul during intercourse. Through this imagery and related material in *Per Amica Silentia Lunae* (1917) and *A Vision*, especially the passages explaining his concept of the Daimon, Yeats develops a complex view of the interplay involved in the relationship between a man and woman and between opposing principles within the psyche during the creative process. In his final book *A Vision*, 1925, where he discusses "The Great Wheel and from Death to Birth," Yeats analyzes an ongoing process which he designates by the term "expiation," thus demonstrating that the forgiveness of sins was still prominent in his mind. In all, the poems and prose statements of this period imply a crucial relationship in Yeats's thinking between the virginity of the soul and the forgiveness of sins: both demand that the lover and artist "try again."

The *Hieros Gamos*

One of Yeats's more didactic poems, "Solomon and the Witch" (1918), provides a framework for his views on human love as a means of near transcendence. Solomon is now finding creative impetus in the physical embrace of his witch, Sheba. Solomon, the prototype of the magus, brings all of Yeats's earlier wishes to be the transforming adept into Sheba's arms. In his Epilogue to *Per Amica Silentia Lunae,* Yeats recalls how reverently in the 1890s he had awaited the moment when Axel would cry out, "I know that lamp, it was burning before Solomon" (My 368). Solomon's experience on the "grassy mattress" (P 176) under the "wild moon" (Jeffares points out the sexual connotations of "wild" in Irish parlance)[2] is now essential to his wisdom. His intellect is mocked in the onomatopoeia and alliteration in the list of things he has "understood." His long discourse explaining what happened to them the night before displays his intellectual acumen and metaphysical bent, but he is in danger of becoming sterile and losing contact with reality if Sheba does not drag him back to earth again. The symbolic resonance in the simplicity of her final speech suggests where true inspiration lies. Significantly, she is the one who calls out in the strange voice that Solomon interprets as indicating that they have achieved a perfect union.

As "Solomon and the Witch" demonstrates, Yeats now presents sexual imagery much more explicitly. His marriage provides one explanation, since Mrs. Yeats is called "Sheba" in an epigram in his journal (M 274). Yet he had used explicit sexual imagery in connection with Solomon and Sheba in "On Woman" (1914) well before his marriage, suggesting that his purpose is not strictly autobiographical. In fact, the vision of love in "The Three Bushes" was already established in his mind by *Responsibilities,* although his later experiences are certainly reflected in the increasingly joyful tone that attends his references to human love. In his work from 1914 on, he explores the analogy between the convictions he has formed about love and the creative process. "On Woman" suggests a parallel between the creative act in Solomon's mind and the sexual act between Solomon and Sheba. Through these two figures, Yeats probes the implications of trying to achieve perfection in both processes.

Solomon's discourse in "Solomon and the Witch," although perhaps a bit too expository for lyric poetry, presents Yeats's views on the effects of perfect sexual union and is, therefore, important to an understanding of Yeats's conclusion about the tragedy of sexual intercourse. Solomon says that the cock cried out through Sheba because:

> he thought,
> Chance being at one with Choice at last,
> All that the brigand apple brought
> And this foul world were dead at last.
> He that crowed out eternity
> Thought to have crowed it in again.

Many notes to Yeats's poems and plays and discussions in his *Autobiography* (written between 1914 and 1935)[3] evidence his fascination with Chance and Choice at this time, but one of the most pertinent here is from "The Cones of Sexual Love" in *A Vision*, 1925: "In all pairs of lovers each is to himself or herself, *Will*, and the other *Body of Fate*.... Love which in this way mirrors the fated and predestined, has three forms of crisis, each at the end of a constituent cone, called the first and second *Critical Moments* and the *Beatific Vision*.... That is to say there is harmonization or the substitution of the sphere for the cone" (V, 1925, 172). In accord with this passage, Sheba sees herself as Will (Choice) and Solomon as Body of Fate (Chance) in her arms at the beginning. He, in turn, says that "a blessed moon last night / Gave Sheba to her Solomon," seeing himself as passive. The three moments of crisis parallel the crowing three hundred years before the fall, the fall itself, and the crowing in of eternity again as they achieve, so Solomon thinks, the Beatific Vision symbolized by the sphere of "a single light." When all the "Cruelties of Choice and Chance" that Solomon mentions are over, they reach a state where they are in perfect harmony: Will and Body of Fate are the same to themselves and each other, paralleling the perfect union between two individuals to the apocalyptic moment when the world is consumed into nothingness in perfect union with God.

As Sheba realizes, however, this moment has not occurred. She brings Solomon squarely back to earth by simply pointing out that "the world stays"; she knows that "the crushed grass where we have lain" keeps the impress of their forms as cones, not as a sphere. She, nevertheless, is the one who comes closest to the transcendent, the one through whom the strange voice cries. Her experience was a moment of crisis, intense enough to be "worth a crow," but not ultimate. Sheba effortlessly accepts that they are still in the fallen world where apple petals "hit the ground." From that world comes her passion to "try again."

In her willingness to repeat the pattern, Sheba illustrates a further comment Yeats makes in "The Cones of Sexual Love": "All *antithetical* life, for *primary* life has but a single movement, is seen as if it were a form of sexual life. It becomes vital through conflict and happy through harmonization, and without either is self-consumed" (V, 1925, 173). The designation of antithetical life as analogous to sexual life is crucial to Yeats's use of the sexual metaphor in relation to the creative process. He had started to develop a connection between the antithetical and the artist in "Discoveries," where he contrasted the saint (the primary) and the sinner or artist (the antithetical). The contrast between the primary and antithetical is, of course, essential in *A Vision*. Generally speaking, the person dominated by the primary is outward-oriented, reasonable, and moral, dedicating himself single-mindedly to others. The antithetical person is inward, divided, and self-reflexive. Although Yeats recognizes that there are primary artists, he definitely sees himself as an antithetical artist, as the theory of the mask in "Anima Hominis" attests. Harper and Hood note that Yeats listed himself in Phase Seventeen, one of the most strongly antithetical phases, in manuscripts relating to *A Vision*, 1925.[4] Thus, the many comments he makes about the antithetical life, the antithetical person, or the antithetical inspiration are especially pertinent to himself as artist.

Two of the points in the comment from "The Cones of Sexual Love" on antithetical life are typical of his view of both sexual relations and the creative process in the antithetical artist. Both become "vital through conflict" and without this conflict are "self-consumed." The conflict between the whirling cones of the two lovers never ends except for brief moments of crisis, such as Solomon and Sheba had experienced the previous night when the two lovers seemed to lose their separate existence and Sheba cried out in a tongue "not his, not mine." For that moment, she lost her antithetical or subjective nature and did not exist reflexively as "I." That moment was short-lived, however; Sheba has clearly returned to an antithetical state, since her speech prior to this description of the cry contains four first-person pronouns.

As Yeats explains in his comments on Blake's "The Mental Traveller" in *A Vision*, 1925, Sheba must resume the sexual conflict: "The woman and the man are two competing gyres growing at one another's expense.... In our system also it is a cardinal principle that anything separated from its opposite—and victory is separation—consumes itself away" (134). The Lady in "The Three Bushes" will achieve her "victory" over her desires by separating herself from physical love, but Sheba senses the source of her creative life and is willing, like the Chambermaid, to engage in all the pain, cruelty, murder, and despair that Solomon delineates as found in the "bride-bed" of Yeats's happiest couple.

Although their interplay is physical and imperfect, many details, in both Sheba's description of the act and Solomon's explanation of it, suggest that Sheba, at least, is closely connected to God through their union. Their intercourse is presented in terms that parallel the *hieros gamos*—the sacred marriage between the woman and God—as described in occult and mythological sources. Yeats had read about this sacred marriage many times and had already created women, such as Edain and the weeping woman in "The Lover mourns for the Loss of Love," who possess the ever-virgin soul that characterizes the woman after this experience. "Solomon and the Witch" represents the first time Yeats depicts the enactment of this marriage, an image pattern crucial to the tragedy of sexual intercourse and later reflected in the relation of the Lover to the Chambermaid.

The parallels between the *hieros gamos*, as described in Frazer, Mead, and other occult and mythological sources, and the interplay between Solomon and Sheba are numerous. The sacred intercourse generally took place in the temple, a place where intercourse would ordinarily be taboo, just as Solomon and Sheba meet in "the forbidden grove." The moon is intricately involved in the *hieros gamos,* since the rite was performed in honor of the moon, originally a male god and believed to be the real husband of all women.[5] A hint of this lingers in Solomon's gratitude that "the blessed moon...gave Sheba to her Solomon." When Sheba describes the moon as "wild" and "wilder," Yeats may be implying that the moon grows more passionate as his human representative lies in Sheba's arms. The mythologists note that later the moon was considered female—the Great Mother, who gives birth to and consorts with her own son. Yeats had, of course, used this symbolism of the moon as virgin-mother from his earliest work. The moon aspect of women was associated with the dark side of the moon,[6] which perhaps accounts for Yeats's designation of Sheba as "witch." Sheba's reference to the "strange tongue" concurs with Frazer's description of intercourse with a stranger as part of the rites of the virgin goddess.[7] The *hieros gamos* was experienced as a death situation,[8] a comparison also made by Solomon in his comments on the murder and despair of love.

In addition, Yeats draws symbolism from the Cabbalistic versions of the *hieros gamos.* Solomon is a fitting choice, not only for his status as magus or priest, but also because part of the Song of Songs was sung in the procession that preceded the Friday night re-enactment of the sacred intercourse between God and his Shekinah. The apple and apple blossoms (in addition to the obvious allusion to Genesis) also parallel the Cabbalistic ritual where the Shekinah is frequently called the field of holy apple trees, which are symbolically fertilized in the union between the King and his Sabbath Bride.[9]

Solomon's reference to Chance and Choice being one, although not taken from traditional *hieros gamos* symbolism, demonstrates that Yeats saw this union as approximating union with God. In his notes to *Calvary,* published in 1921, Yeats indicates that Chance and Choice "exist in God, for if they did not He would have no freedom, He would be bound by His own Choice. In God alone, indeed, can they be united, yet each be perfect and without limit and hindrance" (VPl 790). Solomon's interjection, "though several," in his explanation of the oneness of Choice and Chance, suggests an exact parallel to the sovereignty in unity of these opposing factors in God. Solomon is also describing the consummation to nothingness that will attend the complete reunion of God and his Shekinah: at that moment, "This foul world" will be "dead at last."

In their *hieros gamos,* Solomon and Sheba, as close as they come, do not achieve the world-ending, perfect union. Rather, Sheba's momentary experience of seeming transcendence implies that she has achieved the status of the independent virgin, the self-possessed woman who can never be owned by another. As Mead indicates, she has ensured the virginity of her soul by "congress with God."[10] In her synthesis of the symbolism of the *hieros gamos*, Harding stresses that this virginity is a quality, not a physiological fact. Not all women attain this perpetual virginity: "Woman can only become one-in-herself when she is fully awakened to the possibilities slumbering in her own nature, has experienced what it is to be set afire with passion, carnal and spiritual, and has devoted her powers to the god of instinct. Then when the nonpersonal, the divine energy has been aroused in her, she attains chastity of soul."[11] Sheba clearly experiences all the potentialities within herself and allows the divine energy to flow through her. In the ancient societies, the woman who never attained this psychological virginity was considered a child and dependent on a male.[12] Like counterpart male-female deities, the death of the male would consume her, a pattern paralleling the Lady's death at the death of the Lover in "The Three Bushes." Sheba, in contrast, perceives herself as active and equal in their union.

   Solomon is a substitute for God, but he is not a mere symbol; his physical presence is crucial. Sheba's cry could not be achieved without physical contact with Solomon. Simultaneously, however, her cry proclaims that she will never be engulfed in that union. Passionate involvement is demanded for approaching oneness, but that passion simultaneously guarantees failure to attain that oneness. Yeats had dramatized this pattern in "Words" and in the relationship between Edain and Eochaid in "The Two Kings." The interplay between Solomon and Sheba is his most playful embodiment of this analogy to the creative process. The wholehearted nature of Sheba's attempt to be united with Solomon brings the ecstatic cry, but also keeps her inviolately separate from him, since it allows her to experience her ever-virgin soul. Her plea at the end demonstrates that she has again lost the detached, self-critical stance and is ready for another moment of crisis. As the final word, "again," implies, the pattern is cyclic: they will come very close again, but fail to form the permanent sphere again. Her seemingly transcendent cry really witnesses to her connection to the "grassy mattress" of this world. The closer they come to perfect union, the more poignant is their inability to become a "single light." In Sheba's final exultant cry, nonetheless, the joy of that tragic failure is evident.

   Although Solomon and Sheba are separate persons and their union is physical, their relationship parallels a process within each of them. Several details in this poem, and even more in "On Woman," imply that Yeats is further exploring the androgynous view of the psyche and the possibilities of self-begetting in the artist. Some points already mentioned in connection with the *hieros gamos* have androgynous implications. The Shekinah represents the feminine aspect of God and must be reunited with him for completeness. This union takes place in "the secret inwardness of God himself."[13] The moon, first considered male and then female, is often seen as androgynous since it retains characteristics of both sexes and is thus able to reproduce from itself alone.

In Yeats's version of androgyny, as presented in "On Woman," contact with a separate woman is required before the woman within the poet-lover's psyche can be activated and he can experience creative intercourse with her. From his earliest creative period, Yeats had found that his own mind needed contact with a woman's mind in order to create. In the 1920s his most important correspondent in this vein was Olivia Shakespear, the Diana Vernon of his youth, to whom he wrote many letters about all of his concerns, but most especially his love poetry.

The feminine mind, acting like a womb, gives substance to his thought. The first stanza of "On Woman" sets forth this process:

> May God be praised for woman
> That gives up all her mind,
> A man may find in no man
> A friendship of her kind
> That covers all he has brought
> As with her flesh and bone
> Nor quarrels with a thought
> Because it is not her own. (P 146)

The woman seems quite passive, but the active process of her "giving flesh and bone" to his thought becomes clear in the description of how Solomon "grew wise" when "Sheba was his Queen," in the second stanza. Intercourse between them is required and Sheba is not passive in it. In this, one of his earliest explicit sexual descriptions, Yeats describes the process in terms of the creation of an artifact and then in human terms. The artistic process is primary: the effect is within Solomon who "grew wise." The exterior contact, as for Sheba in "Solomon and the Witch," is a stimulus to interior creativity. And, like Sheba at the end of "Solomon and the Witch," the narrator in "On Woman," knows he must be "led a dance" continuously if he is to give birth to his thought. In *A Vision*, 1925, Yeats says that "exhaustion and creation should follow one another like day and night" (249).

Their oneness is not permanent. Like the iron in the water, which cools itself while warming the water, but is easily extricated from the water, the man and the woman are not fused into a third unifying element. In terms of the moon imagery, the androgynous child of the virgin-mother is not born; rather, the artist re-creates himself:

> The Pestle of the Moon
> That pounds up all anew
> Brings me to birth again—
> To find what once I had.

Then he is driven from his bed, again hungering for that union with a woman which will give birth to his thought. In short, the relationship is triangular: his contact with the exterior woman stimulates and parallels his conflict with the feminine within him, just as the woman awakens contact with God through intercourse with a human man.

"Leda and the Swan" is Yeats's most powerful embodiment of the *hieros gamos* of the artist imaged as woman to his work, as Yeats said in his journal (M 232). Like Sheba in "On Woman," Leda at first seems passive; the artist is overwhelmed by inspiration from without, helpless in the god's grasp. There is no verb, no build up, no logical frame—only the sudden impact of the swan on Leda. The swan's journey and mounting are collapsed into the one ambiguous word "blow," conveying a wind image (inspiration) as well as the violent physical contact. In the first quatrain, the swan dominates, but even here there are subtle hints that Leda will not be merely ravished. Her thighs are "caressed," not forced. Gradually, she and the swan become equal: first, they are both reduced to animal imagery—"her nape caught in his bill" (P 214)—then, the touch of breast to breast raises them both to human level. In terms of the process of attaining psychological virginity, Leda has submitted to the instincts of the god and is allowing his impersonal force to flow through her.

Little by little, Leda becomes more active.[14] The swan seems to be teaching her, arousing her. The second quatrain heightens her involvement. The questions in this quatrain refer to Leda; if the action is to be halted, it will be through her fingers. "Terrified" followed by "glory" conveys awe more than repulsion. The action is not counter, but continuous. Her caressed thighs are now "loosening"—not sundered, but surrendering and softening. Yeats implies that this is his conception of the Leda myth in a revision he made to "The Adoration of the Magi" in 1925, where he speaks of a time when "another Leda would open her knees to the swan."[15] She, like Sheba with Solomon, must match his intensity for true union. In the first question, "how can" implies that she could not possibly push him away, but by the second question, the phrase carries the connotation that she could not possibly want to do so..

The intensest moment of the *hieros gamos*, the moment that parallels Sheba's crowing, occurs when Leda feels "the strange heart beating where it lies." She is now psychologically virgin, and although they are on the brink of their shuddering consummation, he is "strange" to her. The "strange heart" could also refer to her own heart felt in her body as alien, as if she experiences herself from without—an object in the god's embrace.

The juxtaposition of mental distance in the question at the end of this quatrain and the immediacy of the description of the moment of consummation in the next three lines aesthetically enacts the interplay of virginity of soul and physical intercourse as the wellspring of creation. Leda experiences herself both in the immediacy of body and the detachment of "strange heart"; the swan is simultaneously the stranger and one with her. Her experience closely foreshadows the Chambermaid's singing over the Lover, "stranger with stranger / On my cold breast" (P 300). The shudder that climaxes their union is presented without agent. They are both equally passionately involved and coldly detached as the artist allows his work to beget his thought through him.

The entire poem follows the progress of one moment of inspiration, but the imagery suggests the recurring process of creation and exhaustion. In the octave, Zeus dominates, then Leda responds by becoming more active. In the sestet, she is again "mastered," he, in turn, "indifferent." The lines describing the historical consequences of their action recapitulate the sexual act in imagery: "broken wall," "burning tower," and "Agamemnon dead." But the split line juxtaposing the two strong stresses on "dead" and "being" (which can be read as gerund as well as participle) implies that the process, like Solomon and Sheba's union, starts again.

The violent consequences of their union are telescoped into a few phrases, so that the whole process seems to flow inevitably from the "shudder." The whole fall of Troy is made to seem almost inconsequential. Neither Leda nor the Swan can change those concrete effects; what happens within Leda herself is more important. As Yeats noted, "bird and lady took such possession of the scene that all politics went out of it" (VP 828). As Zeus takes possession of Leda in the poem so their images took possession of Yeats. The focus remains on Leda in the last three lines because Yeats's primary concern is the effect of this experience on the antithetical artist, caught in the sexual conflict of her *hieros gamos.*

Yeats is portraying a powerful experience with powerful consequences for the artist. The conjunction between Leda and the Swan closely parallels his depiction of "the moment of the greatest genius possible" in *A Vision.* In the terminology of *A Vision,* Zeus parallels the "Ghostly Self" and Leda the "antithetical man," who can be either man or woman, as the passage shows:

The *Ghostly Self* is as it were shut up in its own marmorean time-less infinity. . . . The man must receive a violent shock from some crisis created by supernatural dramatization. . . . A man feels suddenly for a woman, or a woman for a man. . . . In the one case natural love is brought to the greatest height, and in the other intellectual search, and both reduced to nothing that the soul may love what it hates, accepting at the same moment what must happen and its own being, for the *Ghostly Self* is that which is unique in man and in his fate. This is the moment of the greatest genius possible to that man or woman, and in it a *primary* or *antithetical Arcon* of wisdom is begotten by the *Ghostly Self* upon the soul. (V, 1925, 242-43)

In the poem, the swan's infinity, his sudden desire, the reduction of both swan and Leda to nothingness in the agentless shudder, the indifference to the fall of Troy followed literally by "being," all parallel the moment of genius. Most importantly, the begetting is within the self: the Ghostly Self, which is part of Leda, begets wisdom in her soul.

Yeats's terminology is extremely esoteric in this section of *A Vision*, but this description is crucial to his view of artistic creation. He defines the Ghostly Self as "the permanent self.... It is the source of that which is unique in every man, understanding by unique that which is one and so cannot be analyzed into anything else" (V, 1925, 221). This is the self from before the world began; like Zeus it is beyond time. If the equation of the swan and the Ghostly Self is accepted (further supported by the overtones of Holy Ghost, also imaged as bird),[16] then the process takes place within Leda, although she experiences the Swan as from without. She discovers the unique in herself in her union with the Swan.

The question that almost overwhelms the poet at the end is whether she becomes eternal through her union with her permanent self. The Pauline overtones in "put on" are played upon: has she put on Christ? In alchemical terms, has she become the perfect androgynous union of moon and sun, earth and heaven, male and female? The last word suggests that the moment, although intense, is not ultimate. The artist must "drop" back into the mundane labor of fashioning his inspiration into a poem. The virginity of Leda's soul militates against total reintegration into the androgynous sphere.

Her failure to achieve the perfect androgyny of the reunion of God and his Shekinah is further supported by Yeats's use of Plato's parable on androgyny in "Among School Children." Speaking of himself and Maud Gonne, he comments

> ...and it seemed our two natures blent
> Into a sphere from youthful sympathy
> Or else, to alter Plato's parable,
> Into the yolk and white of the one shell. (P 216)

In Plato's parable, in *The Symposium*, the four-armed, four-legged, circular man-woman (associated with the moon since it is made up of earth and sun) is split in two by Zeus as if he were drawing a thread through an egg. After the fall into the sexes, the male and female seek their former union. They will form the permanent androgynous sphere when permanently reunited.

In Yeats's altered version, male and female, yolk and white come together but retain the ability to separate again. This egg symbolism is clarified in an exchange of letters in 1926 between Yeats and Frank Sturm, an English doctor who wrote to Yeats about *A Vision*. Sturm mentions that "the great work of dissolving the Eagle's Egg is accomplished when the white disappears in the

Yolk, and is enveloped in it." Yeats responded that the dissolving of the white in the yolk is "the soul made divine."[17] Yet, in using Plato's image in "Among School Children" (1927), Yeats keeps the yolk and white separate, although contained in one shell. Unlike the early poet-lover and the later Lady in "The Three Bushes," Yeats is now reluctant to make the human divine. Male and female meet and blend briefly, but neither loses its ever-virgin otherness in a new androgynous being. Like the iron and water in "On Woman," they can be separated from one another. As implied in the *hieros gamos* imagery in "Solomon and the Witch," and made explicit in "Leda and the Swan," the intense conflict of opposites between two individuals and within the artist's psyche approximates ultimate union with God, but the ever-virgin soul simultaneously desires and resists that union. Instead, the individual remains human, caught, as Yeats's view of the Daimon delineates, in "all the cruelties of Choice and Chance."

Daimon, Deception, and Expiation

Yeats's comments on the Daimon are closely intertwined with the continuing evolution of his connection between love and deceit. Both the Daimon and deceit are also related to Yeats's theory of expiation in *A Vision*; thus these concepts are part of his ongoing exploration of the forgiveness of sins and show how this belief is becoming more closely interrelated with his belief in the virginity of the soul during intercourse. His comments on the Daimon, deception, and expiation demonstrate his developing conviction that the poet-lover must accept his sin and affirm his ability to sin again, if he is to engage in a creative struggle with his Daimon.

Per Amica Silentia Lunae includes a recurring emphasis on deceit, Yeats distinguishing two kinds as he had done in his poems and essays between 1900 and 1914. Although passages in *Per Amica Silentia Lunae* dissociate the artist from deceit, ultimately he is not rejecting deceit, but advocating the right kind of deceit. In "Ego Dominus Tuus," referring directly to the artist and using the lover as analogy, Yeats insists that the artist must reject the deceit of rhetoric and sentimentalism, choosing instead the "vision of reality" (My 323) in his mask or antiself. He repeats the same ideas in "Anima Hominis": "The other self, the anti-self or antithetical self . . . comes but to those who are no longer deceived, whose passion is reality" (My 331). Yet the mask is itself a deception in the sense that it is not a mirror but an artifice, a striving on the part of the artist to create his opposite.

Yeats reaffirms the playful, deceiving stance of not giving all to the muse that he had used in self-defense in the years immediately following Maud Gonne's marriage, explaining that he managed to escape five years of creative sterility only "when I mocked in a comedy my own thought" (My 334).

Significantly, the comedy he refers to is *The Player Queen*, where Nona's and Decima's relationship with the poet Septimus is analogous to that of the Lady and the Chambermaid with the Lover in "The Three Bushes."[18] Decima is not as chaste as the Lady (a separate character, the Queen, is the virginal figure in the play), but Decima thinks she can inspire Septimus by denying her body. Right after reciting part of "The Mask," Decima says that Septimus wrote a poem for her after she "had turned him out of bed and he had to lie alone by himself" (VPl 739). Nona knows better and answers that the numbers "were made upon my spine in the small hours of the morning; so many beats a line, and for every beat a tap of the fingers." In this earlier version of the Lover playing tunes between the feet of the Chambermaid, Yeats mocks his own former self-consuming deceit about his source of inspiration. His mocking deceit is self-preserving and creative, however, in contrast to Decima's very rhetorical refusal to admit reality.

He describes the creative kind of deceit in connection with rebirth, sin, and the antiself:

> I think all happiness depends on the energy to assume the mask of some other life, on a rebirth as something not one's self, something created in a moment and perpetually renewed; in playing a game like that of a child where he loses the infinite pain of self-realisation, in a grotesque or solemn painted face put on that one may hide from the terror of self-judgment.... Perhaps all the sins and energies of the world are but the world's flight from an infinite blinding beam. (My 334)

The repeated sinning in an attempt to become "something not one's self" is a deceit since that antiself is most essentially the self. In creating his antiself through his art, the artist creates, as Ille says, not a book but himself. Thus, every new artifact is a means through which the artist begets himself again in a perpetually renewed process dependent upon the right kind of deceit. A deceit that is merely intellectual, such as the Lady's will be, does not involve the right kind of passion. Her rhetorical solution is a self-consuming abstraction through which she refuses to see her connection to the human condition.

Yeats connects this self-preserving deceit to the Daimon. In "Anima Hominis" he says, "I am persuaded that the Daimon delivers and deceives us" (My 336). In this essay, Yeats refers to his Daimon as an "illustrious dead man" (My 335) who seeks his opposite, his mask, through some living man. He had already discovered and communicated with his own Daimon in this sense, Leo Africanus. By "Anima Hominis," his view of the Daimon was shifting, however.[19] For one thing, he was beginning to explore the analogy between the struggle of the individual with his Daimon and the sexual relationship: "Then my imagination runs from Daimon to sweetheart, and I divine an analogy that evades the intellect.... it may be 'sexual love' which is founded on 'spiritual hate,' is an image of the warfare of man and Daimon;

and I even wonder if there may be some secret communion, some whispering in the dark between Daimon and sweetheart" (My 336). Looking back at "Anima Hominis" in a footnote dated February 1924, Yeats says, "I could not distinguish at the time between the permanent Daimon and the impermanent, who may be 'an illustrious dead man,' though I knew the distinction was there. I shall deal with the matter in *A Vision*" (My 335).

A Vision, 1925, contains a section entitled, "The Daimon, the Sexes, Unity of Being, Natural and Supernatural Unity," which demonstrates that the parallel between the warfare of man and Daimon and sexual relations no longer evaded Yeats.[20] He begins the section with a description that closely resembles the passage I have already quoted on Will and Body of Fate from "The Cones of Sexual Love": "The *Will* and the *Creative Mind* are in the light, but the *Body of Fate* working through accident, in dark, while *Mask* or *Image*, is a form selected instinctively for those emotional associations which come out of the dark" (V, 1925, 26-27). Again the pattern parallels Solomon and Sheba. Sheba is repeatedly connected with the dark. In one sense, she is Body of Fate (Chance) to Solomon's Will (Choice). But Yeats has not yet introduced the Daimon into the interplay. When he does so, he adds the suggestion of a third needed to stimulate creativity: "But there is another mind, or another part of our mind in this darkness, that is yet to its own perceptions in the light; and we in our turn are dark to that mind." Thus, the Daimon seems to be both "another" and a part of the individual's mind—a part of the mind that the individual experiences as separate from the self. When Sheba cries out in a "strange voice" at the height of her experience, she has awakened her own Daimon through her intercourse with Solomon.

Her sudden cry illustrates the process of allowing the Daimonic Creative Mind to flow through the individual:

> The daimon carries on her conflict, or friendship with a man, not only through the events of his life but in the mind itself, for she is in possession of the entire dark of the mind. The things we dream, or that come suddenly into our heads are therefore her *Creative Mind* (our *Creative Mind* is her *Body of Fate*) through which her energy, or bias, finds expression.... when however in *antithetical* man the *Daimonic mind* is permitted to flow through the events of his life (the *Daimonic Creative Mind*) and so to animate his creative mind, without putting out its light, there is Unity of Being. (V, 1925, 28)

The artist permits the light of the Daimonic Creative Mind to illuminate the darkness of his or her own Body of Fate (the events of this life) and this light animates and illumines his or her conscious Creative Mind. However, the light of the artist's conscious creative mind is not extinguished. Thus, his mind retains its separate identity in this union and can become separate again. This self-preserving light, a symbolic expression of virginity of soul, guarantees that the process will need to be continued: "He who attains Unity of Being is some man, who, while struggling with his fate and his destiny until every energy of his being has been roused, is content that he should so struggle with no final conquest" (28). The interplay of intercourse and virginity is implied in this passage. Sexual passion spurs the individual on, but this passion also arouses "every energy of his being" so that he refuses to lose his identity and must continue struggling.

The individual is seeking reintegration with his permanent self through his struggle with the Daimon, yet Yeats distinguishes between the Daimon and the Ghostly Self in *A Vision*, 1925. In his definition of the Ghostly Self, he says that it is "the permanent self, that which in the individual may correspond to the fixed circle of the figure, neither man nor *Daimon*, before the whirling of the Solar and Lunar cones" (V, 1925, 221). Once the Ghostly Self enters the realm of sexual desire, he has entered the temporal world of whirling cones and must struggle as Daimon with the temporal self. Right before this definition of the Ghostly Self, Yeats says of the Daimon that "she remains always in the Thirteenth Cycle," keeping an individual under "her tutelage" until "after many cycles man also inhabits the Thirteenth Cycle." She and the individual "are united for twelve cycles, and are then set free from one another" (220-21). As this passage makes explicit, the Daimon must be perceived as of the opposite sex for the interplay to be creative and ultimately redemptive. As in the *hieros gamos*, each individual is engaged in a triangular relationship involving the individual, the other physical partner, and the individual's Daimon also experienced as of the opposite sex.

The struggle with the Daimon continues until the individual achieves the perfection of the Thirteenth Cycle, a spherical perfection Yeats did believe was possible, but only after many reincarnations. With this in mind, "Leda and the Swan" can be seen as an attempt of the Ghostly Self to raise the individual to his permanent perfection in the Thirteenth Cycle, but, because Leda experiences the Swan as her Daimon—alien to herself and in sexual conflict with her—she, like Sheba, is left in the temporal realm and feels the virginity of her soul rather than the perfect harmony of union with her Ghostly Self.

The continued connection with this world through many reincarnations flows from the link between the Daimon, deception, and expiation that Yeats makes later in *A Vision* while discussing the state between death and rebirth. Speaking of the relationship between two people, such as husband and wife, who must play out all possible associations in repeated incarnations, Yeats states that "all strong passions are said to contain 'cruelty and deceit' and so to require expiation" (V, 1925, 233). He adds that we owe our need to continue expiating "not to that other but to our own Daimon which but for 'cruelty and deceit' had found the Daimon of that other." Our own Daimon is caught in the cruelties of the division into sexes—the original sin—and refuses perfect union. Instead, passion is aroused again, as it is in Sheba. A comment earlier in *A Vision* connects deception to the renewal of desire between Solomon and Sheba, their ultimate inability to unite Choice and Chance, and the intensity of their attempt: "Without this continual *discord* through *deception* there would be no conscience, no activity; and it will be seen later that *deception* is used as a technical term and may be substituted for 'desire.' Life is an endeavour, made vain by the Four Sails of its Mill, to come to a double contemplation, that of the chosen *Image*, that of the fated *Image*" (V, 1925, 25).

This process of expiation will eventually bring forgiveness in the form of reintegration with the permanent self, but before that deliverance, the cruelty and deceit of a man's strong passions will prepare him for rebirth. Yeats says that the spirit will "almost certainly pass to human rebirth because of its terror of what seems to be the loss of its own being" (V, 1925, 236). Thus, the self-preserving deceit of the virginity of the soul retains a crucial role in keeping the artist in contact with this world. Yeats himself, in his introduction to *A Vision*, 1925, says that he repeatedly murmured, "I have been part of it always and there is maybe no escape, forgetting and returning life after life like an insect in the roots of the grass" (xiii). So the Lover will be cradled in the arms of the Chambermaid in such total darkness and deception that he still thinks he is with the Lady after a year, while the Chambermaid, much like Daimon to him (as he is to her), will murmur over his dead form her three-fold identification of him with the worm, implying his readiness for rebirth and continued sinning and expiation. Yeats's comment that there is "no escape" from reincarnation suggests a lingering regret in his viewpoint, but he is much more accepting of his return as the "noisy and filthy thing" than he was in "The Dolls."

The deliberate choice of the cruelty and deceit of the temporal self over the harmony of the permanent self because of continued passion is dramatized in "The Hero, the Girl, and the Fool," first published in 1922. The Girl expresses the whole dilemma:

> I rage at my own image in the glass
> That's so unlike myself that when you praise it
> It is as though you praised another, or even
> Mocked me with praise of my mere opposite;
> And when I wake towards morn I dread myself,
> For the heart cries that what deception wins
> Cruelty must keep; therefore be warned and go
> If you have seen that image and not the woman. (VP 447-48)

She wants him to love her temporal self, not her permanent self from before the world was made.

Love militates against merely loving the temporal self, however. As Yeats had written in his journal in 1909, "In wise love each divines the high secret self of the other and, refusing to believe in the mere daily self, creates a mirror where the lover or the beloved sees an image to copy in daily life. Love also creates the mask" (M 145). The Daimon of each of them is seeking the Daimon of the other in order to re-create the perfect self of each. He puts it succinctly in *A Vision*, 1937: "Passionate love is from the *Daimon* which seeks by union with some other *Daimon* to reconstruct above the antinomies its own true nature" (238). There are several kinds of deceit involved. The divination and mirroring of the "high secret self" constitute an ennobling deceit by which each helps to bring the other to union with his or her own permanent self. But their mirrors are, inevitably, distorted, since each has not yet achieved reintegration with his or her own permanent self. The Girl concludes that their perceptions are perforce mixed with deceit because "only God has loved us for ourselves."

To get rid of that deceit they would have to eliminate passion and desire from their relationship. This she refuses to do, saying "But what care I that long for a man's love?" Then the Fool by the Roadside, a choric interpreter, clarifies that the Girl and the Hero will be reincarnated because of the failure of each to find in the other his or her high secret self or Daimon. As Yeats says in *A Vision*, 1937, "that bond may continue life after life, and this is just, for there had been no need of expiation had they seen in one another that other and not something else" (238). Someday, after they have run "from cradle to grave" and "from grave to cradle" many times, they will find "a faithful love, a faithful love,"[21] but a note Yeats attached to "An Image from a Past Life" insists that the cruelty and deceit of imperfect love must precede that moment: "It is therefore only after full atonement or expiation, perhaps after many lives, that a natural deep satisfying love becomes possible, and this love, in all subjective natures, must precede the Beatific Vision" (VP 823). Until the irrevocable union with the Ghostly Self in the Thirteenth Cycle, they will have to love the imperfect image in flesh and blood while always sensing, through the interplay of their Daimons, a residue and promise of their perfect selves.

In these passages in *A Vision*, Yeats repeatedly implies that the way to expiate sin is to sin again and again, reliving all the passions. Solomon describes the necessary process of cruelty and deceit in love:

> For though love has a spider's eye
> To find out some appropriate pain—
> Aye, though all passion's in the glance—
> For every nerve, and tests a lover
> With cruelties of Choice and Chance. (P 177)

Since the culmination of this process is the restoration of the world that preceded "all that the brigand apple brought," Yeats implies that this is the atonement for the primal sin. If Solomon and Sheba had fully expiated their sin, they would be released from recurrence and attain eternity.[22] But they remain "in the wrong" and thus must return to the "forbidden sacred grove": the ultimate forgiveness of the original sin demands that they sin again.

In that attempt, each again discovers the virginity of his or her own soul. Because of the cruelty and deceit of their passion, each of their Daimons remains virginal and is not reunited with the permanent self. In their failure to transcend, they re-enact the original sin of division. Thus, the virginity of their souls is the cause of their continued need for atonement. At the same time, this independent self-possession during bodily love is a prerequisite for their ability to maintain their separate identities in the attempt to become one. Otherwise, their souls, like the early poet-lover's or the Lady's, would consume themselves away in the abstract desire for the ideal image. In short, the virginity of their souls is the mark of the sin of division and the necessary condition for the continued expiation of that sin. The struggle with the Daimon in the darkness of cruelty and deceit will go on for many reincarnations before they become a "single light."

Vehicle and Questioner

The confessional roles of sinner and priest—participant and witness—that Yeats had started to emphasize in *Responsibilities* continue to be important in the context of his evolving theory of expiation. The participant, usually a woman, is intensely involved, like Sheba, but too self-possessed to transcend herself in total union. The detached witness, usually a man, analyzes and judges the passionate involvement, as Solomon does. As in all the other patterns I have analyzed in this chapter, this exchange between two separate individuals parallels and stimulates a process within each individual. This confessional interchange is especially crucial to the creative process in the antithetical artist, such as Yeats. The interchange between participant and witness, or, as Yeats designates them in *A Vision*, "vehicle" and "questioner," allows the division in the psyche of the antithetical artist to be a creative tension that leads to the remaking of the artist, rather than a sterile self-consuming abstraction.

One especially significant description of these roles in relation to the creative process of the antithetical artist occurs in *A Vision*, 1925:

> An *antithetical* inspiration may demand a separation of vehicle and questioner, a relation like that between Priest and Sybil, Socrates and Diotime, wandering magician and his scryer. This relation in its highest form, implies a constant interchange of office and such relations so cross and re-cross that a community may grow clairvoyant.... There must arise in the mind of one, where the bond is between two, a need for some form of truth so intense that the Automatic Faculty of the other grows as it were hollow to receive that truth. (248)

Although Yeats is alluding obliquely to the process by which he received the revelation of *A Vision* through his wife, the interchange between vehicle and questioner is repeatedly dramatized in his poetry of this period, as well. Much of his lyric poetry, especially in *Michael Robartes and the Dancer* (written during the communication of *A Vision*), is in dialogue form. As the title implies, this whole volume is in one sense a dialogue between the vehicle (the dancer or experiencer) and the questioner (Michael Robartes), a wise mediator who analyzes the experience.

Solomon and Sheba, in "Solomon and the Witch," also function in these roles, showing the "constant interchange of office" that Yeats mentions. Sheba is introduced as a Sybil,[23] "And thus declared that Arab Lady," declaiming her experience almost as if Solomon were not present. Solomon, he "who understood," explicates what her experience has revealed. They exchange roles when Sheba calls his interpretation into question by reminding him that "the world stays." In her final speech, she speaks directly to Solomon, witnessing consciously to her former experience, until she grows hungry to become a direct vehicle of truth again. She needs the interchange with Solomon and within herself to facilitate the revelation of the "strange voice" through her. The interchange does not bring an end to division, but she clearly experiences joy at the need to re-create their failure to overcome the sin of division. Yeats is preparing for the pattern in "The Three Bushes" where the Chambermaid questions the Lady as to what sort of man is coming, receives the revelation through her direct experience with the Lover, then again questions how he came there before she becomes vehicle again and delivers her prophecy about the worm. This interchange leads to forgiveness when the Chambermaid recounts her experience in her "full confession." The Priest, the questioner and judge in the confession, becomes vehicle in turn in the planting of the third bush and the final incantatory murmuring of "O my dear, O my dear."

Yeats dramatizes this interchange as between two separate individuals in "Solomon and the Witch"; however, he often images this process as taking place within the strong central "I" figure in his powerfully self-critical poems, such as "The Tower" and "Among School Children." The narrator of "The Tower" functions as a penitent, reviewing his past, questioning himself, and finally finding forgiveness by allowing rejuvenation to flow through him. In Section I, he proclaims his role as questioner of his past: "For I would ask a question of them all" (P 195). He conjures up exempla from those who formerly lived in his tower and from his own creative past, hoping that his personae will reveal to him how to face his own aging. This questioner has trouble in establishing the correct balance implied in the interchange of roles in the passage from *A Vision*. He is too detached from Mrs. French, too painfully involved with Hanrahan. Finally the passion that Hanrahan revives in the narrator allows him to direct his most intense question to himself and see himself objectively (as "you") in the revelation that comes to him:

> Does the imagination dwell the most
> Upon a woman won or woman lost?
> If on the lost, admit you turned aside
> From the great labyrinth out of pride,
> Cowardice, some silly over-subtle thought
> Or anything called conscience once. (P 197)

Through the process of questioning and evaluating the others, he has awakened the Sybil within himself and finally allows her to speak through him. Realizing that his greatest sin was in his relationship with women, he now castigates himself for turning aside from the labyrinth of sexual involvement through his former "over-subtle thought," a form of escapism that he will re-create in the Lady of "The Three Bushes." At present, he shares the ability of Hanrahan to "plunge ... into the labyrinth of another's being," but he senses his continuing attraction to noninvolvement. He recommends a balance between passion and detachment as he remakes his soul in the final section, but he has had to experience the extremes of each before he can reach this balance.

In "Among School Children," Yeats again embodies the interplay of vehicle and questioner in the antithetical artist and compares and contrasts this divisiveness with the oneness of more primary figures. As in "The Tower," the questioner dominates the first part of the poem as the sixty-year-old smiling public man walks "through the long schoolroom questioning" (P 215). The children's eyes in turn question him and he delves into memory to find the self-justification required by both their stares and their similarity to his memory of Maud Gonne. The question that has plagued him again and again in *The Tower* returns: why must he (and Maud Gonne) grow old? He almost exchanges the role of questioner for vehicle, thus becoming oracle to himself, at the end of the third stanza:

> And thereupon my heart is driven wild:
> She stands before me as a living child. (P 216)

But he remains too self-conscious to stop being the questioner and returns to a coolly detached inquiry about her in the next stanza where he sees her face as an art object fashioned consciously by "Quattrocentro finger" rather than as a living reality.

In the first stanzas, his imaginative process is equally conscious and labored. Rather than presenting metaphor directly, he explains the process of analogy to the reader. He does this most markedly in the even-numbered stanzas. The first stanza presents the occasion directly, the second draws an analogy in his memory. He belabors his mental process, saying "I dream of a Ledean body": she is not present and she is only like Leda, rather than the living image of Helen. Later in the stanza, when he mentions the "two natures blent / Into a sphere," he maps out the source of the image, "Plato's parable," and his interpretation of the image, "the yolk and white of one shell." That explanation, as I have indicated, is extremely important, but the poetic process is too consciously analyzed within the poem for any passionate involvement to be conveyed. Then an attempt at directness followed by a return to a discussion is again the pattern in the third and fourth stanzas. Toward the end of stanza four, he mocks his whole imaginative process in the comic alliteration and mock heroic deflation of himself:

> And I though never of Ledean kind
> Had pretty plumage once—enough of that.

At exactly halfway through the poem, he arrives at the empty image of himself as "a comfortable kind of old scarecrow."

The poem seems to have petered out to its natural end. However, the imagery of hollowness used to depict both himself and Maud Gonne in stanza four suggests, in the parallel to his comment on antithetical inspiration, that his mind has grown "hollow to receive the truth." Accordingly, a sharp intensification of the poetic imagery takes place in the fifth stanza and is maintained throughout the rest of the poem. The first stanzas dramatize the difficulty the poet has when he is trying too hard to force his imagination. As a result, he is left, in Coleridge's terminology, in the associative realm of fancy. His evaluative, questioning consciousness is not in contact with a vehicle for truth from beyond his conscious power, as Sheba's and Leda's are. Paradoxically, when he mockingly accepts his powerlessness as the old scarecrow, power flows through him.

The question that constitutes the fifth stanza is quite different from those that preceded it. The poetry is more concentrated and metaphorically direct. Yeats's explanation of "honey of generation" is in a footnote, not in the poem. He is almost overcome by the poignancy of the simultaneous images of himself as infant betrayed into a cradle and as a white-haired sixty-year-old approaching death. This question shows that his need for truth has become intense; he is ready for the revelation. At the same time, however, he is still questioning the value of his birth, if old age and death ensue. In stanza six, he searches for an answer among the great philosophers but the very concrete imagery—"played the taws," "bottom," "golden-thighed," "fingered"— demonstrates that he has already refused an abstract answer. Even the scarecrow image of the futility of their philosophic systems is created with the immediacy of a photograph. The poet is now passionately involved in the poetic process.

He becomes a vehicle in the middle of the seventh stanza, calling out to the self-born Presences as if welcoming them into his embrace, or allowing their creative power to flow through him and leaving his own "enterprise" behind. Then the truth is revealed through him in the last four lines of the last stanza. His tone is oracular and self-assured as if no question remains. The revelation condemns his own approach in the first half of the poem, as well as that of Maud Gonne, mothers, philosophers, and nuns.

Only the tree and the dancer are self-born[24] in an integrated oneness that admits of no division, no aging, no conflict. The harmony within the tree and dancer is complete. The "great-rooted blossomer" is totally simple from root to flower. The dancer's body and the brightening glance of her soul are equally attuned to the music and inseparable. The tree and dancer embody the state of "uncomposite blessedness" that Michael Robartes describes at the end of "Michael Robartes and the Dancer":

> . . . all beautiful women may
> Live in uncomposite blessedness,
> And lead us to the like—if they
> Will banish every thought, unless
> The lineaments that please their view
> When the looking-glass is full,
> Even from the footsole think it too. (P 176)

This kind of labor blossoms and dances in its utter simplicity.

The uncomposite tree is self-born, since its existence requires no intercourse, no conflict with anything outside itself. Yeats describes such a tree[25] at more length in the poem that follows "Among School Children" in *The Tower*, "Colonus' Praise":

> And yonder in the gymnasts' garden thrives
> The self-sown, self-begotten shape that gives
> Athenian intellect its mastery,
> Even the grey-leaved olive-tree
> Miracle-bred out of the living stone;
> Nor accident of peace nor war
> Shall wither that old marvel, for
> The great grey-eyed Athena stares thereon. (P 218)

This tree, miracle-bred without intercourse as Athena was, can never wither, nor is it governed by the realm of accident. The narrator's questions at the end of "Among School Children," which imply division by the very fact that they were asked, would be meaningless to this olive, or to the chestnut and dancer. Yet, these questions are highly significant in characterizing the narrator. He is in near ecstasy, but the questioner within him remains active. He is slightly separated from the tree and the dancer, passionately desirous of sharing their blossoming and dancing labor, but unable to do so completely. The laborious progress of the poem has finally yielded an image of his opposite, but as antithetical artist he cannot yield his consciousness and join in the dance with the single-mindedness of the dancer. The question reasserts itself. In its ambiguity the final question epitomizes the two roles within him. It can be read as meaning that we must give up the need to know one from the other, that we must participate as fully as possible in the experience. Or, if "how can we" is interpreted as "tell us how to," the final question can imply that the ultimate knowledge we can have is the ability to separate the dancer from the dance in objective detachment.

The difference between the dancer and the narrator is crucial to Yeats's views of himself as artist and to the analogy to the tragedy of sexual intercourse in the artistic process. He is strongly attracted to such a self-begotten state. In "Anima Mundi," he describes a rhythmic total self-possession very much like the dancer's: "When all sequence comes to an end, time comes to an end, and the soul puts on the rhythmic or spiritual body or luminous body and contemplates all the events of its memory and every possible impulse in an eternal possession of itself in one single moment" (My 357). Such moments are ultimate; to be self-born is to be in the Thirteenth Cycle, to have achieved reintegration with the Ghostly Self. In the same year Yeats wrote "Among School Children," he revised an early poem "The Countess Cathleen in Paradise," where, as he wrote to Olivia Shakespear in 1927, "the dancer Cathleen has become heaven itself" (L 731). In other words, for Yeats to stop questioning the dancer and join in the dance, he would have to leave the temporal and enter the realm of the eternal, becoming "self-begotten" like the dancer. As he explains in A Vision, he does hope someday, after many cycles, to achieve this perfection, but not for many lives to come.

As antithetical artist, his creative process is one of continual self-begetting, not one through which he is permanently self-begotten. The struggle involved in the slight separation between vehicle and questioner, participant and witness, keeps him always striving to re-create himself. As in the other processes I have been analyzing from this period, the artist is attracted to the self-begotten state, but the divisive virginity of the soul—the conscious separation that marks the antithetical artist—is a pledge of his failure to achieve this oneness. The same self-possession, nevertheless, urges him to keep trying to be reunited with his self-begotten, permanent self.

At times, such as in the last stanza of "Among School Children," Yeats comes close to ecstatic release from the need to know and question. He describes the bliss of such moments in "Anima Mundi" (and later in Section IV of "Vacillation"): "Everything fills me with affection, I have no longer any fears or any needs; I do not even remember that this happy mood must come to an end. It seems as if the vehicle had suddenly grown pure and far extended and so luminous that the images from *Anima Mundi*, embodied there and drunk with that sweetness, would, like a country drunkard who has thrown a wisp into his own thatch, burn up time" (My 365). These spots of time, however pleasant, would be detrimental to an antithetical artist if prolonged, nevertheless. Yeats begins his description of this experience by saying that it sometimes comes upon him when he is reading his own verse and "instead of discovering new technical flaws, I read with all the excitement of the first writing." The self-critical evaluater is silenced: he is uncompositely happy. Yet, such a state would soon lead to stagnancy, unless he were transported permanently to a realm where birth did not require the bruising of the body.

Yeats also dramatizes his strong attraction to such conflict-free moments in "Demon and Beast," in *Michael Robartes and the Dancer.* He portrays a Wordsworthian moment where, in a mood of "aimless joy," he stops beside a little lake to watch two birds and

> Being no more demoniac
> A stupid happy creature
> Could rouse my whole nature. (P 186)

Demon and beast, like all of Yeats's contraries, parallel a whole matrix of oppositions, among which are Daimon or questioner and body or vehicle. For a moment, he is not simultaneously participant and slightly separated, detached questioner. The pain of division ceases and his whole nature responds single-mindedly to the bird.[26]

In the next stanza, however, the self-questioner points out the danger in such experiences:

> Yet I am certain as can be
> That every natural victory
> Belongs to beast or demon,
> That never yet had freeman
> Right mastery of natural things,
> And merely growing old, that brings
> Chilled blood, this sweetness brought.

For the artist of Phase Seventeen, the Daimonic Man, this is self-declension, not self-begetting. He will be merely "withering into eighty years" (My 342) as he accused Wordsworth of doing. He would like this peace to last, just as he is intensely attracted to the blossoming and dancing kind of labor, but he is not yet among the self-begotten, and never will be if he stops questioning. The man with sixty winters on his head whose blood has not chilled into complacency, who still feels compelled to try to separate the tree into "the leaf, the blossom or the bole" and "the dancer from the dance," is continuing to compensate for the "pang of his birth," by re-creating himself continuously in his art.

The primary artist can, perhaps, create from a more unified state that resembles the self-begotten tree in "Colonus' Praise." Directly before the passage describing the separation of vehicle and questioner in the antithetical artist, Yeats characterizes the process in the primary artist: "*Primary* man in certain periods of thought . . . is able 'By dreadful abstinence and conquering penance of the mutinous flesh' to keep his *Automatic Faculty* from desire and fear—hence the symbolic value given to chastity by *primary* philosophers—and so be both vehicle and questioner. His mind has but a single direct movement which may be wholly dominated" (V, 1925, 248). Chastity does not lead to a desirous, violated soul in the primary artist. The souls of primary artists are naturally virginal; they do not need separation followed by violent conjunction, as Sheba and Leda do, to discover the ever-virgin quality of their psyches. Their inspiration can grow, like the olive or chestnut tree, in a single upward movement that is unaffected by the accidents surrounding it. Like the "self-sown" olive tree enclosed "in the gymnasts' garden," the primary thinker needs no intercourse with others, nor need he experience the opposing principles within himself as other.

Both kinds of inspiration are possible, but the individual must follow his true phase. "Demon and Beast" and later the Lady in "The Three Bushes" demonstrate the danger of this chaste approach for the antithetical artist, however. The Lady's mind, in its calculating cleverness and natural bent toward perception of dichotomy, has anything but the single movement that rewards the creative chastity of the primary artist. Vehicle and questioner are clearly separated within her, and her soul is violated with desire and fear; yet she refuses the conflict that would bring lasting inspiration to such an antithetical mind.

To continue being creative, the antithetical artist must beget himself or herself continually by entering into contact with another. Because of the constant interchange of office between vehicle and questioner, imaged so often in Yeats as sexual intercourse, the conflict is never complete. He is always in the process of re-creating himself and evaluating himself as he does so. Yeats reflects the difference between the primary and antithetical approaches in the contrast between the figures in the second and third stanzas in "Colonus' Praise." Athena with her chaste olive tree in the second stanza is contrasted to Demeter, the Great Mother, in the third. The imagery

surrounding Demeter—"drunken by the water," "plucked a flower" (P 218)—
suggests sexual involvement, as does, of course, the mention of her daughter.
She is the sated one, but, as Great Mother, she is also goddess of the
psychologically virginal. Here, she displays the virginity of her soul in her
ability to articulate her loss in song, even as she experiences the grief of it. The
present participles connected to the water suggest that her ever-virgin soul
renews itself continually, but not by isolation. She plucks the flower; she feels
her loss; but she finds inspiration for her song in this process.

The glittering, "abounding Cephisus" by which Demeter sings parallels
Homer's "abounding glittering jet" that springs from "self-delight" (P 200) in
"Meditations in Time of Civil War" (1923). Athena's olive tree and the
chestnut have never known the fall into division and loss that Demeter and
Homer, who has no song but "original sin" in "Vacillation," know. Demeter's
and Homer's self-delighting is not self-born, but the recovered radical
innocence of "A Prayer for my Daughter." This innocence, which depends on
a continual self-begetting process, allows for sweetness in the face of the
violence that surrounds the individual.

In "Meditations in Time of Civil War," Yeats wishes for a self-delighting
sweetness and implies that virginity of soul will help achieve that self-delight.
He longs for an art that, like the moon, is not changeless and connects this
changing, yet not bitter, art to virginity by a series of allusions throughout the
poem. In section I, where the abounding jet appears, he also mentions Juno,
who renewed her virginity repeatedly by bathing in a river. The major allusion
to renewed virginity as the source of sweetness, even in the midst of violence,
occurs in section VI, "The Stare's Nest at My Window." Here, Yeats
repeatedly begs, "O honey bees, / Come build in the empty house of the stare"
(P 205). One important source of this imagery, showing Yeats's ongoing use of
sources that involve mythological figures who are psychologically virginal, is
Porphyry's "On the Cave of the Nymphs," an interpretation of Homer's
cave.[27]

Porphyry says that the priestesses of Demeter were called bees and that
the moon "who is queen of generation was denominated by the ancients as a
bee."[28] Thus, the independent virgin priestesses of the Great Mother, who
regained their virginity through the *hieros gamos*, were symbolized as bees.[29]
Another passage in Porphyry that ends in an especially suggestive phrase
associates fountains and rivers to these women: "fountains and rivers are
proper to aquatic nymphs, and especially to the nymphs called by the ancients
soul...i.e. artificers of sweetness or bees."[30] That they are "artificers of
sweetness" implies that they must build this quality; it is not self-begotten, just
as Yeats, who is longing for the self-abounding spring of sweetness, wants the
bees to build in the house of the stare. Taylor's juxtaposition of
"promiscuously" and "pristine" in the following description of those who are

not overcome by the whirl of generation also suggests regained virginity: "But it is here necessary to observe that they did not promiscuously call all souls descending into the whirl of generation bees; but only those who, while residing in this fluctuating region, acted justly; and who, after being in a manner acceptable to the divinities returned to their pristine felicity."[31] With Porphyry in mind, the fountain and bees in "Meditations in Time of Civil War" imply that the sweetness that Yeats seeks is the renewed virginity of his soul. This is reinforced in the "daemonic images" of the ladies on the backs of unicorns, traditionally associated with virgins, in the last section of the poem. Such a sweetness would not rob him of greatness as he feared in the first section; rather, it would spur him on to seek his full potential.

The references to the bees of Demeter in Porphyry also help explicate the sweetness Yeats attaches to the radical innocence he hopes his daughter will recover in "A Prayer for my Daughter" (1919). This poem is his fullest description of the proper process whereby the antithetical individual can re-create herself or himself without bitterness. He, Maud Gonne, and, as the beginning of the poem implies, the world have grown bitter. His prayer for Anne is a wish that she will find sweetness in the midst of violence. He knows, as he implies in "My Descendants" in "Meditations in Time of Civil War," that he, as her father, cannot give her a self-delighting inner source of sweetness: she will have to beget herself in radical innocence.

The only time he calls her "my" child is at the beginning where he stresses how little protection he can give her against the howling storm. As her father, he has betrayed her into a cradle by giving her life: she has entered the world of division and violence. If she is to sustain herself in the conflict, she will have to develop her own inner strength. In earlier drafts, Yeats had stressed her ancestry, linking her to all her forebears who had slept "under this cradle-hood" and addressing her directly as "my daughter" later in the poem.[32] In the final version, he distances himself by calling her "this young child" in the second stanza and "she" throughout the rest. Her father can neither stop the storm from getting more fierce, as it does in the second stanza, nor implant true innocence and beauty within her.

He stresses that all her virtues should be cultivated, not innate. He hopes she will not be too naturally beautiful, so that she will not overlook the development of kindness and friendship. She will have to learn courtesy since

> Hearts are not had as a gift but hearts are earned
> By those who are not entirely beautiful. (P 189)

He alternates between describing what he hopes she will become and what he and Maud Gonne have done. His own mind has "dried up of late"—the self-abounding spring gone dry. "The loveliest woman born" has bartered that beauty for hatred, rather than cherishing and cultivating it. He hopes that his daughter will "become a flourishing hidden tree"—that she will regain the integrity her father can only gaze upon at the end of "Among School Children."

In the second-to-last stanza, Yeats gives the fullest description in any of his poems of the self-engendering soul. The tone of this stanza is subtly different. He drops the conditional tone of the rest of his prayer. Here, he seems to have a vision of her power if his prayer is answered. Since the stanza that precedes this one ends in a question, his typical pattern of questioner and vehicle is functioning. He has walked and prayed and judged his own past and finally revelation breaks through:

> Considering that, all hatred driven hence,
> The soul recovers radical innocence
> And learns at last that it is self-delighting,
> Self-appeasing, self-affrighting,
> And that its own sweet will is Heaven's will;
> She can, though every face should scowl
> And every windy quarter howl
> Or every bellows burst, be happy still.

He sees her as giving birth to herself again—still surrounded by storm but invincibly happy from within. Her innocence is recovered in the midst of immersion in experience. She is not to be locked in the inexperienced innocence of the Lady in "The Three Bushes" and the early poet-lover. "Recovered radical innocence" involves intercourse with life, as the mention of her bridegroom in the last stanza reinforces, but her self-delighting soul cannot be violated. Her "own sweet will" is that of the independent virgin.

She is united to Heaven's will because she accepts her Chance as her Choice. "Though every face should scowl," she does not rail against the tragedy of alienation. Bloom comments on the solipsistic nature of the virginity of her soul[33]—a judgment that is partially justified. Yeats does imply that the individual is ultimately responsible for forming his or her own soul, as his fondness for the phrase "making my soul" attests. That soul, however, is not cut off from interrelationships with other people, the universe, and God. The child is born into a world of violence and, even after learning that her will is heaven's will, she will confront scowls, wind, and bursting angry bellows. "Arrogance and hatred" will still be sold in the thoroughfares if she cares to barter her innocence and beauty for them. The "self-delighting" soul will definitely have an effect on others and be affected by others—that is the point of the Maud Gonne-Yeats parallel throughout the poem and the mention of her bridegroom at the end. In fact, Yeats, in the fifth stanza, hints that the "glad kindness" of his own young wife may help him to recover some sweetness himself.

Yeats does not suggest that his daughter originally created herself. He addresses his prayer directly to God in the drafts, but downplays what she has been given to emphasize how she cultivates it in the final version. The line "its own sweet will is Heaven's will" could imply a solipsistic self-deification; however, the emphasis on learning to overcome hatred suggests that the sweetness within her is not self-glorifying. If she can accept her place in the universe without bitterness, then this inner sweetness will radiate from her as well, as she dispenses "magnanimities of sound." In this sense, her self-delighting soul is far from solipsistic; it is a necessary prerequisite for turning outward with love.

The three present participles linked to "self" suggest that the process is ongoing. She must continue engendering this self-begetting joy within herself because the storm will not cease, nor can she hide from it. His designation of the soul as "self-affrighting" implies that conflict will continue to arise from within her, as well, but nothing can murder her recovered radical innocence since it can always renew itself. Yeats connects the same process of uniting Chance and Choice and a self-affrighting quality to the art of Dante and Villon in his *Autobiography*:

> The two halves of their nature are so completely joined that they seem to labour for their objects, and yet to desire whatever happens, being at the same instant predestinate and free, creation's very self. We gaze at such men in awe, because we gaze not at a work of art, but at the re-creation of the man through his art, the birth of a new species of man and it may seem that the hairs of our head stand up, because that birth, that re-creation, is from terror. (A 165)

This is the goal of the antithetical artist: to remake himself continuously through his art. As usual, Yeats stands apart, gazing at such self-begetting artists, just as he gazes at the tree, the dancer, and his daughter. The opposing factors in his nature are not so "completely joined." His art is engendered from the slight separation between vehicle and questioner that never fully disappears in his work, but the struggle between them continues to be creative and, in the context of Yeats's theory of atonement and expiation, redemptive. Yeats is still struggling with his own bitterness, but in imagining the process by which his daughter can re-create herself in self-delighting sweetness, he has relived and evaluated his own and Maud Gonne's failures and forgiven their bitterness in the intensity of his vision of his daughter's recovered radical innocence. Literature still functions as the forgiveness of sins for him, but this forgiveness is now an ongoing process, not a cataclysmic transformation. He returns to the questioning mode in the last stanza, as his process of self-begetting and expiating continues.

There is a suggestion of lasting beauty and joy in the last stanza, nevertheless. The happiness his daughter has cultivated within herself, symbolized by the spreading laurel and horn of plenty, clearly outlasts mere natural beauty or the angry bellows of hatred. Like Dante and Villon, she remakes herself into an artifice. This product of regeneration, although not eternal, does last longer than the vegetative world of generation.

Yeats's theory of self-regeneration as a semipermanent artifice—such as the three bushes at the end of that ballad—is most manifest in the golden bird of "Sailing to Byzantium." Here, too, the ongoing interchange of the roles of vehicle and questioner in the antithetical artist keeps that regenerated artifice in the realm of self-begetting mortality, while promising self-begotten immortality. To be gathered into "the artifice of eternity" is awesome, but it does not remove him completely from the world of sin and division.

The bird is not in isolation, nor is there a perfectly androgynous, sexless society in Byzantium.[34] Given Yeats's usual connotations for yawning and stretching,[35] the "drowsy" emperor may be kept awake so that he can engage in sexual relations, but not be "caught in that sensual music" (P 193) of the vegetative world. By crossing the water (a symbol of regeneration in neo-Platonism), Yeats has left the world of the once-begotten—the "fish, flesh, or fowl" that are "begotten, born, and die"—to become a chorus and motivator in a world where the abounding sweetness of the ever-virgin soul can clap and sing in spite of its tattered mortal dress. The emperor and the Lord and Ladies of Byzantium, like the later Lover and the Chambermaid, are inspired to regeneration.

In this sense, they are vehicles of passionate experience while the bird is a detached questioner spurring them on to "try again" to form the indivisible sphere. At the same time, he, too, is a vehicle, "hammered" into his artificial form by experience. The alchemical symbolism of the golden bird attests that the artist imagines himself as coming very close to the total reintegration of his psyche, but like Leda's and Sheba's momentary ecstasy in the *hieros gamos* and the moment of illumination when the conscious mind allows the Daimonic Creative Mind to flow through it, the golden bird's eternity is only an artifice. His tactile form guarantees that his detached, witnessing role is not permanent. Since even golden birds eventually decay, he will once again participate directly in the original sin. The divided nature of the antithetical artist, perpetuated by his ever-virgin soul, will demand the continued interchange of roles between vehicle and questioner as he begets himself continually, singing of what is "to come" before his own release to eternity.

From Bitterness to Blessing

Upon rereading *The Tower* in April 1928, Yeats was "astonished at its bitterness" (L 742). *The Tower* evidences his acceptance of the failure of love to unite the antinomies and implies his concomitant belief in reincarnation, but he can only imagine self-abounding sweetness in the midst of this world for his daughter, not feel it within himself. His self-projection as the golden bird suggests his residual desire to be transmuted to alchemical gold—a desire reinforced by his disgust with the world of "fish, flesh, or fowl." That he has attained resignation, but has not fully reconciled himself to his failure to transform himself and his beloved to golden oneness is most poignantly evident in "A Man Young and Old."

"A Woman Young and Old" was obviously meant to parallel "A Man Young and Old," since both contain eleven short lyrics, both recount the emotional and sexual history of the persona, and both end with an adaption of a chorus from Sophocles; yet "A Woman Young and Old" lacks the rancor of "A Man Young and Old." Although the two sequences were written simultaneously, Yeats kept "A Woman Young and Old" out of *The Tower* and put it in *The Winding Stair* (1929)[1] where its positive attitude matches that of poems such as "A Dialogue of Self and Soul." In fact the pivotal poems of "A Woman Young and Old," "Consolation" and "Chosen," share the diction and viewpoint of the culmination of "A Dialogue of Self and Soul," written in the spring of 1928. "A Man Young and Old," "A Woman Young and Old," and "A Dialogue of Self and Soul" form a transitional unit embodying Yeats's shift from a rather bitter resignation to death to a joyous celebration of reincarnation in this imperfect world.

The last two stanzas of "A Dialogue of Self and Soul" proclaim his attitude at the end of this inner journey:

> I am content to live it all again
> And yet again, if it be life to pitch
> Into the frog-spawn of a blind man's ditch,
> A blind man battering blind men;

> Or into that most fecund ditch of all,
> The folly that man does
> Or must suffer, if he woos
> A proud woman not kindred of his soul.
>
> I am content to follow to its source
> Every event in action or in thought;
> Measure the lot; forgive myself the lot!
> When such as I cast out remorse
> So great a sweetness flows into the breast
> We must laugh and we must sing,
> We are blest by everything,
> Everything we look upon is blest. (P 236)

Yeats, as antithetical artist (one "such as I"), celebrates his need to return to the "frog-spawn" of this world in repeated incarnations. He connects this need to the pattern he was soon to designate as "the tragedy of sexual intercourse": the "fecund ditch" spawns more suffering and divisiveness because of the virginity of soul of the "I" and of "the proud woman not kindred of his soul." By this point, however, Yeats forgives himself for his failure to transcend and finds great sweetness in blessing and being blest by concrete things. He traces the emotional and imaginative journey that brought him to this attitude in his reliving of his most painful memories in "A Man Young and Old," followed by his imaginative projection of the more assured psychological virginity and willingness to sin again of "A Woman Young and Old." Thus, these two sequences embody the same journey and progress to the same convictions as "The Three Bushes" sequence.

"A Man Young and Old"

The narrator's bitterness is especially evident in his first two poems in "A Man Young and Old," where he re-experiences all the frustration and helplessness of his first love for a cold moon-maiden, clearly a figure based on Yeats's interest in mythology and the occult and his love for Maud Gonne. The Man Young and Old, although designated as an "old countryman" (VP 451) when these poems were first published, is a transparent persona through whom Yeats recalls his own relationship with women and with the muse. Through the stone-moon imagery initiated in the first poem, Yeats evaluates the continuing connection between his lifelong interest in mythology and the occult and his creativity in both love and art. By the end of this sequence, the stone image is especially significant, since through it Yeats demonstrates his shift from his early wish as an adept to transform all to perfection to his mature realization that he must nurture the imperfect, transformation-resisting matter of this world.

In "First Love," the woman is the ideal, physically virginal beloved that Yeats connected with both the moon and the Rose in his early poetry and would portray again in the Lady of "The Three Bushes." This first love is now long past, however, as he looks back on the folly of his youth. In the second stanza, he describes the transformation he, as a young adept, hoped to achieve and his inability at that point to accept his failure. He "laid a hand" (P 221) on her, not as a gesture of blessing what she actually was, but in order to transform her "heart of stone" to glowing gold. He was disheartened to find that she remained untransformed stone.

Yeats commented to T. Sturge Moore in 1929 that "sexual desire dies because every touch consumes the Myth, and yet a Myth that cannot be so consumed becomes a spectre."[2] The lover and beloved in "First Love" have both refused to "consume the Myth." She retains her position as reigning goddess, consuming the stars around her rather than responding to his touch. He cannot accept what he finds when he touches her. In the last stanza, they are much like spectres, she still a goddess and he "maundering here, and maundering there / Emptier of thought." The only transformation that took place was the violation of his own soul through his frustrated longing for her.

In this context, the title of the second poem, "Human Dignity," seems ironic, especially since they both still seem to be spectres in the first stanza— she with "no comprehension," he like "a scene / Upon a painted wall" (P 222). The tense has shifted to the present, however. The poet-lover is no longer merely looking back but now reliving all the self-pitying, frustrated, celibate longings of first love. He is sterile and withdrawn, mute about what he longs for most:

> So like a bit of stone I lie
> Under a broken tree.
> I could recover if I shrieked
> My heart's agony
> To passing bird, but I am dumb
> From human dignity.

This broken tree, as well as the shriek that he shuns here, will re-appear in clearly sexual contexts later in the sequence, but at this point he tries to mask his emotional and sexual needs under this false human dignity.

His mute dignity is really a refusal to accept the human condition with all its transience. Rather than identify with the "passing bird" and express his frustration, he recoils into a shell. In 1926, in a provocative essay on "The Cherry Tree Carol," called "The Need for Audacity of Thought," Yeats wrote that the incarnation involves "the indignity of human birth" (UnP 462), which suggests that this man's dignity is an attempt to escape that "indignity." This is not the self-preserving deceit that Yeats had been developing since

"Discoveries," but a self-pitying canker, like the Lady's, that leaves his soul utterly violated, while his body remains frustratedly virginal. He is easy prey for the mermaid who laughingly plucks him from the surface and plunges into the deeps in the third poem.

"The Mermaid" continues to stress his lack of self-possession and the lack of a realistic perspective between lovers. Although this plunge does suggest an allusion to Yeats's first physical love,[3] the "cruel happiness" (P 222) of this mermaid is not simply a parallel to Yeats's early affair with Diana Vernon (Olivia Shakespear). Yeats's repeated protestations of Diana Vernon's great gentleness in his descriptions of her suggest that he is recalling his own continued inability to rid his heart of the image of his moon-maiden (as he recounted in "The Lover mourns for the Loss of Love") rather than portraying Diana Vernon as the mermaid. In mythology, the mermaid is the negative manifestation of the virgin, who lures men to their death.[4] The Irish Cailleac Bare, who is mentioned five times in the different versions of the autobiographical *The Speckled Bird* where the young hero is fascinated with virginity, lives in water and drags her male victims to their deaths under the waters.[5] This figure is associated with the young Yeats's fear of being engulfed and losing his creative impulse in a sexual relationship; however, her power comes from the man's attraction to physical virginity.

The young man, like Michael, the hero of *The Speckled Bird*, is controlled by his longing for the moon-maiden. He is still projecting all the blame onto her: she is cruel; he is totally passive, a victim. The mermaid's action symbolizes the negative effect of that frustratedly celibate relationship on the young Yeats, as he is drowned in longing, while afraid to drink. This is not the fecund ditch that he will choose at the end of "A Dialogue of Self and Soul"; rather, he is submerged in a romantic dream world—otherwise the mermaid would have no control over him.

He shifts from being prey to being hunter in "The Death of the Hare," finally beginning to take some responsibility for his actions. He has been torturer, as well as victim. He has ensnared the hare, just as the mermaid engulfed him. If the woman equated symbolically with the hare alludes to Iseult Gonne, as the hare does in "Two Songs of a Fool," this memory seems to be out of order in the man's recollection, but Yeats is not presenting his emotional history with historical accuracy. He balances the young man who seems powerless in connection with the moon-maiden with a lover who uses his own power to master a wild young woman. He enjoys his power to change her, until he realizes how destructive that bridling is. He is brought back abruptly from his misconceptions by the untransformed image of primary suffering in "the death of a hare" (P 223).

The first four poems, which deal with his youth, have all involved transformation. He is transfigured to a lout in the first, to a stone in the second, to a dead body in the third, to a hunter in the fourth. She, meanwhile, is moon, mermaid, hare. At the end of "The Death of the Hare," his focus is returned to untransformed matter, but when he shifts to his old age in "The Empty Cup," the persona continues his alchemical allusions: he has not yet abandoned his hope that he can transmute the stone to gold.

These alchemical allusions are especially significant since Yeats used such references in his earlier sequences about his relationship with his beloved. In *The Wind among the Reeds*, a set of interrelated sequences in which Yeats uses Aedh, Robartes, and Hanrahan as his principal mouthpieces, he explores his power as an adept in relation to his ideal beloved. The eight poems in the "Raymond Lully and his wife Pernella" sequence that begins *The Green Helmet and Other Poems*, are supposedly spoken by an adept to his virginal *soror mystica*. The group of poems about Maud Gonne in *The Wild Swans at Coole* are again filled with alchemical symbolism, such as the phoenix. Although Yeats has achieved a resigned attitude in both the Raymond Lully sequence and the poems in *The Wild Swans at Coole*, he has not fully affirmed the failure of the love between Maud Gonne and himself. He seems to have put their relationship resignedly into the past in "His Phoenix," but her image surfaces, still violating his soul, in "A Deep-sworn Vow." He comes much closer to celebrating his loss of her in the poems relating to old age in "A Man Young and Old."

The empty cup he describes in the fifth poem suggests many symbolic allusions—the grail, the cups that the nymphs are connected with in Porphyry, or, in general terms, the womb. This poem was sent to Olivia Shakespear in a letter with a comment about the wasted opportunities of youth. The situation and biographical parallel is the same as in "The Lover mourns for the Loss of Love" and "A Deep-sworn Vow": his yearning for the moon goddess (Maud Gonne) interfered with his pleasure with Diana Vernon. The second half of the poem where he bemoans how dry the cup now is could merely reinforce his repeated lamentations over his decrepit body in *The Tower*. The once full cup also relates to his alchemical quest, however. As Keith points out, this poem is reminiscent of a passage in the *Autobiography* where an "old white-haired Oxfordshire clergyman" tells Yeats how he once made the elixir of life and put it away on a shelf.[6] The old alchemist concludes, "I meant to drink it when I was an old man, but when I got it down the other day it had all dried up" (A 184). The crazed, sleepless state that the persona admits to at the end of "The Empty Cup" implies that Yeats, like the old alchemist, still hopes that the alchemical transformation is possible.

The autumnal man dissociates himself from his youth, referring to his younger self in the third person. He is not yet able to celebrate his continued defeat as the dry bone will a few years later in "Three Things." Yeats told Olivia Shakespear that he was adding poems to this series "upon the old man and his soul as he slowly comes to understand that the mountains are not solid, that all he sees is a mathematical line drawn between hope and memory"

(L 720). He has not crossed that line between hope and memory in "The Empty Cup." His resentment and remorse toward his youth, which colored the first four poems dealing with his younger days, continue in this first poem about his old age. His bitterness implies that his hope is not dead, that he still regrets the wasted opportunities of his youth.

In the pivotal poem in the sequence, "His Memories," he not only accepts his own past as past, but begins to revel in his failure. The bald sexuality of this lyric contrasts to the mythological and symbolic allusions in the preceding poems. Yet, in another sense, this is the most obscure poem in the sequence, given the designation of the "old countryman" in the original title. Why should an old countryman have Helen of Troy in his arms? Yeats often spoke of the likeness between Irish and Greek mythology—a point he drives home by using a chorus from Sophocles as the endpiece to this sequence. In this poem, however, the abrupt introduction of Helen can only be explained as an autobiographical reference. He obscures the reference to this physical relationship with Maud Gonne by the use of the persona, but, since Yeats always equated Maud Gonne with Helen, there is no reason to think he does not do so here.[7]

Most specifically, this allusion ties in with Yeats's identification of Helen and Maud in "No Second Troy" in the Raymond Lully sequence, written during their second period of spiritual marriage, the time during which they had their brief affair. Their physical consummation is the moment that climaxes "His Memories." This moment is intensified by the alchemical interpretation of "The Empty Cup," since that poem, in addition to referring to his inability to give himself to Diana Vernon because of Maud Gonne, may also allude to the memory of his union with the moon maiden. The night when "the first of all the tribe lay there" (P 224) was the moment when the young alchemist created the elixir, the night of his sacred marriage in the forbidden grove, the passionate antithesis of his sterile recoil under the same tree in "Human Dignity."

Before re-creating that moment, however, the old man describes how his body is now "broken like a thorn." The Lady in "The Three Bushes" will refuse physical love because she is disgusted to be "like a dumb beast in a show." This old man has become a "holy show" through the violence and harsh intensity of his carnality, but he is not "dumb" as the Lady fears she will become, and as the young man was in "Human Dignity." The moment is described with gusto:

> The first of all the tribe lay there
> And did such pleasure take—
> She who had brought great Hector down
> And put all Troy to wreck—
> That she cried into this ear,
> "Strike me if I shriek."

The references to "buried" Hector and "that none living knows" in the first stanza are echoed in the last stanza of "The Three Bushes." This old man, in contrast to the Lady and in comparison to the Lover, Chambermaid, and Priest, knows where the roots of his thorn tree lie—in his physical, passionate, but transient union with even his ideal beloved. His most sacred memory is just that, a memory, not a hope. The elixir did not bring eternal youth; the arms where "beauty lay" are now "like the twisted thorn."

The poem is a crucial autobiographical revelation in Yeats's description of his own experience of "the tragedy of sexual intercourse," since this is the only poem where he refers to his physical relationship with Maud Gonne. The intensity of the physical experience, as with Leda and Sheba, underlines both the proximity to oneness and the impossibility of two ever becoming one. He testifies to the dividedness of his own response by describing only her pleasure and referring to himself objectively and dissociatedly as "this ear." He is confessing the moment that was simultaneously his greatest success and most disillusioning failure. He relives the moment when he discovered the virginity of his own soul in the midst of his *hieros gamos* and by so doing starts to accept his failure.

In the next four poems, Yeats looks back upon and relives imaginatively, not self-pityingly, his young hopes, allowing them to be turned into memories. Having accepted his antithetical, divided, lunatic nature, he remembers "The Friends of His Youth" with laughing resignation. Now that his soul-violating hopes have become memories, the moon maiden has become a much more prosaic Madge (probably a shortened form of <u>Maud Gonne</u>), whereas the young lover is remembered not as the broken stone, but as the strutting peacock, Peter.

Yet, alchemical stone symbolism pervades this lyric. Peter, whose name means "rock," embodies Yeats himself as a young occultist who thought he could transform the stone to gold. In *A Vision*, 1925, Yeats connects his Golden Dawn motto—DEDI—with Peter: "The Wheel is in this way reversed, as St. Peter at his crucifixion reversed by the position of his body the position of the crucified Christ: 'Demon est Deus Inversus' " (27). Ellmann associates Yeats's motto with his desire to transform himself to spiritual perfection:

> The order dwelt a great deal upon this rebirth of the individual . . . and compared it to the alchemical transmutation of base metal into gold, which they considered symbolical of the change of the dross of matter into the pure spirit of the perfected man. Yeats bound himself by a solemn oath to work towards the transmutation, using his order name (Demon Est Deus Inversus—a demon is an inverted God), which was itself an indication of man's dual nature.[8]

Yeats's use of Peter in "The Friends of His Youth" and "Summer and Spring" fits into a symbolic pattern suggesting that the older Yeats accepts the fact that he did not transmute matter into spirit: his nature remains dual.

Yeats may be playing upon the symbolism of Peter that he had known since his days with Madame Blavatsky, whose *Secret Doctrine*, with a chapter entitled "Daemon Est Deus Inversus," is the most likely source of Yeats's Golden Dawn name. Blavatsky stresses that Peter, who is addressed by Christ as Satan, is the adversary:[9] he is DEDI. Most significantly, Blavatsky connects Peter to the stone-birth imagery that pervades this poem and is the basis of "Summer and Spring." She points out that Peter is the stone on which the church is built, but Kronos is sure to swallow this rock one day as he swallowed Jupiter-lapis; following this, Peter, like Jupiter, will come forth again.[10]

In the first stanza of "The Friends of His Youth," Madge, clearly identified with the moon maiden and with Helen, nurses a stone, thinking it a child. Madge displays the result of her union under the thorn tree. She, the moon, which is associated in Plato's parable with the androgynous pair who unite heaven and earth, does not give birth to the androgynous Christ, but to the untransmuted virgin matter of stone. In this context, Peter, also the untransmuted rock, is laughably pretentious when he proclaims, "I am the King of the Peacocks" (P 224). The double shriek at the end of the poem focuses again on the night under the thorn, suggesting that both of them have accepted the indignity of human birth, since even though he shrieks from pride, he does enter wholeheartedly into the experience.

The same mythological pattern underlies "Summer and Spring." The lovers have engaged in their *hieros gamos*, hidden by night under a thorn tree, like Solomon and Sheba in the sacred grove. At the moment when they tried to achieve the perfect alchemical, psychological, and spiritual union, Peter (not Christ) is reborn:

> We sat under an old thorn-tree
> And talked away the night,
> Told all that had been said or done
> Since first we saw the light,
> And when we talked of growing up
> Knew that we'd halved a soul
> And fell the one in t'other's arms
> That we might make it whole;
> Then Peter had a murdering look. (P 224-25)

They have tried to efface the original sin of division which occurred when they were betrayed into cradles, but Peter's murdering look following their union shows that they are still in the fallen world where the cruelty and deceit of passion demands further expiation. Peter, who is an unexorcized part of the old man's youth, is still the adversary—the Daimon. Union with the feminine does not yield an indivisible androgynous sphere. Yet, the extremely enigmatic ending of this poem implies that Yeats can affirm his antithetical, and thus always dual, nature:

> O what a bursting out there was,
> And what a blossoming,
> When we had all the summer-time
> And she had all the spring!

The pronouns make the lines obscure: who are "we" and why is that "we" separated from "she"? The poem is one stanza of sixteen lines. The pronoun "we" appears five times in the first half of the poem. The reader presumes it refers to the persona and his beloved, as the old man builds up to the crucial line eight: "That we might make it whole." But the verb in this line is conditional; the wholeness is still a hope. What follows in the second half of the poem is the poet's memory of what actually occurred. Peter, in symbolic terms the untransformed stone, reappears as if born from their union. Peter is the adversary who will not allow the "aimless joy" of the primary as described in "Demon and Beast" to remain. Demon and beast are locked in combat again in the "bursting out" and "blossoming" at the end. "We" refers both to the two lovers and to "I" and his "Daimon," Peter. Unlike the Lady in "The Three Bushes" and Aedh in *The Wind among the Reeds*, the Man Young and Old is willing to wrestle with his Daimon, although the juxtaposition of "we" and "she" at the end indicates that he has not overcome the alienation between himself and his own Daimon and by so doing found the Daimon of the other. His Daimon is still imaged as masculine; the fertile interplay that Yeats describes as "sporting with the Daimon" requires that the conscious mind experience the Daimon as of the opposite sex.

Yet their conflict will not end in sterile annihilation. Only separation would cause each to "consume itself away" and stop the "blossoming" that results from their imperfect union. In fact, the old man's struggle is the ongoing source of his strength. What could have engulfed him when he harbored his hope for transmutation now has no power over him. In "The Secrets of the Old," he offhandedly says:

> Madge tells me what I dared not think
> When my blood was strong,
> And what had drowned a lover once
> Sounds like an old song. (P 225)

No longer the passive, unself-possessed lad whose longing could drown him, he has discovered the irrevocable duality of his nature, but knows that the "bed of straw / Or the bed of down" where the gyres continue competing is the source of his song.

Yet, for all the pleasure he refers to, he accepts his essential solitude. Referring literally to himself and his two mistresses, he says, "We three make up a solitude." He then alternates his recollections of the two affairs in the odd and even lines in the last stanza, collapsing them into one[11] and implying that the effect on himself is the most important factor:

> How such a pair loved many years
> And such a pair but one,
> Stories of the bed of straw
> Or of the bed of down.

The whole sequence suggests a triangular relationship between the poet-lover, the exterior woman, and the antiself or Daimon (in this sequence, Peter), who is aroused but remains virginal in the interplay. That the Daimon is not of the opposite sex perhaps helps to explain the old man's inability to bless his memories to the extent of being ready to live them again willingly. The Man Young and Old can celebrate death in the chorus "From 'Oedipus at Colonus'" at the end of his sequence, but he still feels that "never to have lived is best" (P 227). In the second-to-last poem, the last spoken by the old man, Yeats suggests that the man has not found his "self-abounding" sweetness because he has not developed the feminine within himself. However, he proclaims both his willingness to develop the feminine within him and his acceptance of his connection to the untransformed stone as the source of his song in the last image in "His Wildness": "Being all alone I'd nurse a stone / And sing it lullaby" (P 226).

"A Woman Young and Old"

Yeats finds this inner source of sweetness by exploring the feminine within himself in his imaginative projection of a woman's emotional and sexual history in "A Woman Young and Old." Some critics have noticed the likenesses between this woman and Olivia Shakespear;[12] however, that parallel is not so closely drawn as the biographical parallels to Maud Gonne, Olivia Shakespear, and Yeats himself in "A Man Young and Old." Rather, Yeats creates a fairly ideal set of experiences for this woman. Through his lengthiest lyric probing of experience from a feminine point of view, Yeats epitomizes much of his vision of the virginity of the soul and its effect on the possibility of unity between lovers and of integrity within the individual. The changing attitude of the Woman Young and Old typifies the evolution from a violated soul in an inviolate body to a violated body with an inviolate soul. In other words, she embodies the progression from a cold, naive physical virgin—like the Lady of "The Three Bushes"—to a passionate, experienced, psychological virgin—like the Chambermaid. In this evolution, she also demonstrates a shift from the residue of bitterness in "A Man Young and Old" to the attitude of forgiveness, blessing, and joyful willingness to sin again at the end of "A Dialogue of Self and Soul." She comes as close as is humanly possible to solving the antinomies and, because she has done so, looks forward confidently to someday achieving the oneness where her soul will no longer be virginal.

Looking back at her early reactions to love, she recalls and portrays, without self-pity or blame, her own extremes before she learned the wisdom she tells to the sages in "Consolation." In the first two poems, she dramatizes her earliest attraction to the disembodied. She perceives the supposedly profligate lover, to whom her father objects in "Father and Child," in images reminiscent of a fairy lover beckoning to her from the other world, as the Sidhe did in Yeats's earliest poems. The girl justifies her attraction by saying that "his hair is beautiful / Cold as the March wind his eyes" (P 270). Since the whole sequence draws heavily on Platonic symbolism, Yeats implies that the young girl still remembers her lover from before she was born. Her father's objection to the man because of his ill-repute, however, suggests how naive the girl's perception of the relationship between human men and women is. She has not yet felt the passion that will make her prefer an earthly lover to an image from a past life.

The girl's childish self-deception that she can re-create her permanent self by means of a few dabs of makeup undercuts her declaration of devotion to the disembodied ideal in "Before the World was Made." Her soul seems capriciously uninvolved:

> What if I look upon a man
> As though on my beloved,
> And my blood be cold the while
> And my heart unmoved?
> Why should he think me cruel
> Or that he is betrayed?
> I'd have him love the thing that was
> Before the world was made. (P 270-71)

Here the young girl closely prefigures the Lady, hoping that she can be a nonphysical inspiration—although the Lady, who never outgrew this position, is more sophisticated and knows that more physical food must be offered to her Lover. The girl and the Lady, moreover, share the rationalization that their attempt to be nonphysical lovers is not a betrayal of their partners.

This young woman, however, eventually chooses intercourse with life and learns what the Chambermaid will also know. First, the young woman goes to the opposite extreme from her first position, because she has a lingering disgust toward physical sexual love. She describes the conflict within herself in "First Confession":

> I long for truth, and yet
> I cannot stay from that
> My better self disowns,
> For a man's attention
> Brings such satisfaction
> To the craving of my bones. (P 271)

Her confession sounds much like the Lady's admission that "What hurts the soul / My soul adores," except that the young woman is at the opposite pole from the Lady in her actions. This young woman has lost her physical virginity, but she thinks that her soul is uninvolved.

She has not achieved independent virginity of soul through the full experience of her potentialities in her *hieros gamos*, but has tried to deceive even herself into thinking that she can find satisfaction by indulging in physical love while remaining uninvolved emotionally. Although she does not realize it, her soul is utterly violated and dehumanized by her cold attitude. She is physically woman, but far from whole psychologically. She is dissociated from herself, not really recognizing and proclaiming that her physical relationship in the briar—parallel to Helen's experience under the thorn in "A Man Young and Old"—is the source of her strength. As she indicates at the beginning of "Her Triumph," her actions were not redemptive at the time she recalls in "A First Confession." At this point, she is futilely chained to "the dragon's will" (P 271) of merely repetitive physical passion: the sins she confesses do not bring her closer to her integral self. She is trapped in the vegetative cycle that Yeats described in the first stanza of "Sailing to Byzantium." She tries to shun responsibility at the end of "A First Confession," refusing to face and answer "those questioning eyes / That are fixed on me."

She is freed from the dragon's will, but must accept responsibility for her own choice in "Her Triumph." Her freedom is attained through the discovery of her virginal soul in her *hieros gamos*. Perseus, himself born of a virgin impregnated by a god, functions as the substitute for God in her sacred intercourse.[13] Only when she meets her rightful man who can master her coquetry and make her see that love is more than a game does she become a responsible woman:

> And then you stood among the dragon-rings.
> I mocked, being crazy, but you mastered it
> And broke the chain and set my ankles free.

She stands equal to her liberator at the end, now an independent psychological virgin for whom "the miraculous strange bird shrieks" as it did for Sheba.

She stands beside her rightful lover, but she experiences strangeness in their relationship. This is not the easy dissembling of her earlier coquetry, but the mature preservation of her self-identity even in a wholehearted relationship. Paradoxically, her triumph over the craving of her bones is also the guarantee of her failure to find full satisfaction in love. This bird announces the miracle of her own regeneration into the redemptive realm of "what is past, passing, and to come." She has connected her prior self with her passionate, and passing, self. Her façade of noninvolvement is shattered; she accepts that she must see life as more than a "casual improvisation" and her passion becomes truly atoning.

At present, she rejoices that she has not yet completed her reintegration with her permanent self and must expiate the original sin of division by repeating it. She tells the sages in "Consolation":

> How could passion run so deep
> Had I never thought
> That the crime of being born
> Blackens all our lot?
> But where the crime's committed
> The crime can be forgot. (P 272)

Through her, Yeats makes his clearest statement of the interrelation of birth, intercourse, and sin. Like Crazy Jane, the Woman Young and Old is willing to be rent in order to be whole. The crime of being born into the darkness of this world is forgotten momentarily in the pleasure between lovers and forgiven in their willingness to commit the crime again.

Her ability to provide this consolation without being engulfed herself depends upon the virginity of her soul. She passionately enters the re-enactment of the fall into division, which caused the dichotomy between the ever-virgin soul and the body, but simultaneously sees herself as objectively separate and as more permanent than the act and its consequences. Her passion runs deep, yet she senses that her lot existed before it was "blackened" and that she will someday return to the inextinguishable light. Until that time, she enters as passionately as possible into the consolation. She has accepted the inevitable fact and the consequences of her own birth, and thus maintains her sovereign individuality—the virginity of her soul—in seeking and giving solace.

The mention of our "lot" connects "Consolation" and the next lyric, "Chosen," with the last stanza of "A Dialogue of Self and Soul." In all three, Yeats alludes to Plato's parable of the souls lined up before Lachesis, in the interim between death and rebirth, choosing their "lots"[14] in the next incarnation. Since the Woman Young and Old disagrees with Plato to some extent, the sages she instructs in "Consolation" may be the Platonists. Plato describes an orderly process where a rational choice is possible, if the soul learns to weigh the good and evil of sample lives. Many make unfortunate choices, but others choose well. Plato does not emphasize the moment of birth and does not equate birth and intercourse, as Yeats does. Orpheus, for example, is allowed to become a swan without being conceived in a woman. The Woman Young and Old rejects such a rational, non-physical progression to a new incarnation. She fully accepts the indignity of human birth. She knows that her passion disrupts the harmony of Plato's spindle and that all our lot is blackened at birth inevitably.

"Blackens" also ties in with the darkness and blindness that Yeats consistently connects with conception and birth. Living persons are in the dark, as Yeats stresses by repeating "blind" four times in the last section of "A Dialogue of Self and Soul." Paradoxically, however, as is clear in "Chosen," daylight accompanies this blindness. The dark mother earth, who offers "the maternal midnight of her breast" (P 272) to her lover, must choose daybreak herself. This interplay of light and darkness is similar to the imagery Yeats used to explain the relationship between the Daimon and the conscious mind and between the lovers in "Solomon and the Witch." The Woman Young and Old chooses to join the light while retaining the darkness of her passion in that light. The return of temporal daybreak signifies her failure to attain the inextinguishable light of release from this world.

Yeats's astrological image in the first stanza of "Chosen" is reminiscent of Plato's description of the rebirth of the souls, except that, in keeping with the whole sequence and his typical approach, Yeats puts the image in sexual terms. Plato says that the souls drink from the river of forgetfulness, then rebirth follows in the middle of the night when they are driven upwards like shooting stars. In "Consolation" the Woman Young and Old has reached the plain of forgetfulness and has drunk from the stream. In "Chosen" she is at the moment of midnight and instantly the moment of oblivious consolation passes and she is shot upward to another daybreak:

> Scarce did he my body touch,
> Scarce sank he from the west
> Or found a subterranean rest
> On the maternal midnight of my breast
> Before I had marked him on his northern way,
> And seemed to stand, although in bed I lay.
>
> I struggled with the horror of daybreak
> I chose it for my lot. . . .

Because they touch, the myth is consumed; the moment of perfect balance when, as she indicates later in the second stanza, the cones seem "changed into a sphere" is passing as soon as it is reached.

Yeats suggests the Woman's double role as participant and witness, as physical lover and spiritual virgin, as subjectively involved and objectively judging. She is struggling passionately to achieve and maintain the sphere of union with her lover while she simultaneously views herself and him as other and removed, in the last two lines of the first stanza. She is in bed with him (symbolically he is the sun), yet as he metaphorically passes the center of gravity of the "maternal midnight of her breast," she perceives him as already moving away from her while she seems to shoot upward like Plato's souls into a standing position.

She and the lover who awakened her independence in "Her Triumph" have found the moment to which the bird beckoned them, but the virginity of her soul that was a prerequisite for her entering into love as more than a game reveals itself in a deliberate and inevitable betrayal of her lover at the height of their union. She is passionately involved, yet analyzing and distancing as she articulates the whole experience using the past tense. The moment of her "utmost pleasure" in the second stanza is even further removed since it is an answer to a hypothetical question within the narrative of the past. She is not reliving the moment passionately as she does in the first stanza. Having re-experienced the intensity of her inner conflict, she calmly accepts the loss of their momentary illusion of oneness.

The imagery in "Chosen" closely parallels Blake's engraving of the lustful in Circle Two of *The Inferno*, "The Whirlwind of Lovers" (see fig. 1), which Yeats had designated as "the most perfect and most moving, and must always haunt the memory with a beauty at once tender and august."[15] Both the "whirling Zodiac" and the sphere are paralleled in the engraving. The static, eternal union of Paolo and Francesca in the sun, imaged almost like a halo over Virgil's head (an analogue to the "learned astrologer"), matches the moment of perfect union the Woman Young and Old will describe in "A Last Confession" when her Sun need not whirl back to a temporal daybreak. The flame arising from the prostrate figure of Dante showing the upright, separating figures of Paolo and Francesca reaching out to each other suggests the same kind of radical shift from supine to erect that the Woman Young and Old experiences. The gyrating motion of the whirlwind which touches the feet of the prostrate figure forms another sphere where the lovers entwine and separate continuously moving in and out of the constantly shifting sphere caused by their unsatisfied passions. That mutable sphere is the one that the Woman Young and Old chooses, although as "A Last Confession" makes clear, she looks forward to the inextinguishable light of union in the eternal

Figure 1. "The Whirlwind of Lovers"
Engraving by William Blake for Dante's *Divine Comedy*
(Reproduced by permission of the Tate Gallery, London)

sun. The daybreak she chooses is transient, but as the faces of Blake's figures attest, offers her consolation.

The prostrate figure from which the lovers rise is reminiscent of the dead knight from whom the kissing lovers in the Rose tree grew on the cover of *The Secret Rose*. That early vision was one-dimensional, however. Yeats's later convictions are better portrayed by the complexities of Blake's print. Both the whirling sphere and the static sphere are possible, but the human figure is, at present, enrooted in the gyre of multiplicity, repeatedly begetting herself rather than attaining self-begotten oneness. The indistinctness of the naked figures at the beginning and the end of the whirlwind hint at the Lover's cyclic regeneration as the worm in "The Three Bushes." This whirlwind brings countless repetitions of the sin of division while always guaranteeing that the eternal sphere is not ultimately unattainable.

The daybreak the woman chooses is, of course, inevitable, but her ability to choose is real. Like My Self at the end of "A Dialogue of Self and Soul," she is willing to live it all again. A comparison of "Chosen" and "His Memories," the sixth and pivotal lyrics in "A Woman Young and Old" and "A Man Young and Old" respectively, reinforces that the woman's greater affirmation of life brings her closer to the conclusion of "A Dialogue of Self and Soul" than the man. The poems are structured similarly. In both, the lover looks back upon the most significant moment of love that each experienced in the prime of life. Both poems build up to that moment, depicted almost as if it were a separate, static icon at the end of the poem. The reader is conscious that the moment of near ecstasy is over before it is described. Both narrators have a tendency to portray the union in terms of the pleasure that the partner experienced in the narrator's embrace, while seeing themselves as struggling or broken.

Since the poems are so parallel, the subtle differences between them point out the essential differences in the attitudes of the Man Young and Old and the Woman Young and Old. The man dissociates himself much more drastically from the pleasure of the experience. Most of his emphasis is on his present decrepit condition, now a source of mockery as far as women are concerned. He recalls the pleasure that Helen took from him and how she cried into "this ear" almost as if his body were dismembered. He has difficulty in perceiving and affirming the continuity from within himself between the former lover and the present twisted thorn, so his bitterness remains partially unresolved. The Woman Young and Old also experiences duality within herself, but this realization does not deter her from finding continuity and a form of integrity in her acceptance of her present self while she looks forward to complete integrity someday. She recalls the pleasure as well as the horror of the experience, internalizing both and accepting that she will not resolve the tension within her until her final release.

Her choice is ultimate in its intensity, but one that will have to be repeated again and again, since she brings her darkness into that daybreak. Thus, in "Parting," she once again offers the "dark declivities" (P 273) of her dragon body to her lover, as Yeats re-emphasizes the cycle of seeming union followed by return to fragmentation. The lovers reverse roles in the process: in "Chosen" "He" seeks only rest, while "She" chooses daybreak; in "Parting" "She" longs for rest, while "He" faces the inevitable betrayal of daybreak.

The creative tension of the combined experience of virginity and intercourse becomes more difficult to maintain as the Woman gets older. In "Her Vision in the Wood," she relives her *hieros gamos* "at wine-dark midnight in the sacred wood" (P 273). Now her passion rises more slowly; she must tear at her body to bring forth blood before she can experience what she toyed with so effortlessly in "A First Confession." Finally, she re-experiences "love's bittersweet." She recognizes that the man is her "heart's victim and its torturer" as they continue their passionate struggle—each inevitably unrequited because of the virginity of each soul. Her fall before him is reminiscent of the gesture that precedes forgiveness in Yeats's earliest works, such as *John Sherman*. He, in a pattern reminiscent of Blake's "The Mental Traveller," is now young whereas the implication in the first poem was that the very young woman was attracted to a more experienced man. As in Blake's poem, the cycle will continue repeating itself, until the final release that she describes at the end of her next lyric.

The Woman Young and Old summarizes the whole evolution of Yeats's attitude and experience as poet-lover when she recounts her history as a lover in "A Last Confession." In the first stanza, she remembers that, like the young Yeats in relation to Maud Gonne and Aedh in relation to the Rose, she loved in misery when she gave only her soul. Next, she "loved bodily" (P 275), but found that her soul was inviolate:

> To think his passion such
> He fancied that I gave a soul
> Did but our bodies touch,
> And laughed upon his breast to think
> Beast gave beast as much.

This, too, is reminiscent of Yeats's experience, particularly at the beginning of the twentieth century when he learned the self-preserving deceit he described in "Discoveries" and embodied in poems such as "The Mask."

At the end of "A Last Confession," the woman looks forward to the ultimate moment when her rightful man will penetrate her naked soul:

> But when this soul, its body off
> Naked to naked goes,
> He it has found shall find therein
> What none other knows,

And give his own and take his own
And rule in his own right;
And though it loved in misery
Close and cling so tight,
There's not a bird of day that dare
Extinguish that delight.

She will be released from the "whirling Zodiac" into the eternal sun. She and her lover will be irrevocably one and each will find "his own" or "her own" in the union of their Daimons. He will find his permanent self in union with her and she hers in his eternal embrace. This will be the last confession because they will have finished their expiation and obliterated the original sin.

As she is well aware, she has not reached this stasis, however. The implication is that she would never have reached the stage where she could even project what the perfect union would be like if she, like the early poet-lover and the later Lady, had not fully experienced both the passion of intercourse and the virginity of her soul in the utmost pleasure she has had in this life. She would have remained cold and miserable if she had loved only with her soul and would still be chained to the dragon's will if she had indulged the craving of her bones without recognizing the virginity of her soul. Both the sphere and the renewed struggle of "Chosen" are essential to her vision at the end of "A Last Confession." She can imagine the eternal moment when the gulf between the one and the many is bridged and her soul is no longer virginal because she has experienced the tragedy of almost, but not quite, achieving that oneness already. Unlike the Man Young and Old, she is fully confident that she will achieve that oneness someday; her vision of perfection is stated in terms of "when" it will occur, rather than "if" it will. That confidence allows her to affirm her past and face "living it all again" with much more sweetness and less remorse than the Man Young and Old. In "Meeting," she awaits the "sweeter word" (P 276) of their final meeting while she concurrently experiences the hatred that requires their rebirth before they can "discard this beggarly habiliment."

Like Antigone in the endpiece, the Woman Young and Old prays and sings even as she weeps at the bitter sweetness that sends her "into the loveless dust" (P 276) from which she will have to continue reascending until her love is strong enough to "overcome the Empyrean." Her focus is unflinchingly held on the dust from which she came and to which she descends only to start the cycle again, just as the Chambermaid will focus on the same cycle through the symbolism of the worm. The Woman Young and Old can already "nurse a stone" and has shown the Man Young and Old how to do so. The Woman Young and Old knows that her choice of daybreak returns her to the untransformed matter of this world, but the self-delighting sweetness of her psychological virginity assures that her present misery will be ultimately redemptive. In fact, Yeats seemed to believe that the feminine artist's reservoir of sweetness was twice that of the masculine artist. Warning her against the bitterness of propaganda and lamenting his own tendency to bitterness in his youth, Yeats wrote to Ethel Mannin several years after he wrote "A Woman Young and Old " and "A Man Young and Old," "You are doubly a woman, first because of yourself and secondly because of the muses, whereas I am but once a woman" (L 831). Yeats's imaginative projection of the feminine psyche in "A Woman Young and Old" allows him to share in that double reservoir of sweetness, just as his intellectual exchanges with women in letters and conversation had always fostered his creativity.

Yet the Woman Young and Old is not "uncomposite" as Robartes claims beautiful women are in "Michael Robartes and the Dancer" and as the dancer is at the end of "Among School Children." She embodies a composite blessedness—one attainable by the antithetical artist—in which she accepts the imperfection of her present life and is willing to repeat all its successes and failures. Thus, she prepares the antithetical poet for his conclusion to "A Dialogue of Self and Soul." The playful, self-possessed tone of even her first lyrics demonstrates her willingness to endure once more all "the toil of growing up" (P 236) that My Self also embraces, but that Peter seemed to resent in "Summer and Spring." She has no desire to be delivered from "the crime of death and birth," as My Soul advocates. Yeats subtly reinforces this at the end of her sequence by referring to Antigone as "Oedipus' child" in the chorus' exultant declaration of the mixed feelings from which their song flows:

> Pray I will and sing I must,
> And yet I weep—Oedipus' child
> Descends into the loveless dust.

The speaker of this chorus, like the Priest at the end of "The Three Bushes," does not participate bodily in the woman's struggle, but witnesses, understands, and blesses her case, recognizing that his ability to sing depends on her ability to continue her bittersweet struggle. The chorus's proclamation "Sing I must" underlines Yeats's reaffirmation that "literature is the forgiveness of sins" by its contrast to the last statement of My Soul in "A Dialogue of Self and Soul":

> For intellect no longer knows
> *Is* from the *Ought*, or *Knower* from the *Known*—
> That is to say, ascends to Heaven;
> Only the dead can be forgiven;
> But when I think of that my tongue's a stone. (P 235)

My Soul is also a nonparticipating figure, but does not recognize its need to focus on life as the source of its song. Because it looks to heaven rather than the dust its tongue becomes frozen and its song dies out. My Soul's mistake is in believing, like the early poet-lover in "He wishes his Beloved were Dead," that "only the dead can be forgiven." The chorus at the end of "A Woman Young and Old" has learned from her experience that only the living can be forgiven, because only the imaginative re-enactment of the crime of being born constitutes the forgiveness of sins. Only the living can be forgiven, since only they can repeat their sins.

My Self fully accepts the need for ongoing forgiveness and projects himself into the roles of both penitent and priest in his final speech. The role of penitent, still reflected in his measuring "every event in action or in thought" in the final version, was even more evident in the earliest printed version. In 1929, the first two lines in the last stanza read:

> Content to trace that misery to its source,
> Count every sin of action or of thought. (VP 479)

Then he reverses roles, in a pattern similar to that of vehicle and questioner in *A Vision*, and, as priest, forgives himself. The two roles are balanced perfectly in the third line of the last stanza: "Measure the lot; forgive myself the lot." This forgiveness, as the rest of this poem and "A Woman Young and Old" have demonstrated, is accomplished through the "charter to commit the crime once more." He must witness detachedly what he has done and relive it imaginatively and passionately.

The only poems in which Yeats ever used the word "crime" are "Consolation," written in June 1927, and "A Dialogue of Self and Soul," written between July and December 1927. In both, the narrator, like the Heart in "Vacillation," claims the right and need to repeat the original sin of being born with its concomitant fall into division and passion and simultaneously judges herself or himself as comforted and forgiven by doing so. My Self has learned the sweetness that the Man Young and Old paves the way for and the Woman Young and Old models. He blesses his own past, present, and future and his blessing overflows onto everything else. My Self's tongue is not a stone, just as the Heart is not "struck dumb" in "Vacillation." Like the ballad of the Abbé de Bourdeille, their songs flow from their conviction that the willingness to repeat the crime is creative and ultimately redemptive.

6

The Purgatorial Journey

Ironically, by choosing reincarnation in the "blind man's ditch," My Self has chosen the only path that will eventually give him access to the inextinguishable light. Often, as is evident in "A Woman Young and Old," Yeats employs the obvious but very fitting pattern of going from darkness to light, especially from dusk to dawn, as an analogy to a purgatorial process between death and rebirth. His use of dusk to dawn imagery allows him to dovetail his frequent use of sexual intercourse as a parallel to artistic creation with the purgatorial process, as he does in his comments on expiation in *A Vision*, thus further demonstrating the interrelationship between the tragedy of sexual intercourse and the forgiveness of sins.

As is evident from the passages on expiation I have already quoted, Yeats's view of the period between death and rebirth involves reliving passionate moments that still retain some "cruelty and deceit." He also indicates, although in a rather confused manner, that two people might be required to experience relationships they had failed to experience in their former lives. Yeats gives an elaborate listing and description of the stages that he envisioned as occurring between death and rebirth in both versions of *A Vision*; however, the specific stages are not so crucial to his use of Purgatory as a parallel to the creative process in his lyric poetry as they are to his plays. The basic pattern of experiencing and re-experiencing all the possible passions and relationships between lover and beloved is more pertinent to his lyric poetry.

His choice of Purgatory as an analogy signifies that the process is ultimately redemptive, not merely repetitive. Dorothy Wellesley reports a dialogue with Yeats that includes a succinct description of his view of Purgatory:

> I once got Yeats down to bed-rock on these subjects and we talked for hours. He had been talking rather wildly about the after life . . . . "And after that," I asked, "what happens next?" He replied: "Again a period which is Purgatory. The length of that phase depends upon the sins of the man when upon this earth." And then again I asked: "And after that?" I do not remember his actual words, but he spoke of the return of the soul to God. (LP 195)

My Self's return to the fecund ditch, like the Lover's return as the worm, is not futilely repetitive, but a presently divided prerequisite for the final return to oneness.

Crazy Jane

Purgatorial images are particularly prevalent in the Crazy Jane sequence. Years earlier, Yeats had said, in "If I Were Four-and-Twenty" (1919), that he would like to "associate that doctrine of purgatory, which Christianity has shared with Neo-Platonism, with the countryman's belief in the nearness of his dead 'working out their penance' in rath or at garden end" (Ex 267). Through Crazy Jane and Jack, whose ghost wanders the nearby roads at night, Yeats brings Purgatory and the countryman and woman together. As the sequence unfolds, it becomes clear that the road that they both travel is a purgatorial road and that the virginity of Jane's soul and her willingness to sin again are crucial both to her continued journey on that road and to her final destination.

Her desire to curse the Bishop under the oak at midnight in Poem I suggests that she wants to return to the spot where she and Jack experienced the symbolic death of the *hieros gamos* and where Jack will return to claim her once again. Her request that she be brought to the oak implies that she may be too weak to walk there, but wants to be there to die, an implication strengthened by her mention of "midnight upon the stroke" and the tomb in the first stanza. The rest of the sequence can be read as a flashback to the experience and emotions she has had in this life and brings to the moment of death. Crazy Jane does not give her history from youth to old age in order as the Woman Young and Old does. Jane is old throughout the sequence, but re-experiences her sacred intercourse with Jack imaginatively several times within the course of her songs. She is consistently independent and psychologically virginal:[1] clearly no man could own her. Jack had her virginity under the oak, but he will find her virginal when she returns to him under the oak.

The first refrain, "All find safety in the tomb" (P 255) conveys a certain amount of ironic ambiguity in the context of Yeats's view of Purgatory. By confessing and reliving her past as she recounts it in this sequence, Jane is atoning and finding, through literature, the forgiveness of sins. She may thus find safety in the tomb, having lived her Purgatory already. Her anger and passion, however, imply that her expiation is far from complete. Jack, too, has not found safety in the tomb; rather, he "wanders out into the night," bidding her join him. The last stanza suggests that Jack beckons her to the Druid oak so that, like Solomon and Sheba in the sacred grove, they can "try again" to expiate the original sin of division:

> Jack had my virginity,
> And bids me to the oak, for he
> (*All find safety in the tomb.*)
> Wanders out into the night
> And there is shelter under it,
> But should that other come, I spit:
> *The solid man and the coxcomb.*

Her self-preserving rage and Jack's still-hungry pursuit suggest that neither of them will find repose, even in death.

Poem II, a highly enigmatic reproval of Jane, contrasts two kinds of creation, which, in the light of a comment Yeats made in his *Autobiography*, could be interpreted as two processes necessary to bring about the re-creation of the self during the purgatorial period. The speaker in "Crazy Jane Reproved" contrasts "those dreadful thunder-stones, / All that storm that blots the day" (P 256) with an even more heaven-shaking process:

> To round that shell's elaborate whorl,
> Adorning every secret track
> With the delicate mother-of-pearl,
> Made the joints of Heaven crack.

Yeats uses the same imagery in describing the creation of the macrocosm in his *Autobiography*: "Is it not certain that the Creator yawns in earthquake and thunder, but toils in rounding the delicate spiral of a shell?" (A 164). He also depicts the inner re-creation of the permanent self in two contrasting processes that parallel the "thunder-stones" and the "secret track" of the shell: "I know now that revelation is from the self, but from that age-long memoried self, that shapes the elaborate shell of the mollusc and the child in the womb . . . and that genius is a crisis that joins the buried self for certain moments with our trivial daily mind" (A 164). Later in the same paragraph, Yeats says that artists who join the two selves achieve "the re-creation of the man through the art, the birth of a new species." The speaker in this poem admonishes Crazy Jane that she will need more than the stroke of midnight (the thundering moment of crisis) if she wants to reunite her two selves and find the "whole" she longs for in the first stanza of the next poem.

In "Crazy Jane on the Day of Judgment," Jane again describes the moment of crisis when she lay open to the storms that "blot the day":

> "Naked I lay,
> The grass my bed;
> Naked and hidden away,
> That black day";
> *And that is what Jane said.* (P 257)

But she is only physically naked, like the Woman Young and Old in the second stanza of "A Last Confession." She has not revealed her buried self; it is still "hidden away" in her darkness. The image of "that black day" is Yeats's most concentrated expression of the paradox of daybreak and darkness that attends rebirth. Jane describes one kind of death—that of sexual intercourse—as she faces the judgment that awaits her approaching death. Neither, however, is an ultimate moment that will be followed by the inextinguishable light. Since Jack and many others have taken her body, it must be her soul that remains "unsatisfied"; the virginity of her soul keeps her on this side of the gulf. Yeats wrote the Crazy Jane poems between 1929 and 1931; she is his most immediate embodiment of his statement to Sparrow in 1931 that "the tragedy of sexual intercourse is the perpetual virginity of the soul"[2] and she demonstrates how that tragedy requires and constitutes the forgiveness of sins.

She and Jack have not yet found their buried selves in each other; their skeins are still bound together, each calling the other to expiation and reincarnation in Poem IV, "Crazy Jane and Jack the Journeyman." The purgatorial image is most developed in this poem, the central poem in Jane's seven lyrics. Jane sets up an image of unwinding a skein between dusk and dawn in the first stanza:

> The more I leave the door unlatched
> The sooner love is gone;
> For love is but a skein unwound
> Between the dark and dawn. (P 258)

The unraveling of the skein suggests a parallel to the more intricate of the two processes of creation in the second poem. If the skein can be carefully unwound, she will uncover her buried self and achieve the state that the Woman Young and Old describes in the last stanza of "A Last Confession."

The second stanza depicts such an ultimate moment when the soul returns to God:

> A lonely ghost the ghost is
> That to God shall come;
> I—love's skein upon the ground,
> My body in the tomb—
> Shall leap into the light lost
> In my mother's womb. (P 258)

If all the cruelty and deceit of their interpenetrating gyres is expiated, then Jane will return to her permanent self, her image from before she was betrayed into her mother's womb. Yeats's repetition of "ghost" suggests an echo of the

Ghostly Self from *A Vision*, 1925. If Jane could achieve this state, she would be reunited to that Ghostly Self in the Thirteenth Cycle and never need to return to this world through rebirth.

Jane's designation of this ghost as "lonely," while encapsulating Plotinus's view of the culmination of the soul's journey when "alone it returns to the Alone,"[3] also conveys her dissatisfaction with that projected state of perfection. At present, she prefers to remain "all unsatisfied," choosing the repetition of the crime with Jack rather than the return to God. The second stanza projects a future and remote possibility; her present state is portrayed in the third. She will find no safety in the tomb this time. She and Jack are still unraveling their passion. Her ghost must walk with his, joining him under the blasted oak to sin again after death.

The image of how they are joined suggests an allusion to the end of "A Man Young and Old" and implies that their continued expiation is bringing them closer to the state described in the second stanza. Jane says:

> The skein so bound us ghost to ghost
> When he turned his head
> Passing on the road that night,
> Mine must walk when dead.

Jack turned away into death after his "gay goodnight," but his spindle is so intricately interwoven with hers that the turning of his head delicately tugs hers along—an image analogous to the forming of the shell in Poem II. Her buried self is touched and brought closer to the surface as she responds to the now gentler movement of the "roaring, ranting journeyman." She is already traveling with her journeyman on the purgatorial road.

Fittingly, she commits the atoning crime again and again between dusk and dawn in "Crazy Jane on God":

> That lover of a night
> Came when he would,
> Went in the dawning light
> Whether I would or no;
> Men come, men go,
> *All things remain in God.* (P 258)

The refrain suggests the origin and goal of her journey as well as the ultimately redemptive power of her experiences. It conveys both the seeming insignificance and the ultimate value of human action.

In the next stanza, Jane introduces an apocalyptic image; this Armageddon is not ultimate, however. The shades of the armed men and the neighing horses are in the same purgatorial middle state as Jack and Jane.

They point to the final cataclysm while re-enacting their former attempts to get through the narrow pass. The band of horsemen encounter a more individual apocalyptic scene in the third stanza:

> Before their eyes a house
> That from childhood stood
> Uninhabited, ruinous,
> Suddenly lit up
> From door to top:
> *All things remain in God.*

This scene closely parallels the lighted house and horsemen in the later play *Purgatory*.[4] Here, as in the play, the image is connected with the repetition of the interrelated crimes of birth, intercourse, and death. In *Purgatory*, as in the preceding poem in this sequence, the main characters envision the ultimate moment as a self-begotten re-creation where they become both agent and issue of their own conception and thus bring the inextinguishable fire of the apocalypse, ending the darkness, cruelty, deceit, and passion of the purgatorial process of expiation. In both instances, the conflagration is not yet complete. However, as the refrain stresses, the re-enactment of the primal sin paradoxically brings the sinners closer to their return to God.

Jane celebrates her purgatorial journey in the last stanza. The road image connects her repeated intercourse with the interwoven skeins of the last stanza of the preceding poem:

> I had wild Jack for a lover;
> Though like a road
> That men pass over
> My body makes no moan
> But sings on:
> *All things remain in God.*

She has become the road that leads Jack, other men, and herself to the immortal light. Her confidence that this purgatorial road brings her to God parallels the Chambermaid's assurance that "God's love" protects the Lover in her bed. The ambiguity toward sexual love that led to the ambivalence of the raveling image and the spiring worms in the grave of "The Man who dreamed of Faeryland" and the almost paralyzing awe of the naked self cast out on the purgatorial road at the end of "The Cold Heaven" have been replaced by Crazy Jane's confidence that her song emanates from the passionate and purgatorial journey over that road.

The purgatorial road is the place where Jane meets the Bishop in "Crazy Jane Talks with the Bishop." The Bishop sees death as moral finality threatening ultimate judgment. Thus, he joins My Soul in "A Dialogue of Self and Soul" in advocating a disembodied perspective. A comment Yeats makes in "An Indian Monk" explains the Bishop's indignation, its connection to his view of death, and the contrasting view of Crazy Jane:

> Our moral indignation, our uniform law, perhaps even our public spirit, may come from the Christian conviction that the soul has but one life to find or lose salvation in: the Asiatic courtesy from the conviction that there are many lives. There are Indian courtesans that meditate many hours a day awaiting without sense of sin their moment, perhaps many lives hence, to leave man for God. For the present, they are efficient courtesans. (EI 436)

Crazy Jane confidently awaits her "heavenly mansion" (P 259), knowing that now she must repeatedly experience the interrelationship of "fair and foul." She senses that the repeated rending of her body that she describes at the end of "Crazy Jane on God" is the only process that will bring her to unity and integrity. Like the Woman Young and Old and the Chambermaid, Jane knows that her experience of human love with its paradoxical interplay of passion and virginity is the only path to eternal love.

Her declaration to the Bishop in the last stanza summarizes what the psychological virgin learns. The stiff woman in the first two lines who is "intent" on love suggests the physical virgin, like the Lady, who wants to love only with her soul. But that approach is a mere negation that consumes itself away, as Yeats subtly implies by using a lower case "l" for this love and a capital for the "Love" that has "pitched his mansion in / The place of excrement." Lasting "Love" must be learned, as Jane says in the preceding stanza, in "bodily lowliness." The only way to achieve both the sphere where two become irrevocably one—"sole"—and the integrity of the permanent self—"whole"—is to engage repeatedly in imperfect human love.

Yeats implies that this Love parallels divine love. The image of Love pitching his mansion in the place of excrement is analogous to the Holy Spirit overshadowing Mary (the old woman on whom Crazy Jane was patterned was called "Cracked Mary")[5] with the resultant birth in the stable. "Nothing" that is "sole" and "whole" recalls the Cabbalistic idea that when God and his Shekinah are fully united all will be subsumed to nothing. Clearly, Jane must continue to leave the door unlatched if she is to find this divine love. The rending will not effect her transformation until time is gone, however. If the purgatorial state follows death and gives way to either rebirth or release, then death, for all the poignance of parting, is not an ending. Physical death, including her own, is insignificant in comparison to the continuous journey through division to wholeness.

The Bishop is a necessary foil to Jane, keeping her hatred at a purifying level of intensity. He functions as a questioner increasing her need for truth until she becomes a vehicle for her oracular declaration in the last stanza. In fact, Crazy Jane quotes one of the figures that Yeats included as an example of vehicle—Diotime,[6] who cries to Socrates in the *Symposium*, "must that be foul which is not fair."[7] Since Diotime's point is that love is the mean between mortality and immortality, the allusion supports the purgatorial nature of love. The Bishop, one of Yeats's final embodiments of his own pontificating and dogmatic tendencies, dramatizes that Yeats still recognizes this side of himself, just as he had in the early coxcomb William Howard in *John Sherman*. He puts an even finer edge on his self-forgiving mockery of his coolly detached antithetical tendencies by describing the unappealing Bishop through a woman's eyes in the first poem. In the pattern of questioner and vehicle, the Bishop embodies Yeats's past and present as much as the sensual Jane does. Then, as is typical in this pattern, Jane, in turn, becomes questioner in the final poem, trying to understand the dancers as she stands apart and watches.

She concludes the sequence by making very clear, in Poem VII, that the passion to "try again" is more important than death:

> Did he die or did she die?
> Seemed to die or died they both?
> God be with the times when I
> Cared not a thraneen for what chanced
> So that I had the limbs to try
> Such a dance as there they danced—
> *Love is like the lion's tooth.* (P 260)

As long as she can attempt to dance the purifying, purgatorial dance of love with all the cruelty and deceit that the strangulation and drawn knife of the first two stanzas dramatize, she will be tortured by the "lion's tooth" and goaded on to achieving the light lost in her mother's womb.

The refrain in this last poem, as in the others, is italicized, suggesting that it is spoken in a different tone and distancing it from the verses. This technique, used by Yeats throughout his career, gives the impression of a mysterious and omniscient narrator who evaluates and comments on Jane's experience. The attitude of this choric voice evolves as Crazy Jane recounts her past so that by the end of the sequence they both find forgiveness and blessing, embodying the double blessing at the end of "A Dialogue of Self and Soul" and paralleling the understanding between the Priest and the Chambermaid in "The Three Bushes." Thus, for both of them, this interchange is a purgatorial process.

As the songs progress, the narrator becomes more sympathetic, whereas Jane recognizes her own failure more clearly, although never faltering in her self-affirmation. The ambiguity of the refrains in the first poem suggests that the narrator is keeping his judgment open-ended. I have already indicated the ambiguity of "*All find safety in the tomb*"; the second refrain, "*The solid man and the coxcomb*," is equally two-edged. Jane would presumably find Jack the solid man and the goose-skinned Bishop the coxcomb; yet, the Bishop called Jack a coxcomb and the living Bishop is literally more solid than the ghost of Jack. The second poem, "Crazy Jane Reproved," could be interpreted as spoken by the narrator, since the tone does not fit either Crazy Jane or the Bishop. If so, the narrator is pointing out to Jane (who tries to dismiss him with "*Fol de rol, fol de rol*") that she must find more than sound and fury under the oak. He listens and affirms her more accurate confession in "Crazy Jane on the Day of Judgment," where she recognizes that not the Bishop, but the virginity of her own and Jack's souls kept her love unsatisfied. The dialogue nature of this confession is underlined by the repetition of "Jane said" and "said he" at the end of the alternating stanzas. The second refrain, "'*That's certainly the case,' said he*," relates especially closely to the attitude of the Priest in "The Three Bushes," who understands "her case" when the Chambermaid confesses the same failure of love to him.

In "Crazy Jane and Jack the Journeyman"—Jane's most profoundly confessional poem in the sense that Jane reveals the continuing source of her sin and intention to continue sinning—the choric figure remains silent, letting her ravel up in words the bond between her ghost and Jack's. Then the narrator offers blessing and sacramental affirmation for her body's continued song in the refrain, "*All things remain in God*," in "Crazy Jane on God." Next, he allows the Bishop to goad her into confessing what a proud woman such as herself does in love. In the last poem, the narrator witnesses that he himself has been affected by hearing and understanding Jane's case. His whispered, complacent first refrain, "*All find safety in the tomb*," has evolved to the terrifying realization that "*Love is like the lion's tooth*." He now recognizes that love is an ongoing process in which there is no repose.

Yeats implies that the Priest in "The Three Bushes" is blessed when he looks long in the Chambermaid's face and understands her case, just as the narrator is given Jane's revelation at the end of "Crazy Jane Talks with the Bishop" and is blessed with a better understanding of the bitter sweetness of love. The narrator is ultimately part of Jane's own psyche, her Daimon with whom she must struggle until she is released from the purgatorial process. That her Daimon has also gone through a purgatorial process guarantees that her confession has truly brought her closer to the ultimate forgiveness of sins when love will be able to take the "whole / Body and soul" (P 257).

Ribh

Crazy Jane's experiences and longings evidence the paradoxical nearness to and distance from God that characterize the purgatorial journey. Yeats wrote to Olivia Shakespear in 1926, "The mystic way and sexual love use the same means—opposed yet parallel existences" (L 715). The processes of human love and union with God are analogous, but each takes place on a different side of the "gulf between the one and the many, or . . . God and man,"[8] as Yeats told Sparrow. In the mid 1930s, Ribh, another figure engaged in a purgatorial journey up Mount Meru, dramatizes how the artist must be in touch with each of the parallel processes. Like lovers, such as Crazy Jane and the Chambermaid, the artist must be aware of and develop both his virginity of soul, which keeps him on the side of the many, and his vision of the divine, which projects him imaginatively onto the side of the one.

Ribh, like the Priest in "The Three Bushes," is a choric, mediating figure. At present, he is not participating directly in either the sexual or mystical experiences he witnesses; he views each from a middle ground and understands both imaginatively and empathetically. He can thus delineate the parallel between perfect human love and divine love, stressing the oneness, androgyny, and self-begotten nature of both. Recognizing that the virginity of his own soul keeps him in the realm of multiplicity, he affirms this fragmented world in a manner that prepares for the third bush that the Priest plants on the Chambermaid's grave. Ribh's "Supernatural Songs" suggest that the illusion of oneness that the three bushes create is crucial if the purgatorial journey is to lead the three lovers to perfect unity, but that the lovers' songs, at present, flow from their separate roots sunk in the darkness and deception of their ongoing multiplicity.

Ribh, a Druidic Christian, who echoes "pre-Christian thought" (VP 857), indicates both how much Yeats's views of the poet as adept have changed since his early view of the noninvolved dreamer, and how important the analogy between the priest-adept and the artist remains to him. Ribh, in contrast to Aedh, is an adept who understands and participates imaginatively in passionate experience. He closely prefigures the Abbé de Bourdeille, who listens sympathetically to the Chambermaid's confession because, as his name implies, he has participated in similar cases in his time. Such a choric, questioning figure, balanced by the many figures who participate directly in physical love, is still an important aspect of the antithetical artist's psyche. The passionate lover must listen to the ascetic with "tonsured head" within himself or herself in order to create a work of art. The artist must contain both Ribh and Crazy Jane, Priest and Chambermaid: their dialogue transforms the creative tension of the antinomy into song.

Ribh first reports his vision of perfect human love, in "Ribh at the Tomb of Baile and Aillinn." His description is obviously based on Swedenborg:[9]

> The miracle that gave them such a death
> Transfigured to pure substance what had once
> Been bone and sinew; when such bodies join

> There is no touching here, nor touching there,
> Nor straining joy, but the whole is joined to whole;
> For the intercourse of angels is a light
> Where for its moment both seem lost, consumed. (P 284)

Through death, Baile and Aillinn attain a state much like the one Solomon described (but could not maintain) in "Solomon and the Witch." There is a slight difference in the depictions, however. Solomon remarks that "two things, / Though several, are a single light" (P 177), giving prominence to the individual sovereignty of each in the embrace. Ribh does not deny the fact that each is really becoming his or her truest self, since they only "seem" lost. As Yeats had said in "Anima Mundi," "they make love in that union which Swedenborg has said is of the whole body and seems from afar off an incandescence. . . . This running together and running of all to a centre, and yet without loss of identity, has been prepared for by their exploration of their moral life" (My 356). Nonetheless, Ribh emphasizes the loss of each separate identity at the moment of union.

As Yeats had indicated in *A Vision*, 1925, the fear of the loss of his unique identity sends the spirit back to this world rather than into the final release. In *A Vision*, 1937, Yeats insists that the inability "to lose and keep his identity" (52) is what keeps a lover from solving the antinomy in the marriage bed. Instead, the lover "falls asleep. That sleep is the same as the sleep of death." In "The Three Bushes," the symbolic death is soon followed by the physical death of the Lover, but as Crazy Jane delineates, mere physical death cannot end the antinomy. The passionate sense of their own identity will lead the Lover, the Chambermaid, Crazy Jane, A Woman Young and Old, Sheba, Leda, and My Self back to the conflict of the antinomies again.

Baile and Aillinn have experienced a different kind of death, however. Ribh says that "the miracle that gave them such a death" is the cause of their transfiguration to pure substance. Unlike the figures mentioned above, Baile and Aillinn have achieved their final release. Before this ultimate death, they were completely "purified by tragedy"—no further expiating purgatorial experience is necessary. The Lover dies on the anniversary of his first meeting with the Chambermaid, but the implication of his dying deceived is that he will be reborn. Baile and Aillinn meet on the anniversary of their miraculous death, not to continue expiating, but to delight in the total oneness they have attained.

Ribh proclaims that his asceticism has prepared him to witness their light while retaining his own identity—emphasized by the "I" and "my" of the last line. Since his perception of their perfect circle of light is "somewhat broken by the leaves," the darkness of his imperfect identity keeps him from joining them. As Yeats says in "The Holy Mountain" (1932), "Darkness is the causal body of existence" (EI 463). If Ribh found his permanent self, he would find God, since Yeats also says in "The Holy Mountain" "a God is but the Self" (EI 461). Leaving his need for purification behind him, Ribh would be "transfigured to pure substance" and become divine, rather than paralleling the divine on this side of the gulf by creating artifices of eternity. However, there would be no one to mediate the vision to other humans: the light would consume his ability to report the tale if it were not somewhat broken. Ribh's subsequent songs indicate that, although he looks forward to achieving the pure light someday, he, as artist, prefers to remain slightly in the dark at this point.

He continues in his role of mediator, reporting his view of the perfect union of masculine and feminine in divine love in the first stanza of "Ribh denounces Patrick." The second stanza stresses the analogy between temporal love and divine intercourse: "Natural and supernatural with the self-same ring are wed. / As man, as beast, as an ephemeral fly begets, Godhead begets Godhead" (P 284). As the reference to the Smaragdine Tablet indicates, this correspondence is a basic tenet of occultism, one Yeats had been familiar with from his youth. In the second half of the poem, however, Ribh clarifies that human love does not perfectly parallel divine love:

> Yet all must copy copies, all increase their kind;
> When the conflagration of their passion sinks, damped by the body or the mind,
> That juggling nature mounts, her coil in their embraces twined.
>
> The mirror-scaled serpent is multiplicity.

Human love cannot maintain the conflagration of two into one. The passion "sinks," a foreshadowing of the Lover sunk in rest on the Chambermaid's breast. Or, as Yeats puts it in *A Vision*, "the Lover falls asleep." Then the "contrapuntal serpent" that the Lady describes to the Chambermaid is heard hissing in the lovers' union. The two processes are parallel, but opposed: human lovers remain on the side of the many. Their intercourse fails to be the intercourse of angels, one of the marks of which, as Swedenborg designates, is that there are no offspring from the union.[10] In terms of the opposition Yeats had wrestled with in "The Dolls," both the dolls and the "noisy filthy thing" are signs of multiplicity. Both works of art and children point out the failure of the creative and sexual processes to achieve divine simplicity. Referring to this poem, Yeats wrote to Olivia Shakespear, "We beget and bear because of the incompleteness of our love" (L 824).

If the union were perfect, they would beget and bear themselves, not separate offspring. God's intercourse is eternally in process and eternally completed: God is and remains but three. In Cabbalistic[11] and Platonic terms, the male and female perpetually combine to produce the androgyne—the Christ, in alchemical terms. He and She have united to beget a third who consists of themselves. No further proliferation is necessary, or even possible. There is no before or after, no alternation of desire and exhaustion. Nothing is needed to spur them on or save them from oblivion: God is eternally self-begotten.

Yeats explains that the Indian mystics, in imitation of God, are careful not to procreate:

> A man and woman, when in sexual union, transfigure each other's images into the masculine and feminine characters of God, but the man must not finish, vitality must not pass beyond his body, beyond his being. There are married people who, though they do not forbid the passage of the seed, practice, not necessarily at the moment of union, a meditation, wherein the man seeks the divine Self as present in his wife, the wife the divine Self as present in the man. (EI 484)

The end of the passage glosses Ribh's statement that couples "share God that is but three." If each could truly find the divine Self through his or her intercourse with the other, each would find his or her Daimon's matching masculine or feminine counterpart to make up the permanent androgynous self.

Ribh describes such a self-begotten ecstasy where "my soul had found / All happiness in its own cause or ground" (P 285) in "Ribh in Ecstasy." In that state he is uninterested in communicating to other generations:

> What matter that you understood no word!
> Doubtless I spoke or sang what I had heard
> In broken sentences.

This statement is reminiscent of a comment about those who achieve the Ghostly Self or beatitude: "We may even while we live hear their voices when in a state of trance, but speaking detached or broken sentences, and that which they say is always the greatest wisdom attainable by the soul" (V, 1925, 237). Such "broken sentences" are an attempt to translate the ineffable. In this moment, already past, that Ribh recounts, he had become pure vehicle; demon and beast were quieted and he knew with direct apprehension that "Godhead on Godhead in sexual spasm begot / Godhead."

Yet Ribh, so essentially connected to the dark in his first song, cannot remain in that self-begotten ecstasy of pure light. Darkness intervenes:

> . . . Some shadow fell. My soul forgot
> Those amorous cries that out of quiet come
> And must the common round of day resume.

The same paradox of light and darkness that functions in "Chosen" and "Crazy Jane and Jack the Journeyman" appears here. The shadow that falls is daybreak. After he has lost the vision, Ribh tries again to describe the other side of the gulf in "There," but he is reduced to formulaic repetition[12] of traditional images of heaven, that imply that his inspiration has failed him. He can no longer function as pure vehicle, pronouncing what he heard in his moment of ecstasy. He now mouths not the "broken sentences" that transcend communication, but far too pat aphorisms.

He recognizes that the virginity of his soul keeps him from being permanently among the self-begotten in "Ribh Considers Christian Love Insufficient." Since he cannot love as God does, he will take the opposite road—hatred. Yeats's concept of hatred here is closely associated with his view of cruelty and deceit in his comments on expiation. Just as the lovers work toward a perfect love by experiencing the imperfections of their present love, so by concentrating on the impurities of the human condition, Ribh will sense, by contrast, what constitutes the pure state:

> From terror and deception freed it can
> Discover impurities, can show at last
> How soul may walk when all such things are past,
> How soul could walk before such things began. (P 286)

The virgin-bride imagery in the third stanza is crucial to Yeats's view that the tragedy of the soul is ultimately salvific. Ribh proclaims:

> Then my delivered soul herself shall learn
> A darker knowledge and in hatred turn
> From every thought of God mankind has had.
> Thought is a garment and the soul's a bride
> That cannot in that trash and tinsel hide:
> Hatred of God may bring the soul to God.

In one sense, the soul, in Blakean fashion, rejects all orthodox constructs of God. Once free of these false illusions, the soul is naked and open to God. At the same time, the imagery suggests that the virgin soul is brought to God by turning violently away from him, by trying to hide from him and retain her virginity. If the soul continues in her virginal struggle to keep God from penetrating her, however, God will eventually master her. Her abhorrence of being violated by God paradoxically strips her and readies her for God's mastery at "the stroke of midnight."

Ribh describes the ultimate moment in the fourth stanza:

> At stroke of midnight soul cannot endure
> A bodily or mental furniture.
> What can she take until her Master give!
> Where can she look until He make the show!
> What can she know until He bid her know!
> How can she live till in her blood He live!

This is the moment Yeats describes in "Anima Hominis" when he says that "the ringers in the tower have appointed for the hymen of the soul a passing bell" (My 332). The soul, utterly devoid of all physical and intellectual "furniture"—stripped of even the self-preserving virginity that brought her to this point—has reached the irrevocable moment when she is completely reintegrated into her permanent self and the identity her conscious mind has known "seems lost." Ribh's last four lines prophesy the same experience between the soul and her master that the Woman Young and Old looks forward to when her soul will go "naked to naked" and "He" will "rule in his own right" (P 275).

But such experience is, of course, exactly what Yeats renounced in "A Dialogue of Self and Soul." Ribh, like the Woman Young and Old and Crazy Jane, realizes that at present he must choose to stay in the penultimate step. Right now, he, as artist, will "study hatred with great diligence, / For that's a passion in my own control." He will act out of the self-preserving virginity of his own soul, still ironically unable to yield to his permanent self for fear that he will lose his identity as he knows it. He will continue to produce "furniture" or artifice in the world of things and multiplicity.

Continuing to designate the soul as "She," which he images as the moon, and God as "He," imaged as the sun, Ribh further develops the implication that the soul of the antithetical artist comes very close to being subsumed into God, but that her virginity keeps her from submitting to her master, in "He and She." If the soul, like the moon, "dared" (P 287) stop her constant waxing and waning to rest in the stasis of the sun, she would lose her separate identity and her song would stop. But she, in the pattern Yeats described in *A Vision*, 1925, fears the loss of her transient identity and so returns to creation. Like Crazy Jane's body, nevertheless, the antithetical soul sings on. Retaining her own identity, she continually flies to and from the sun.

The key line that indicates how closely she parallels God, yet how great a chasm separates them because of the soul's virginity is "I am I, am I." Yeats told Olivia Shakespear that this short lyric conveyed his "centric myth" (L 723), referring to the recurring phases of the moon and also implying that a myth ending "I am thyself" was essential to his vision. This myth is recorded in his conversation with Sparrow in 1931: "He [Yeats] quoted a story of Hafiz, of a man who knocked on the door of his beloved, 'Let me in' and was told to go away; he knocked again and was again sent away; he knocked a third time and was asked 'Who are you?' 'I am thyself' 'Enter'. The whole of life, the world itself arises out of the opposition of these two."[13] Using imagery that relates to the master giving and taking his own at the end of "A Last Confession" and the unlatched door that Crazy Jane uses to describe intercourse, Yeats implies that the opposition between virginity and intercourse creates life in this world; conversely, when the lover penetrates the virgin soul, he can say "I am thyself" and the opposition ends. Some passages in Yeats's essays in the 1930s, particularly those on Indian mysticism, employ both moon imagery and the phrase "I am thyself" and thus gloss this seemingly simple lyric. He relates the two in "The Holy Mountain": "He that moves towards the full moon may, if wise, go to the Gods . . . or if to the Brahma's question 'Who are you?' he can answer 'Yourself,' pass out of those three penitential circles . . . and so pass out of all life" (EI 469). At the full, the moon can say "I am thou" to the sun and their opposition and the soul's need for reincarnation ends. Another passage ties together the moon, the sun, and the bride imagery in Ribh's preceding poem:

> As the first and last crescents are nearest the Sun, the visionary must have seen in those cycles a conflict between Moon and Sun, or when Greek astronomy had reached India, between a Moon that has taken the Sun's light into itself, "I am thyself," and the Moon lost in the Sun's light, between Sun in Moon and Moon in Sun. The Eastern poet saw the Moon as the Sun's bride; now in solitude; now offered to her Bridegroom in a self-abandonment unknown to our poetry. (EI 470)

Like the intercourse of angels, total union of sun and moon creates a pure light that involves mastery without loss of identity. In full union with the sun, the moon (or soul) achieves a stasis that is "objectless because objects are lost in complete light" (EI 462-63). To summarize the pattern that relates to "He and She" from these passages: the perfect union of the self and the other (the ability to say "I am thyself") creates pure light, is noncyclic, and is objectless.

Since Yeats was so familiar with the formula indicating perfect union, his alteration to "I am I" must be significant.[14] The soul cannot say "I am you" because of her self-preserving virginity. She remains on the parallel, but opposed, course, unable to unlatch the door completely and bridge the gulf between the human and the divine. In her hatred of God and his mastery, she affirms herself instead. She will not abandon the darkness that causes her earthly existence. She will not return to the light lost in her mother's womb. Her return, like My Self's, is to the original source of division, even as she, with all of creation, trembles at her closeness to the return to her unfallen self. Her "sweet cry" suggests a carry-over from the allusion to Porphyry's equation of honey bees and the virgin moon goddesses and a link with the Chambermaid making her "body sweet" in preparation for the Lover.

At present, the soul is happy to stay on the side of the many, remaking herself in her song, although as Ribh points out in "The Four Ages of Man," the artist's self-preserving struggle will not endure the final stroke of midnight. Then the soul will lose her virginity and the source and impetus of her song.

The inverted repetition of the phrase is subtly important, as well. The second "am I" is an echo, implying the cyclic process that the soul is still engaged in. "Am I" could also be interpreted as a question, as the antithetical artist continues the struggle within. She comes very near to uttering the ineffable biblical "I am," but for her there is a new beginning and she must try again to express herself. Unlike the Lady who finds shame in her imperfect "I am" in her first song, this soul accepts the division and darkness that characterize her earthly existence.

The repetition of "I" three times is symbolic of the parallel and of opposition to God, also. This is not the completeness of "God that is but three," as Ribh said in "Ribh denounces Patrick," but the multiplicity occasioned by the virginity of the soul. Another lyric, "Three Things" (1929), more explicitly conveys the incompleteness of earthly threes in a manner that contrasts to the objectlessness of eternity. The title itself indicates how important objects are to the speaker's existence. The bone-woman is dreaming back through her life as a preparation for rebirth.[15] The moment described in the third stanza, when she meets her "rightful man" (P 264) at dawn recalls the moment in her former incarnation when she chose the horror of daybreak. She almost achieved the moment that the Woman Young and Old envisions at the end of "A Last Confession," but her yawning implies the pattern that Yeats spoke of in *A Vision* when he said we fall asleep and thus do not solve the antinomy. Her stretching and yawning is both precoital and postcoital; exhaustion and desire follow each other other inexorably as long as she is not released from the cycle, as long as she is rooted in the world where the roots of the three bushes will be planted. The woman created her artifice of eternity when she met her rightful man face to face, imaging the reunion of the androgynous pair, just as the three bushes give the illusion of oneness. But the things that constitute that artifice will fragment again, just as the woman is now a dried bone on the shore.

The placement of the bone on the shore, together with the woman's desire to retain things, suggests a foreshadowing of the girl singing on the shore at the beginning of "The Soul in Judgment" in the later version of *A Vision*: "My imagination goes some years backward, and I remember a beautiful young girl singing on the edge of the sea in Normandy words and music of her own composition. She thought herself alone, stood barefooted between sea and sand; sang with lifted head of the civilisations that had come and gone, ending every verse with the cry: "O Lord let something remain" (219-20). Both the bone and the young girl are in a purgatorial state between two lives, but shunning neither. They are convinced, with Crazy Jane, that "All things remain in God" yet they resist the return of all things to God at this point. The singing soul of the artist in "He and She" is also in a middle ground, as symbolized by the position of the moon between earth and heaven. She refuses to sever her connection with either earth or sun.

In the remaining songs in the sequence, Ribh stresses the feminine in God, the seeming eternity of passion, the continuing struggle of the soul with God, and the astrological patterns that predict and reflect the recurrence of civilizations. Like the Woman Young and Old and Crazy Jane, Ribh seems profoundly confident that his struggle with God will eventually bring him into the pure, self-begotten, divine light he has witnessed and reported to others. At present, nonetheless, he is content to continue his purgatorial journey up Mount Meru, celebrating the dawn that shows that "his glory and his monuments are gone" (P 289).

The Wild Old Wicked Man

One of the last figures Yeats portrays as living and reliving the purgatorial process between dusk and dawn is "The Wild Old Wicked Man." This lyric includes four figures who resemble each of the four characters of "The Three Bushes." Through them, Yeats reaffirms his views on the virginity of the soul during intercourse and the forgiveness of sins with all the implications of these convictions for the lover and the artist. The action in "The Wild Old Wicked Man" also recapitulates the historical journey that brought Yeats to these conclusions, as does the progress in "The Three Bushes." Thus, "The Wild Old Wicked Man" offers a final summary of the vision of love and art in "The Three Bushes" in the same manner that that sequence traces Yeats's evolution throughout his career.

The Wild Old Wicked Man is a much more aware and deliberate lover than the Lover in "The Three Bushes." The epithet "wild" obviously carries a sexual connotation. His sexuality, like the Woman Young and Old's, Crazy Jane's, and the Chambermaid's, aligns him with God:

> "Because I am mad about women
> I am mad about the hills,"
> Said that wild old wicked man
> Who travels where God wills. (P 310)

That he is drawn to the hills by both God and lust suggests that he has experienced his *hieros gamos* and is ready to repeat the experience. Although Ribh certainly witnessed to the virginity of his soul, the Wild Old Wicked Man represents Yeats's first clear embodiment of a masculine lover who is conscious of his sacred marriage and resultant psychological virginity. He is aware of his connection to both God and women. He is not ignorant of what kind of women fill his physical need as the Lover is, nor does someone else murmur of God's love over his inert figure. The active and passive roles are reversed in that he has found his "proper food" and would have his lady share in the banquet:

> "I have what no young man can have
> Because he loves too much,
> Words I have that can pierce the heart,
> But what can he do but touch."

Because he has discovered the virginity of his soul in his *hieros gamos*, he is no longer violated by the longing of loving "too much" and has the self-possession necessary to touch another's heart. He, like all the other psychological virgins Yeats has depicted, can join in a deeper love than mere bodily love, but not be consumed by that love.

The first woman he meets and offers his love to is much like the Lady. This woman, a final expression of figures such as The Man Who Dreamed of Faeryland, the Rose, Aedh, the adept in the poems in *The Green Helmet and Other Poems*, the younger version of both the Man and the Woman Young and Old, and My Soul in "A Dialogue of Self and Soul," chooses to disdain human love in anticipation of heavenly love. The wild old man will not settle for a strictly spiritual relationship as the younger Yeats and all these personae did, however:

> "Kind are all your words, my dear
> Do not the rest withhold.
> Who can know the year, my dear,
> When an old man's blood grows cold?"

Yet she holds to her very orthodox chastity, fingering her beads in homage to "the old man in the skies." Her beads imply her Catholicism and suggest an allusion to Maud Gonne, whose religion was partly responsible for her refusal to requite Yeats's love. In a sense, this part of the poem functions as a final answer to the question that Yeats posed in "King and No King" at the height of his second period of spiritual marriage with Maud Gonne. In that earlier poem, Yeats had asked if her faith gave her assurance that "the blinding light beyond the grave" would compensate for lost opportunities for human love. This Maud Gonne figure, like the Lady, retains her faith that it will. Since "the old man in the skies" is a counterpart to the Wild Old Wicked Man, this woman seems to love the old man's permanent self, his image from before the world was made, rather than his human embodiment. But he is no longer under the control of his longing for her and chooses to be the coarse old man. Fittingly, however, the old man acknowledges once more that only her refusal brought other women into his arms.

This woman is not allowed to have it both ways, as the Lady does to some extent in her successful deception of the Lover. The old man is conscious that she cannot give him proper food and quickly turns to more willing lovers:

> "Go your ways, O go your ways,
> I choose another mark,
> Girls down on the seashore
> Who understand the dark;
> Bawdy talk for the fisherman;
> A dance for the fisher-lads
> When dark hangs upon the water
> They turn down their beds."

The description of these women is reminiscent of Yeats's depiction of the muses in *A Vision*, 1937: "But Muses resemble women who creep out at night and give themselves to unknown sailors and return to talk of Chinese porcelain . . . virginity renews itself like the moon" (V, 1937, 24). These girls are psychological virgins who renew their own virginity through intercourse with strangers. Their placement on the seashore suggests that, like the girl at the beginning of "The Soul in Judgment" and the bone-woman in "Three Things," they are between two worlds engaging in a purgatorial dance. Ironically, by immersion in human intercourse they are finding the old man in the skies more successfully than the woman with her beads, just as the Chambermaid, not the Lady, finds forgiveness in "The Three Bushes."

In the next stanza, the Wild Old Wicked Man suggests that his virginity, like theirs, is renewed in this embrace:

> "A young man in the dark am I,
> But a wild old man in the light,
> That can make a cat laugh, or
> Can touch by mother wit
> Things hid in their marrow-bones
> From time long past away,
> Hid from all those warty lads
> That by their bodies lay."

His *hieros gamos* has brought him to near oneness, so his repetition of it is regenerative. He is not merely doing the dragon's will like "all those warty lads."[16] He is a young man in the dark because his sin is redemptive, but his psychological virginity does not free him from the process of aging and death: he is still old at daybreak. By wholeheartedly taking part in physical love while being conscious that this is not the whole, he can bring himself closer to his permanent self from "time long passed away," although like all these purgatorial figures, the old man must choose the paradoxical darkness of dawn.

Yeats subtly suggests that the old man is finding his deepest self through these encounters by using the phrase "am I." At the same time, he stresses that the old man has not found his pure light by connecting darkness to his "I am." Yeats repeats this phrase very effectively in the last stanza to show that the old man is not yet self-begotten: "a coarse old man am I." He knows that he is a "right-taught man" to whom the "stream of lightning" will one day bring the inextinguishable daybreak where candles are not needed—but not yet. Now he chooses to repeat the crime where it is committed, knowing that the virginity of his soul will someday be penetrated by his permanent self.

Until that ultimate daybreak, he delights in the consolation afforded by his repeated sinning. Through his portrayal of the Wild Old Wicked Man, Yeats suggests that the Man Young and Old has found the life-affirming, self-abounding sweetness of the Woman Young and Old within himself. He is both Chambermaid and Lover, celebrating and blessing both the suffering and pleasure he experiences. He knows and affirms, through the virginity of his soul, that he is on the "second-best" road, but that designation implies that his is the regenerating, purgatorial journey that parallels God's love, not the mere repetition of the "warty lads."

The refrain, "*Day-break and a candle end*," adds the suggestion of a fourth figure, similar to the Priest in "The Three Bushes." This voice is detached and choric, understanding the confession that the old man makes and responding with both judgment and compassion. The deflated phallic image in "candle end" suggests that the refrain implies an ironic tone toward the boasting old man.[17] On the other hand, the voice could be interpreted as blessing and affirming the old man's willingness to be reduced once again on his way to the release of the final dawn. This refrain, like the worm image in "The Chambermaid's Second Song," reflects both the endless round of daybreak and darkness (birth, death, and rebirth) and the paradox of daybreak bringing the darkness of this world. The irony of the Lady's designation of herself as the "daytime lady" while refusing intercourse with life is underlined once more.

The refrain fragments the old man's tale, breaking in to dramatize that he is still in the world of multiplicity. At the same time, it ties his tale together and gives a suggestion of mysterious continuity that neither the old man nor the choric voice understands fully at this point. The choric voice could issue from the man himself, as if he stepped back and encapsulated the fragmentation that characterizes his experience in a more enigmatic and objective voice before continuing his self-affirming confession. Both the old man and the choric voice—the passionate self and the Daimon—are part of the same psyche, but that psyche is still tragically fragmented.

The interplay between the refrain and the verses creates a technical parallel to the tragedy of love. The refrain is neutral in itself, virginally unaffected in its perfect repetition. Yet it conveys an increasing response to the old man's self-revelation as his song progresses. The final repetition of the refrain is especially significant. Yeats has built a technical suggestion of completeness in the strong rhyme and even meter of the last stanza. The old man seems satisfied in his second-best consolation. Then he slightly fragments this aesthetic finality by the last repetition of the enigmatic refrain, suggesting that aesthetic unity will give way to fragmentation once more.

Even within the last stanza, traditional formal perfection and imperfect individuality play against each other. Yeats maintains the strong rhythm and fundamental singsong that he demanded in ballads, but he disrupts that form slightly in the imperfect rhyme between "I" and "awhile." As in his portrayals of love or the integration of the self, Yeats resists perfection of the work as much as he does perfection of the life. Paradoxically, the near perfection of his work flows from its slight imperfection—the string is often tuned ever so subtly off pitch in Yeats's greatest lyric poems by means of half rhymes, concentrated diction, and truncated syntax. The individual virginity of the poet's soul refuses to be swallowed by the impersonal infinity of the perfection of traditional forms, while he simultaneously re-creates as nearly perfect an embodiment of the perfection of traditional forms as he can.

He connects the interplay between traditional form and individuality to the antinomy between the one and the many in his conversation with Sparrow. Sparrow reports that "the essence of poetry was for him [Yeats] putting the personal into a static form, which he compared to the metaphysical antinomy of the individual and the infinite, the many and the one."[18] In "A General Introduction for My Work" (1937), Yeats advocates traditional form over free verse using imagery reminiscent of the virginity of the soul during intercourse: "The maid of honor whose tragedy they sing must be lifted out of history with a timeless pattern, she is one of the four Marie's, the rhythm is old and familiar, imagination must dance, must be carried beyond feeling into the aboriginal ice. Is ice the correct word? I once boasted, copying the phrase from a letter of my father's, that I would write a poem 'cold and passionate as the dawn'" (EI 523). Traditional form (the one) calls the poet and the reader to the Self beyond the everyday warm, changing, painful life (the many). Its ice is "aboriginal": its form recalls a virginal time before division into imperfection and predicts the return to such an eternal oneness. But this ice is "beyond feeling"; it is attained by intercourse with the pain of life that brings the cold and passionate dawn of psychological virginity. It is the technical correlative to the daybreak that the Woman Young and Old, Crazy Jane, Ribh, the Chambermaid, and the Wild Old Wicked Man choose. The too-easy parroting of traditional form, used as an escape from life, as Yeats had tended to do in his earliest works, is not the pattern he praises here.

The formal and the individual must struggle with one another as they do in "The Wild Old Wicked Man" for a truly creative pattern to emerge: "The contrapuntal structure of the verse, to employ a term used by Robert Bridges, combines the past and present.... The folk song is still there, but a ghostly voice, an unvariable possibility, an unconscious norm. What moves me and my hearer is a vivid speech that has no laws except that it must not exorcize the ghostly voice" (EI 524). Traditional form ("the ghostly voice") and the individual's "vivid speech" interact without either being consumed, although one or the other may dominate, as is true in the confessional interchange between vehicle and questioner, light and darkness, passion and detachment.

As I suggested briefly in chapter 1, "The Three Bushes" sequence epitomizes the unresolved, contrapuntal interchange between formal unity and individual fragmentation. Both the ghostly voice and the individual voice are heard in each verse and in each repetition of the refrain. The ballad is in a traditional form, yet Yeats uses imperfect rhyme in over half of the stanzas in his final version, clearly counterpointing the traditional folk voice with his own voice. The refrain, "O my dear, O my dear," also reflects the interplay between the traditional and the individual. Not only is it a refrain from a traditional Gaelic ballad, but Yeats also quotes a similar phrase, "O my child, O my dear" (EI 460, 478), as that heard by an Indian mystic as a sign of union with the divine. Thus, even the traditional associations conflict, since the Gaelic ballad is earthy. Yeats was very fond of "O my dear" as a personal utterance and repeats it frequently in his letters to Dorothy Wellesley. Since he was writing "The Three Bushes" and sending copies of the poems to her in those letters, he is, at times, quoting his own literary artifice when he uses the phrase. The refrain is two-edged, since the repetition of the phrase suggests both balanced stasis and cyclic duality. The ambiguity within the refrain is not resolved: the ghostly voice continuously calls the individual to wholeness, while the individual repeatedly effects the fragmentation which is paradoxically necessary to permanent wholeness.

The counterpoint of wholeness and fragmentation is repeated on a larger scale in the contrast between the formal unity of the ballad and the piecemeal effect of the songs. Within the songs, moreover, Yeats builds to a suggestion of aesthetic perfection in "The Lady's Third Song," then returns to fragmentation by "The Chambermaid's Second Song." In chapter 1, I commented on the ambiguity that surrounds the Lover's poetic ability. That ambiguity is indicative of his lasting creativity: both the choppiness of his individual voice in the stanza that refers to him in the ballad (which images disunity in the midst of the traditional unity of the ballad form) and the artifice of eternity that he creates in his exquisite song (which images unity in the midst of the prevailing fragmentation of the songs) are essential to his poetic ability.

In the context of the whole sequence, Yeats leaves a final impression of fragmentation and incompleteness. However, the poet will start the process again, building other artifices of eternity that will in turn fragment. Just as the Chambermaid and Priest create the emblematic artifice of eternity by planting the intertwining three bushes, so the Wild Old Wicked Man can fashion a work of art out of his present fragmentation without negating its multiplicity. The formal unity of that work of art, like his second-best consolation, almost releases him from the chaos of fragmentation, but because it fails slightly, he, as artist as well as lover, must "try again." Yet his artifices of eternity, like the repetition of the sin of division, are part of the purgatorial process that leads to eventual wholeness.

In one of his last conversations with Dorothy Wellesley, Yeats summarized the process by which the return to aesthetic wholeness is effected by the experience of fragmentation: "The Greek Drama alone achieved perfection; it has never been done since; it may be thousands of years before we achieve that perfection again. Shakespeare is only a mass of magnificent fragments" (LP 213-14). Shakespeare's "magnificent fragments" and Yeats's artifices of eternity are redemptive failures in the purgatorial process of regaining perfection. The Wild Old Wicked Man, like Yeats in "The Circus Animals' Desertion," knows that "complete" images grow "in pure mind" (P 347) but that this process parallels the sterile intellectual separation that ultimately consumes the Lady. He must return to the place where "all the ladders start"—a woman's breast where he was nursed and where he re-enacts the crime of being born. His continued song requires contact with fragmented things—"old kettles, old bottles, and a broken can / Old iron, old bones, old rags"—as he returns to the bottom rung of poetic intensity, like the Chambermaid at the end of "The Three Bushes," and pays the price demanded by "the raving slut / Who keeps the till."

The Wild Old Wicked Man will continue to forget the crime where it is committed, embodying Yeats's own intention as he expressed it to Olivia Shakespear: "I shall be a sinful man to the end, and think upon my death bed of all the nights I wasted in my youth" (L 790). As he declares in "Politics," the final word in his lyric poetry,[19] if he were a young poet again, he would shun politics and make up for that wasted youth: "But O that I were young again / And held her in my arms" (P 348). His final passionate cry is his pledge that he is willing to "live it all again." He has come full circle from the cry, toward the end of *The Wind among the Reeds*, of the man who thinks

> . . . that his head
> May not lie on the breast nor his lips on the hair
> Of the woman that he loves, until he dies. (P 73)

The young Yeats, like the Lady and the first woman in "The Wild Old Wicked Man," reluctantly believed My Soul's dictum that "only the dead can be forgiven"; the aged Yeats, like the Chambermaid and the Wild Old Wicked Man, knows that only living and reliving—plunging wholeheartedly into intercourse with life—can bring forgiveness and blessing.

His consolation will only last "awhile": daybreak will return. That new day, however, offers one more opportunity to try to overcome the antinomy between the one and the many and to celebrate his failure to do so in another song. The final complete sentence of Yeats's that Wellesley records is "I feel that I am just beginning to understand how to write" (LP 214). He, like so many of the personae he created, rejoices that he is still on the purgatorial road. The Wild Old Wicked Man continues on his journey, finding the ultimate forgiveness of sins by the repeated experience of the virginity of his soul during intercourse—a failure that is both the tragedy and the redemption of love and art.

Notes

Chapter 1

1. The most pertinent reference for this study is in the Preface, "Music and Poetry," to *Broadsides: A Collection of New Irish and English Songs*, ed. Dorothy Wellesley and W. B. Yeats (Dublin: Cuala Press, 1937; reprint ed., Shannon: Irish University Press, 1971), n. p.

2. Vivienne Koch, *W. B. Yeats, The Tragic Phase: A Study of the Last Poems* (Baltimore: Johns Hopkins Press, 1951), p. 131.

3. Gloria C. Kline, *The Last Courtly Lover: Yeats and the Idea of Woman* (Ann Arbor: UMI Research Press, 1983), p. 157.

4. Jon Stallworthy, *Vision and Revision in Yeats's Last Poems* (Oxford: Clarendon Press, 1969), pp. 80–81, makes a convincing case that the two ballads were independently written after a discussion of the basic plot. Thomas Henn, *The Lonely Tower: Studies in the Poetry of W. B. Yeats*, 2nd ed. (New York: Barnes and Noble, 1965), p. 330, and A. Norman Jeffares, *A New Commentary on the Poems of W. B. Yeats* (Stanford University Press, 1984), p. 367, hold that Yeats's version is derived from Wellesley's.

5. Wellesley's full ballad appears in *Broadsides*, No. 9, September 1937. It was printed with neither mention of the source nor a priest in the ballad. When it was reprinted in a shorter version, an ascription identical to Yeats's was added in an errata.

6. Arra Garab, "Fabulous Artifice: Yeats's 'Three Bushes' Sequence," *Criticism* 7 (1965): 238. I am indebted to Garab's article, as well as Edward Partridge, "Yeats's 'The Three Bushes'—Genesis and Structure," *Accent* 17 (Spring 1957): 67–80.

7. Garab designates Pierre de Bourdeille (1540–1614), a chronicler who died after falling from a horse, as a possible historical name Yeats used. If so, the change to "Michel" must be for a purpose.

8. Stallworthy, *Vision and Revision*, pp. 84–85, 95, 98.

9. Ibid., p. 86.

10. Ibid., p. 87.

11. Most commentators find a symbol of the unity not possible in life in the contiguous burial of the three lovers: Garab, pp. 238–39; Partridge, p. 76, and Daniel Hoffmann, *Barbarous Knowledge: Myth in the Poetry of Yeats, Graves, and Muir* (New York: Oxford University Press, 1967), p. 52.

12. Various interpretations have been put forth explaining who speaks the refrain. Koch, p. 130, favors a fourth, unknown voice. Partridge, p. 75, and Stallworthy, *Vision and Revision*, p. 111, suggest that different figures from the ballad speak the refrain in different stanzas. Partridge, p. 76, also says that "we, the chorus" sing the refrain.

13. Quoted in A. Norman Jeffares, *W. B. Yeats: Man and Poet* (New York: Barnes and Noble, 1966), p. 267. Also recorded by William Rothenstein, *Men and Memories: Recollections 1872–1938*, abridged by Mary Lago (London: Chatto and Windus, 1978), p. 195; Wellesley, LP 192; and George Brandon Saul, *Prolegomena to the Study of Yeats's Poems* (Philadelphia: University of Pennsylvania Press, 1957), p. 147. Garab, p. 247, Kline, p. 162, and Partridge, p. 79, connect this statement to "The Three Bushes." Commentators who discuss this statement in relation to other works or to Yeats's works in general include the following: Harold Bloom, *Yeats* (New York: Oxford University Press, 1970), pp. 253, 327; David Clark, *Yeats at Songs and Choruses* (Amherst: University of Massachusetts Press, 1983), p. 29; Koch, p. 135; Bernard Levine, *The Dissolving Image: The Spiritual-esthetic Development of W. B. Yeats* (Detroit: Wayne State University Press, 1970), p. 52; J. Hillis Miller, *Poets of Reality: Six Twentieth-Century Writers* (Cambridge: Belknap Press, 1965), p. 95; Joyce Carol Oates, *The Edge of Impossibility: Tragic Forms in Literature* (New York: Vanguard Press, 1972), p. 180.

14. Quoted in Lady Augusta Gregory, *Seventy Years*, ed. Colin Smythe (New York: Macmillan, 1974), p. 351.

15. Jeffares, *Man and Poet*, pp. 267–68.

16. Curtis Bradford, "Yeats and Maud Gonne," *Texas Studies in Language and Literature* 3 (1962): 461 and Virginia Moore, *The Unicorn: William Butler Yeats's Search for Reality* (New York: Macmillan, 1954), p. 38. Maud Gonne had been involved in an affair with Lucien Millevoye, but "sexual love soon began to repel her" (M 133).

17. A good summary statement of the image of the magus is provided by E. M. Butler, *The Myth of the Magus* (Cambridge University Press, 1979).

18. C. A. Burland, *The Arts of the Alchemists* (New York: Macmillan, 1968), p. 118.

19. Philippe-Auguste Villiers de L'Isle-Adam, *Axel*, trans. Marilyn Gaddis Rose (Dublin: Dolmen Press, 1970), p. 170.

20. Bradford, "Yeats and Maud Gonne," pp. 461, 465–66. Moore, p. 197, dates the second spiritual marriage from June 1908 to January 1909. The discrepancy seems to be caused by different datings of a crucial diary entry discussed below.

21. *Letters to W. B. Yeats*, ed. Richard J. Finneran, George Mills Harper and William Murphy (New York: Columbia University Press, 1977), p. 202.

22. Conrad Balliet, "The Lives—and Lies—of Maud Gonne," *Eire-Ireland* 14 (Fall 1979): 41–42. Balliet, who does not date the journal entry itself, accepts Bradford's dating of the affair. Moore, p. 202, dates the entry January 21, 1909; Bradford, "Yeats and Maud Gonne," p. 465, dates it June 21, 1909. Given Yeats's handwriting, the disagreement is understandable; however, Bradford's other evidence, particularly the fact that Maud Gonne joined Yeats in London during May and June of 1909, suggests that June is correct.

23. Thomas Parkinson, "Yeats and the Love Lyric," *James Joyce Quarterly* 3 (Winter 1966): 115–16.

24. Bradford, "Yeats and Maud Gonne," p. 473.

25. Garab, pp. 242, 247, finds the resolution of the antinomies in the Lady's "verbal magic." Helen Vendler, *Yeats's VISION and the Later Plays* (Cambridge: Harvard University Press, 1963), p. 132, also finds that the Lady's "poetic sleight of hand" unites spirit and flesh.

26. Conversation with Sparrow, quoted above, and V, 1937, 214.

27. John Dryden, *The Poetical Works of John Dryden*, ed. George Noyes (Cambridge: Riverside Press, 1950), p. 189.

28. Moore, p. 202; Bradford, "Yeats and Maud Gonne," p. 465; Richard Ellmann, *Golden Codgers: Biographical Speculations* (New York: Oxford University Press, 1973), pp. 107-8n.; Richard Ellmann, *Yeats: The Man and the Masks* (New York: W. W. Norton, 1978), p. 192.

29. Balliet, p. 42.

30. Partridge, p. 78. Yeats explicitly suggests this connection between worms, death, and reincarnation in "The Phases of the Moon."

31. Stallworthy, *Vision and Revision*, p. 104.

32. Garab, p. 244.

33. Partridge, p. 78.

34. Stallworthy, *Vision and Revision*, pp. 103-5.

35. A. G. Stock, *W. B. Yeats: His Poetry and Thought* (Cambridge University Press, 1961), p. 236, holds that the Lover finds oneness in his rest.

36. Gregory, p. 351. The statement appears in a list of Yeats's sayings at the end of a chapter in which the earliest reference is to 1897 and the latest to 1904.

37. LP 64, 80, 100, 111, 113; Stallworthy, *Vision and Revision*, p. 81.

38. Commentators on Yeats's theory of Purgatory include: Douglas Archibald, *Yeats* (Syracuse University Press, 1983), pp. 188-89; Harbans Rai Bachchan, *W. B. Yeats and Occultism: A Study of His Works in Relation to Indian Lore, the Cabbala, Swedenborg, Boehme, and Theosophy* (London: Books from India, 1976), pp. 120-29, 203; Clark, *Yeats at Songs and Choruses*, pp. 51-52; Vendler, Chapter 3; F. A. C. Wilson, *W. B. Yeats and Tradition* (New York: Macmillan, 1958), pp. 137-61, 216-23, 231-43.

Chapter 2

1. Bachchan, pp. 127-28, gives an extensive list of Yeats's use of this idea, but begins the list with *Per Amica Silentia Lunae* (1917).

2. Edward Engelberg, " 'He too was in Arcadia': Yeats and the Paradox of the Fortunate Fall," in *In Excited Reverie: A Centenary Tribute to William Butler Yeats, 1865-1939*. Ed. K. G. W. Cross and A. Norman Jeffares (New York: Macmillan, 1965), p. 92.

3. Finneran, ed., JS 26.

4. Giorgio Melchiori, *The Whole Mystery of Art: Pattern into Poetry in the Work of W. B. Yeats* (London: Routledge and Kegan Paul, 1960), p. 262.

5. H. P. Blavatsky, *Collected Writings, 1888: The Secret Doctrine* (Adyar Madras, India: The Theosophical Publishing House, 1978), 1: 392-93.

6. Finneran, ed., JS 26, also connects her name to "Mary Cronan," the girl to whom the earliest extant letter by Yeats is addressed.

7. Ibid., p. 22.

8. W. B. Yeats, ed., *Fairy and Folk Tales of the Irish Peasantry*, 1888; reprint in *Fairy and Folk Tales of Ireland* (Gerrards Cross, Buckinghamshire: Colin Smythe, 1973), p. 76.

9. Finneran, ed., JS 27–30; Ellmann, *Man and Masks*, p. 79; Henn, p. 26; Moore, pp. 184–85.

10. Yeats revised this line, making it echo "Innisfree," for the 1895 edition. All references to earlier printed versions and titles, as well as dates of publication, of the poems are taken from VP. Dates of composition are from Richard Ellmann, *The Identity of Yeats* (New York: Oxford University Press, 1954), pp. 287–94.

11. Suzette Henke, "Yeats's *John Sherman*: A Portal of Discovery," *Canadian Journal of Irish Studies* 8 (June 1982): 31.

12. Miller, *Poets of Reality*, p. 78, points out that wandering is the dominant motif of Yeats's early works.

13. Ellmann, *Identity*, p. 73.

14. In his Preface to *Letters to the New Island*, ed. Horace Reynolds (Cambridge: Harvard University Press, 1934), p. xii, Yeats says that as a young man he only stopped reading Boehme for fear he would do nothing else.

15. Jacob Boehme, *Three Principles*, xiii, 38, quoted in *Personal Christianity, A Science: The Doctrines of Jacob Boehme*, ed. Franz Hartmann (1891; reprint ed. New York: Macoy Publishing Co., 1919), p. 235. Since Yeats used another book compiled by Hartmann (see Thomas Leslie Dume, "William Butler Yeats: A Survey of His Reading" [Ph. D. dissertation, Temple University, 1950], p. 120) at the same time that he was reading Boehme, he may have used Hartmann's handy anthology of Boehme. If so, Hartmann's chapter entitled, "Incarnation—The Celestial Virgin" probably strongly influenced Yeats's depiction of the Rose. Even if he did not use Hartmann, he did own a copy of *The Three Principles of the Divine Essence* (Moore, p. 97).

16. Boehme, *Forty Questions*, xxxvi, 12, in Hartmann, p. 235.

17. Boehme, *Three Principles*, xviii, 98, in Hartmann, p. 237.

18. Jeffares, *New Commentary*, p. 23.

19. Dume, p. 132.

20. A. E. Waite, *Lives of the Alchemystical Philosophers* (London: George Redway, 1888), pp. 95–118.

21. Yeats put the first two lines quoted here into question form much later, when revising this poem for a 1929 edition. His hindsight enabled him to capture the ambivalence of his early attraction to and repulsion from physical love.

22. The fullest list of allusions is provided by F. A. C. Wilson, *Yeats's Iconography* (New York: Macmillan, 1960), pp. 248–54.

23. Yeats says that Blake does distinguish a "kind chastity" for the "sake of the Lord," YE-B 1: 398.

24. Bradford, "Yeats and Maud Gonne," p. 456.

25. The following ten poems, designated by their numbers in VP, were assigned to Aedh: 44, 52, 58, 63, 64, 65, 66, 73, 74, 75.

26. Three poems were assigned to Robartes: 54, 56, 62.

27. Three poems were assigned to Hanrahan: 55, 69, 72.

28. Yeats refers to *The Golden Bough* in his note to "The Valley of the Black Pig," VP 809.

29. James George Frazer, *The Golden Bough: A Study in Magic and Religion* (New York: Macmillan, 1951), I, 1: 30–31; IV, 1: 38.

30. Donoghue, ed., M 86n.; and Ellmann, *Man and Masks*, p. 157, connect this poem to Olivia Shakespear (Diana Vernon). However, since it was first published as the song of Aedh's severed head to Dectora in "The Binding of the Hair," I agree with Allen Grossman, *Poetic Knowledge in the Early Yeats: A Study of THE WIND AMONG THE REEDS* (Charlottesville: University Press of Virginia, 1969), p. 112, that this is the inaccessible woman.

31. Jeffares, *Man and Poet*, p. 102, dates the affair 1895; Donoghue, ed., M 88n., dates it in 1896 since Yeats states that they met in Woburn Buildings. Yeats says that he wrote "The Shadowy Horses" (an earlier title for "He bids his Beloved be at Peace") and two other poems (not designated) for Diana Vernon (M 86).

32. L. C. Parks, "The Influence of Villiers de L'Isle-Adam on W. B. Yeats" (Ph. D. dissertation, University of Washington, 1959), pp. 27–28.

33. Grossman, pp. 155–56.

34. Donoghue, ed., M 74n.

35. Frazer, I, 1: 35–37.

36. Ibid., IV, 1: 40–46.

Chapter 3

1. David Clark, Michael Sidnell, and George Mayhew, *Druid Craft: The Writing of THE SHADOWY WATERS* (Amherst: University of Massachusetts Press, 1971), show that Yeats had been working on this drama from as early as 1883.

2. *Shadowy Waters*, VP p. 750, ll. 59–60, 65–66; p. 765, ll. 354–55.

3. 1906 version, ll. 146–47. Allt and Alspach include a chart listing only forty lines as repeated in whole or part in the later version, VP, p. 220.

4. Clark et al., *Druid Craft*, p. 299.

5. Parks, p. 99.

6. This suggests that Olivia Shakespear (Diana Vernon) was partly the model for Dectora, as noted in Clark et al., *Druid Craft*, pp. 144–45.

7. James Runnels, "Mother, Wife, Lover: Symbolic Women in the Work of W. B. Yeats" (Ph.D. dissertation, Rutgers University, 1973), Chapter 4.

8. Bloom, p. 143 and Clark et al., *Druid Craft*, p. 15.

9. Bloom, p. 139.

10. Miller, *Poets of Reality*, p. 83, calls this passage a "crucial reversal."

11. Edward Engelberg, *The Vast Design: Patterns in W. B. Yeats's Aesthetic* (University of Toronto Press, 1964), p. 59, notes that Yeats's move away from writing lyrics during these years was itself a self-preservation.

12. Bradford, "Yeats and Maud Gonne," p. 461.

13. Ellmann, *Man and Masks*, p. 176.

14. Finneran, ed., P 698.

15. Allt and Alspach cross-reference this refrain in a note to "The Three Bushes," VP 569. Stallworthy, *Vision and Revision*, p. 81, also connects the two ballads.

16. Bradford, "Yeats and Maud Gonne," p. 467.

17. Quoted from Balliet, p. 41, up to "sweetheart. . . ." From "Always . . ." on taken from Moore, pp. 202–3.

18. Parkinson, "Yeats and the Love Lyric," pp. 115–16.

19. Philip Marcus, "Incarnation in 'Middle Yeats,'" in *Yeats Annual*, no. 1, ed. Richard J. Finneran (Dublin: Gill and Macmillan, 1982), p. 75, notes that this line may be a Dionysian counterpoint.

20. David Clark, "Stretching and Yawning with Yeats and Pound: 'Three Things,'" in *Yeats at Songs and Choruses*, pp. 43–64, connects similar actions to sexual arousal.

21. The first eight poems in *The Green Helmet and Other Poems* were grouped under the title "Raymond Lully and his wife Pernella" in the original edition, "Raymond Lully" being an error for Nicholas Flamel, VP 253.

22. Jeffares, *New Commentary*, p. 89.

23. Bradford, "Yeats and Maud Gonne," p. 466.

24. Marcus, "Incarnation," p. 73, connects Eochaid to Maud Gonne's husband.

25. Moore, pp. 105–6.

26. G. R. S. Mead, *Thrice-Greatest Hermes: Studies in Hellenistic Theosophy and Gnosis* (London: The Theosophical Society, 1906), 1: 218.

27. James Lovic Allen, "Life as Art: Yeats and the Alchemical Quest," *Studies in the Literary Imagination* 14 (Spring 1981): 32–33 and Parkinson, "Yeats and the Love Lyric," p. 115.

28. Waite, p. 107.

29. This combination of detachment and involvement is discussed at length in Engelberg, *The Vast Design* and in Thomas Whitaker, *Swan and Shadow: Yeats's Dialogue with History* (Chapel Hill: University of North Carolina Press, 1964).

30. Conrad Balliet, "W. B. Yeats: The Pun of a Gonne," *Modern British Literature* 4 (Spring 1979): 45.

31. Henn, p. 93.

32. "Is the Order of R.R. & A.C. to Remain a Magical Order?" printed in George Mills Harper, *Yeats's Golden Dawn* (New York: Barnes and Noble, 1974), p. 266.

33. Ibid., p. 270.

34. For example, "Baile and Aillinn," "The Grey Rock," and "The Three Beggars."

35. See especially "The Happy Townland," "The Withering of the Boughs," and "Running to Paradise."

36. Peter Ure, *W. B. Yeats* (New York: Grove Press, 1964), pp. 57–58.

Chapter 4

1. Thomas Parkinson, "This Extraordinary Book," in *Yeats's Annual*, no. 1, ed. Finneran, p. 204.

2. Jeffares, *New Commentary*, p. 141.

3. Joseph Ronseley, *Yeats's Autobiography: Life as Symbolic Process* (Cambridge: Harvard University Press, 1968), pp. 20, 32.

4. Harper and Hood, eds., V, 1925, Notes, p. 21.

5. Esther Harding, *Woman's Mysteries, Ancient and Modern: A Psychological Interpretation of the Feminine Principle as Portrayed in Myth, Story, and Dreams*, rev. ed. (New York: G. P. Putnam's Sons, 1971), pp. 91–92. Harding's synthesis draws from the same sources with which Yeats was familiar.

6. Ibid., p. 122.

7. Frazer, I, 1: 30.

8. Erich Neumann, *The Great Mother: An Analysis of the Archetype*, trans. Ralph Manheim (Princeton University Press, 1974), p. 318.

9. Gershom G. Scholem, *On the Kabbalah and Its Symbolism*, trans. Ralph Manheim (New York: Schocken Books, 1965), pp. 140–42.

10. Mead, 1: 218–19.

11. Harding, p. 148.

12. Ibid., pp. 124–26.

13. Scholem, p. 138.

14. Ellmann, *Identity*, p. 177; J. F. Adams, "'Leda and the Swan': The Aesthetics of Rape," *Bucknell Review* 12 (December 1964): 51, 55, 56; and Thomas Parkinson, *W. B. Yeats: The Later Poetry* (Berkeley and Los Angeles: University of California Press, 1964), pp. 137–42.

15. *The Secret Rose: A Variorum Edition*, ed. Philip Marcus, Warwick Gould, and Michael Sidnell (Ithaca: Cornell University Press, 1981), pp. 166–67n.

16. Yeats specifically connects the Ghostly Self to the Holy Ghost in V, 1925, 236.

17. Frank Pearce Sturm, *His Life, Letters, and Collected Work*, ed. Richard Taylor (Urbana: University of Illinois Press, 1969), p. 28.

18. Vendler, *Yeats's VISION*, p. 131.

19. Harper and Hood, eds., V, 1925, Notes, pp. 67–68; Moore, pp. 287– 88, 368; and James Olney, "Sex and the Dead: *Daimones* of Yeats and Jung," *Studies in the Literary Imagination* 14 (Spring 1981): 43–60.

20. Parkinson, "This Extraordinary Book," p. 195.

21. Yeats quotes this speech by the Fool at the beginning of "The Gates of Pluto," in V, 1925, 219.

22. Olney, pp. 56–57, assumes that Solomon and Sheba did achieve the "prelapsarian condition."

23. Wilson, *Yeats's Iconography*, pp. 76–77, says that Sheba becomes a receptacle of knowledge.

24. Frank Kermode, *Romantic Image* (New York: Macmillan, 1957), p. 102.

25. Clark, *Yeats at Songs and Choruses*, p. 151.

26. Peter Ure, "Yeats's Demon and Beast," in *Yeats and Anglo-Irish Literature: Critical Essays by Peter Ure*, ed. C. J. Rawson (Liverpool University Press, 1974), pp. 106–12.

27. George Mills Harper and Kathleen Raine, eds. *Thomas Taylor the Platonist: Selected Writings* (Princeton University Press, 1969), p. 296, note that Yeats probably read the version printed in 1895 and reprinted in 1917. Wilson, *Yeats and Tradition*, p. 211, discusses how important Yeats thought this essay was. Yeats refers to Porphyry's bees as early as 1900 in "The Philosophy of Shelley's Poetry."

28. Porphyry, in *Taylor*, p. 307.

29. Frazer, I,1: 37, notes that the image of Artemis at Ephesus was decorated with bands of bees. Neumann, *The Great Mother*, p. 267, also connects "the virginity of the goddess [Demeter], i.e., her independence of the male," with bees.

30. Porphyry, in *Taylor*, p. 307.

31. Ibid., p. 308.

32. Jon Stallworthy, *Between the Lines: Yeats's Poetry in the Making* (Oxford: Clarendon Press, 1963), pp. 31, 38.

33. Bloom, p. 253, calls it "solipsistic" in a general comment on virginity of soul. In reference to "A Prayer for my Daughter," p. 327, he implies the same solipsism.

34. Helen Vendler, "The Byzantine and Delphic Oracle Poems" (Paper read at the Fifth Annual LeMoyne Forum on Religion and Literature, Syracuse, New York, November 5, 1982).

35. Clark, *Yeats at Songs and Choruses*, p. 45.

Chapter 5

1. Yeats said that he left "A Woman Young and Old" out of *The Tower* "for some reason I cannot recall" (VP 831).

2. W. B. Yeats and T. Sturge Moore, *Their Correspondence: 1901–1937*, ed. Ursula Bridge (London: Routledge and Kegan Paul, 1953), p. 154.

3. Jeffares, *New Commentary*, pp. 259–60.

4. Ann Bedford Ulalov, *The Feminine in Jungian Psychology and in Christian Theology* (Evanston: Northwestern University Press, 1971), p. 206.

5. O'Donnell, ed. *The Speckled Bird*, p. 136n.

6. W. H. Keith, "Yeats's 'The Empty Cup,'" *English Language Notes* 4 (March 1967): 209.

7. Balliet, "The Lives . . . Maud Gonne," p. 42. See also John Unterecker, *A Reader's Guide to William Butler Yeats* (New York: Octagon Books, 1980), p. 195, and Ellmann, *Golden Codgers*, p. 108n.

8. Ellmann, *Man and Masks*, p. 96.

9. Blavatsky, 2: 337.

10. Ibid., 2: 341.

11. John Somer, "Unageing Monuments: A Study of W. B. Yeats' Poetry Sequence, 'A Man Young and Old,'" *Ball State University Forum* 12 (Autumn 1971): 33.

12. For example, Samuel Hynes, "All the Wild Witches: The Women in Yeats's Poems," *Sewanee Review* 85 (Fall 1977): 581.

13. The sources of this allusion in paintings are discussed in Clark, *Yeats at Songs and Choruses*, Chapter 4.

14. My references to Plato are taken from *The Dialogues of Plato*, trans. Benjamin Jowett (New York: Random House, 1937), 1: 877–79.

15. Yeats, ed., *The Poems of William Blake* (1905; reprint ed., Cambridge: Harvard University Press, 1969), xlvi.

Chapter 6

1. Kline, p. 47, agrees that Crazy Jane is a virgin in the ancient sense of the term.

2. Both Saul, p. 147, and Clark, *Yeats at Songs and Choruses*, p. 29, connect Yeats's statement about the "tragedy of sexual intercourse" to this poem. Sharon Decker, "Love's Mansion: Sexuality in Yeats's Poetry," *Modern British Literature* 4 (Spring 1979), p. 28, holds that this poem presents the same themes as "The Three Bushes."

3. *The Essence of Plotinus: Extracts from the Six Enneads and Porphyry's Life of Plotinus*, based on the translation by Stephen MacKenna, compiled by Grace H. Turnbill (New York: Oxford University Press, 1948), p. 222.

4. In describing a similar occurrence in "The Words upon the Window-pane," Yeats lists many instances of how the "timeless individuality" of the dead lives on and claims that "the Irish country-woman did see the ruined castle lit up" (Ex 369).

5. Unterecker, p. 226.

6. V, 1925, 248.

7. Plato, trans. Jowett, 1: 318; M. L. Rosenthal and Sally M. Gall, *The Modern Poetic Sequence: The Genius of Modern Poetry* (New York: Oxford University Press, 1983), pp. 126–27.

8. Jeffares, *Man and Poet*, p. 267.

9. Yeats explicitly connects the phrase "intercourse of angels" to Swedenborg (L 805).

10. Emanuel Swedenborg, *Delights of Wisdom concerning Conjugial* [*sic*] *Love after which follow Pleasures of Insanity concerning Scortatory Love* (Boston: T. Harrington Carter and Otis Clapp, 1843), #51, p. 52.

11. Bachchan, pp. 164–68, claims that Yeats must have reread Mathers's *Kabbala Unveiled* right before composing "Supernatural Songs."

12. Peter Ure, "Yeats's Supernatural Songs," in *Yeats and Anglo-Irish Literature*, ed. C. J. Rawson, pp. 128–29.

13. Jeffares, *Man and Poet*, p. 267.

14. Bachchan, p. 78, equates "I am I" and "I am you."

15. Clark, *Yeats at Songs and Choruses*, pp. 51–52.

16. Yeats wrote to Dorothy Wellesley that warts were considered a sign of sexual power by the Irish peasantry (LP 69).

17. Koch, p. 35.

18. Jeffares, *Man and Poet*, p. 267.

19. Curtis Bradford, "Yeats's *Last Poems* Again," in *The Dolmen Press Yeats Centenary Papers MCMLXV*, ed. Liam Miller (Dublin: The Dolmen Press, 1968), p. 286, and Finneran, ed., P 676.

Selected Bibliography

Works by Yeats

Yeats, William Butler. *Autobiography*. New York: Macmillan, 1953.
_____. *The Collected Poems of W. B. Yeats*. Definitive Edition. New York: Macmillan, 1956.
_____. *Essays and Introductions*. New York: Macmillan, 1961.
_____. *Explorations*. London: Macmillan, 1962.
_____. *John Sherman and Dhoya*. Edited by Richard J. Finneran. Detroit: Wayne State University Press, 1969.
_____. *The Letters of W. B. Yeats*. Edited by Allan Wade. New York: Macmillan, 1955.
_____. *Letters to Katharine Tynan*. Edited by Roger McHugh. New York: McMullen Books, 1953.
_____. *Letters to the New Island*. Edited by Horace Reynolds. Cambridge: Harvard University Press, 1934.
_____. *Memoirs: The Autobiography—First Draft; Journal*. Edited by Denis Donoghue. New York: Macmillan, 1973.
_____. *Mythologies*. New York: Collier Books, 1974.
_____. *The Poems*. Edited by Richard J. Finneran. New York: Macmillan, 1983.
_____. *The Secret Rose: A Variorum Edition*. Edited by Philip Marcus, Warwick Gould, and Michael J. Sidnell. Ithaca: Cornell University Press, 1981.
_____. *The Speckled Bird*. Edited by William H. O'Donnell. Canada: McClellan and Stewart, 1976.
_____. *Uncollected Prose*. Vol. 1: *First Reviews and Articles, 1886-1896*. Edited by John P. Frayne. New York: Columbia University Press, 1970; Vol. 2: *Review Articles and Other Miscellaneous Prose, 1897-1939*. Edited by John Frayne and Colton Johnson. New York: Columbia University Press, 1976.
_____. *The Variorum Edition of the Plays of W. B. Yeats*. Edited by Russell K. Alspach and Catherine C. Alspach. New York: Macmillan, 1969.
_____. *The Variorum Edition of the Poems of W. B. Yeats*. Edited by Peter Allt and Russell K. Alspach. New York: Macmillan, 1957.
_____. *A Vision*. 1937. A Reissue with the Author's Final Revisions. New York: Macmillan, 1956.
_____. *A Critical Edition of Yeats's A VISION (1925)*. Edited by George Mills Harper and Walter Kelly Hood. London: Macmillan, 1978.
_____, ed. *Fairy and Folk Tales of Ireland*. Gerrards Cross, Buckinghamshire: Colin Smythe, 1973.

_____, ed. *Poems of William Blake*. Cambridge: Harvard University Press, 1969.

Yeats, William Butler and Ellis, Edwin, eds. *The Works of William Blake—Poetical, Symbolic, and Critical*. 1893. Reprint. New York: AMS Press, 1973.

Yeats, William Butler and Moore, T. Sturge. *Their Correspondence 1901-1937*. Edited by Ursula Bridge. London: Routledge and Kegan Paul, 1953.

Yeats, William Butler and Ruddock, Margot. *Ah, Sweet Dancer: A Correspondence*. Edited by Roger McHugh. New York: Macmillan, 1970.

Yeats, William Butler and Swami, Shree Purohit. *The Ten Principal Upanishads*. London: Faber and Faber, 1937.

Yeats, William Butler and Wellesley, Dorothy. *Letters on Poetry*. New York: Oxford University Press, 1940.

Yeats, William Butler and Wellesley, Dorothy, eds. *Broadsides: A Collection of New Irish and English Songs*. Dublin: Cuala Press, 1937. Reprint. Shannon: Irish University Press, 1971.

Works about Yeats and Other Works

Adams, J. F. "'Leda and the Swan': The Aesthetics of Rape." *Bucknell Review* 12 (December 1964): 47-58.

Allen, James Lovic. "Life as Art: Yeats and the Alchemical Quest." *Studies in the Literary Imagination* 14 (Spring 1981): 17-42.

Archibald, Douglas. *Yeats*. Syracuse University Press, 1983.

Bachchan, Harbans Rai. *W. B. Yeats and Occultism: A Study of His Works in Relation to Indian Lore, the Cabbala, Swedenborg, Boehme, and Theosophy*. London: Books from India, 1976.

Balliet, Conrad. "The Lives—and Lies—of Maud Gonne." *Eire-Ireland* 14 (Fall 1979): 17-44.

_____. "W. B. Yeats: The Pun of a Gonne." *Modern British Literature* 4 (Spring 1979): 44-50.

Beum, Robert. *The Poetic Art of William Butler Yeats*. New York: F. Ungar, 1969.

Blavatsky, H. P. *Collected Writings, 1888: The Secret Doctrine*. Adyar Madras, India: The Theosophical Publishing House, 1978.

Bloom, Harold. *Yeats*. New York: Oxford University Press, 1970.

Boehme, Jacob. *Personal Christianity: A Science: The Doctrines of Jacob Boehme*. Edited by Franz Hartmann. 1891. Reprint. New York: Macoy Publishing Company, 1919.

_____. *Six Theosophic Points and Other Writings*. Translated by John Rolleston Earle. Ann Arbor: University of Michigan Press, 1958.

Bornstein, George. *Yeats and Shelley*. University of Chicago Press, 1970.

_____. "Yeats's Romantic Dante." *Colby Library Quarterly* 15 (June 1979): 93-113.

Bradford, Curtis. "George Yeats: Poet's Wife." *Sewanee Review* 57 (July-September 1969): 385-404.

_____. "Yeats and Maud Gonne." *Texas Studies in Language and Literature* 3 (1962): 452-74.

_____. *Yeats at Work*. Carbondale and Edwardsville: Southern Illinois University Press, 1965.

Burland, C. A. *The Arts of the Alchemists*. New York: Macmillan, 1968.

Butler, E. M. *The Myth of the Magus*. Cambridge University Press, 1979.

Clark, David. *Yeats at Songs and Choruses*. Amherst: University of Massachusetts Press, 1983.

Clark, David; Sidnell, Michael; and Mayhew, George. *Druid Craft: The Writing of THE SHADOWY WATERS*. Amherst: University of Massachusetts Press, 1971.

Coxhead, Elizabeth. *Daughters of Erin: Five Women of the Irish Renascence*. London: Secker and Warburg, 1965.

_____. *Lady Gregory: A Literary Portrait*. New York: Harcourt, Brace, and World, 1961.

Cross, K. G. W. and Jeffares, A. Norman, eds. *In Excited Reverie: A Centenary Tribute to William Butler Yeats, 1865-1939*. New York: Macmillan, 1965.

Decker, Sharon. "Love's Mansion: Sexuality in Yeats's Poetry." *Modern British Literature* 4 (Spring 1979): 17–32.

Donoghue, Denis. *William Butler Yeats*. New York: Viking Press, 1971.

Dryden, John. *The Poetical Works of John Dryden*. Edited by George Noyes. Cambridge: Riverside Press, 1950.

Dume, Thomas Leslie. "William Butler Yeats: A Survey of His Reading." Ph.D. dissertation, Temple University, 1950.

Ellmann, Richard. *Golden Codgers: Biographical Speculation*. New York: Oxford University Press, 1973.

————. *The Identity of Yeats*. New York: Oxford University Press, 1954.

————. *Yeats: The Man and the Masks*. New York: W. W. Norton, 1978.

Engelberg, Edward. *The Vast Design: Patterns in W. B. Yeats's Aesthetic*. University of Toronto Press, 1964.

Finneran, Richard J., ed. *Yeats Annual*. No. 1. Dublin: Gill and Macmillan, 1982.

Finneran, Richard J.; Harper, George Mills; and Murphy, William, eds. *Letters to W. B. Yeats*. New York: Columbia University Press, 1977.

Flannery, Mary Catherine. *Yeats and Magic: The Earlier Works*. New York: Barnes and Noble, 1978.

Frazer, James George. *The Golden Bough: A Study in Magic and Religion*. 3rd ed. New York: Macmillan, 1935.

Frye, Northrop. "The Top of the Tower: A Study of the Imagery of Yeats." *Southern Review* 5 (1969): 850–71.

Garab, Arra. "Fabulous Artifice: Yeats's 'Three Bushes' Sequence." *Criticism* 7 (1965): 235–49.

Gregory, Lady Augusta. *Lady Gregory's Journals 1916–1930*. Edited by Lennox Robinson. New York: Macmillan, 1947.

————. *Seventy Years*. Edited by Colin Smythe. New York: Macmillan, 1974.

Grossman, Allen R. *Poetic Knowledge in the Early Yeats: A Study of THE WIND AMONG THE REEDS*. Charlottesville: University Press of Virginia, 1969.

Gwynn, Stephen, ed. *Scattering Branches: Tributes to the Memory of W.B. Yeats*. New York: Macmillan, 1940.

Hall, James and Steinman, Martin, eds. *The Permanence of Yeats*. New York: Collier Books, 1961.

Harding, Esther. *Woman's Mysteries, Ancient and Modern: A Psychological Interpretation of the Feminine Principle as Portrayed in Myth, Story, and Dreams*. Rev. ed. New York: G.P. Putnam's Sons, 1971.

Harper, George Mills. *Yeats's Golden Dawn*. New York: Barnes and Noble, 1974.

————, ed. *Yeats and the Occult*. Canada: Macmillan, 1975.

Harper, George Mills, and Raine, Kathleen, eds. *Thomas Taylor the Platonist: Selected Writings*. Bollingen Series LXXXVIII. Princeton University Press, 1969.

Henke, Suzette. "Yeats's *John Sherman*: A Portal of Discovery." *Canadian Journal of Irish Studies* 8 (June 1982): 25–35.

Henn, T.R. *The Lonely Tower: Studies in the Poetry of W.B. Yeats*. 2nd ed. New York: Barnes and Noble, 1965.

Hinkson, Katherine Tynan. *The Middle Years*. London: Constable and Company, 1916.

Hoffman, Daniel. *Barbarous Knowledge: Myth in the Poetry of Yeats, Graves, and Muir*. New York: Oxford University Press, 1967.

Hone, Joseph. *W.B. Yeats 1865–1939*. New York: Macmillan, 1943.

Hynes, Samuel. "All the Wild Witches: The Women in Yeats's Poems." *Sewanee Review* 85 (Fall 1977): 565–82.

Jeffares, A. Norman. *The Circus Animals: Essays on W.B. Yeats.* Stanford University Press, 1984.

———. *A New Commentary on the Poems of W.B. Yeats.* Stanford University Press, 1984.

———. *W.B. Yeats: Man and Poet.* New York: Barnes and Noble, 1966.

———. *Yeats, Sligo and Ireland: Essays to Mark the 21st Yeats International Summer School.* Irish Literary Studies. No. 6. Gerrards Cross, Buckinghamshire: Colin Smythe, 1980.

Keith, W.H. "Yeats's 'The Empty Cup.' " *English Language Notes* 4 (March 1967): 206–10.

Kermode, Frank. *Romantic Image.* New York: Macmillan, 1957.

Kline, Gloria C. *The Last Courtly Lover: Yeats and the Idea of Woman.* Ann Arbor: UMI Research Press, 1983.

Koch, Vivienne. *W.B. Yeats, The Tragic Phase: A Study of the Last Poems.* Baltimore: Johns Hopkins Press, 1951.

Levenson, Samuel. *Maud Gonne.* New York: Reader's Digest Press, 1967.

Levine, Bernard. *The Dissolving Image: The Spiritual-esthetic Development of W.B. Yeats.* Detroit: Wayne State University Press, 1970.

MacBride, Maud Gonne. *A Servant of the Queen: Reminiscences.* London: Oxford University Press, 1941.

Mead, G.R.S. *Thrice-Greatest Hermes: Studies in Hellenistic Theosophy and Gnosis.* 3 vols. London: The Theosophical Society, 1906.

Melchiori, Giorgio. *The Whole Mystery of Art: Pattern into Poetry in the Work of W.B. Yeats.* London: Routledge and Kegan Paul, 1960.

Milhail, E.H., ed. *W.B. Yeats: Interviews and Recollections.* London: Macmillan, 1977.

Miller, J. Hillis. *Poets of Reality: Six Twentieth-Century Writers.* Cambridge: Belknap Press, 1965.

Miller, Liam, ed. *The Dolmen Press Yeats Centenary Papers MCMLXV.* Dublin: The Dolmen Press, 1968.

Moore, Virginia. *The Unicorn: William Butler Yeats's Search for Reality.* New York: Macmillan, 1954.

Neumann, Erich. *The Great Mother: An Analysis of the Archetype.* Translated by Ralph Manheim. Bollingen Series XLVII. Princeton University Press, 1974.

Oates, Joyce Carol. *The Edge of Impossibility: Tragic Forms in Literature.* New York: Vanguard Press, 1972.

O'Driscoll, Robert and Reynolds, Lorna. *Yeats and the Theatre.* Canada: Macmillan, 1975.

Olney, James. "Sex and the Dead: *Daimones* of Yeats and Jung." *Studies in the Literary Imagination* 14 (Spring 1981): 43–60.

Parkinson, Thomas. *W.B. Yeats: The Later Poetry.* Berkeley and Los Angeles: University of California Press, 1964.

———. "Yeats and the Love Lyric." *James Joyce Quarterly* 3 (Winter 1966): 109–23.

Parks, L.C. "The Influence of Villiers de L'Isle-Adam on W.B. Yeats." Ph.D. dissertation, University of Washington, 1959.

Partridge, Edward B. "Yeats's 'The Three Bushes'—Genesis and Structure," *Accent* 17 (Spring 1957): 67–80.

Plato. *The Dialogues of Plato.* Trans. Benjamin Jowett. 2 vols. New York: Random House, 1937.

Plotinus. *The Essence of Plotinus: Extracts from the Six Enneads and Porphyry's Life of Plotinus.* Based on the translation by Stephen MacKenna. Compiled by Grace H. Turnbill. New York: Oxford University Press, 1948.

Rajan, Balanchandra. *W.B. Yeats: A Critical Introduction.* London: Hutchinson University Library, 1969.

Reid, B.L. *William Butler Yeats: The Lyric of Tragedy.* Norman: University of Oklahoma Press, 1961.

Rhys, Jocelyn. *Shaken Creeds: The Virgin Birth Doctrine, A Study of Its Origins.* London: Watts and Company, 1922.

Robinson, Lennox, ed. *The Irish Theatre.* London: Macmillan, 1939.

Ronseley, Joseph. *Yeats's Autobiography: Life as Symbolic Pattern.* Cambridge: Harvard University Press, 1968.

Rose, Marilyn Gaddis. *Katherine Tynan.* Lewisburg: Bucknell University Press, 1974.

————. "Yeats's Use of *Axel.*" *Comparative Drama* 4 (Winter 1970–71): 253–64.

Rosenthal, M.L. and Gall, Sally M. *The Modern Poetic Sequence: The Genius of Modern Poetry.* New York: Oxford University Press, 1983.

Rothenstein, William. *Men and Memories: Recollections 1872–1938.* Abridged by Mary Lago. London: Chatto and Windus, 1978.

Rudd, Margaret. *Divided Image: A Study of William Blake and W.B. Yeats.* London: Routledge and Kegan Paul, 1953.

Runnels, James Alan. "Mother, Wife, Lover: Symbolic Women in the Work of W.B. Yeats." Ph.D. dissertation, Rutgers University, 1973.

Saul, George Brandon. *Prolegomena to the Study of Yeats's Poems.* Philadelphia: University of Pennsylvania Press, 1957.

Scholem, Gershom G. *On the Kabbalah and Its Symbolism.* Translated by Ralph Manheim. New York: Schocken Books, 1965.

Somer, John. "Unageing Monuments: A Study of W.B. Yeats's Poetry Sequence, 'A Man Young and Old.'" *Ball State University Forum* 12 (Autumn 1971): 28–36.

Spanos, William V. "Sacramental Imagery in the Middle and Late Poetry of W.B. Yeats." *Texas Studies in Language and Literature* (1962): 214–27.

Spitzer, Leo. "On Yeats's Poem 'Leda and the Swan.'" *Modern Philology* 51 (1954): 271–76.

Stallworthy, Jon. *Between the Lines: Yeats's Poetry in the Making.* Oxford: Clarendon Press, 1963.

————. *Vision and Revision in Yeats's Last Poems.* Oxford: Clarendon Press, 1969.

Stock, A.G. *W.B. Yeats: His Poetry and Thought.* Cambridge University Press, 1961.

Sturm, Frank Pearce. *His Life, Letters, and Collected Work.* Edited by Richard Taylor. Urbana: University of Illinois Press, 1969.

Swedenborg, Emanuel. *Delights of Wisdom concerning Conjugial* [sic] *Love after which follow Pleasures of Insanity concerning Scortatory Love.* Boston: T. Harrington Carter and Otis Clapp, 1843.

————. *Heaven and Its Wonders and Hell, from Things Heard and Seen.* Translated by J.C. Ager. Standard Edition. 1812. Reprint. New York: Swedenborg Foundation, 1980.

Trowbridge, Hoyt. " 'Leda and the Swan': A Longinian Analysis." *Modern Philology* 51 (1953): 118–29.

Ulalov, Ann Beford. *The Feminine in Jungian Psychology and in Christian Theology.* Evanston: Northwestern University Press, 1971.

Unterecker, John. *A Reader's Guide to William Butler Yeats.* New York: Octagon Books, 1980.

Ure, Peter. *W.B. Yeats.* New York: Grove Press, 1963.

————. *Yeats and Anglo-Irish Literature: Critical Essays by Peter Ure.* Ed. C.J. Rawson. Liverpool University Press, 1974.

Vance, Thomas. "Dante, Yeats, and Unity of Being." *Shenandoah* 17 (1966): 73–86.

Vendler, Helen Hennessey. "The Byzantine and Delphic Oracle Poems." Paper Read at Fifth Annual LeMoyne Forum on Religion and Literature, November 5, 1982, at LeMoyne College, Syracuse, New York.

————. *Yeats's VISION and the Later Plays.* Cambridge: Harvard University Press, 1963.

Villiers de L'Isle-Adam, Philippe-Auguste. *Axel.* Translated by Marilyn Gaddis Rose. Dublin: Dolmen Press, 1970.

Wade, Allan. *A Bibliography of the Writings of W.B. Yeats.* 3rd ed. Revised and edited by Russell K. Alspach. Suffolk: Rupert Hart-Davis, 1968.

Wain, John, ed. *Interpretations: Essays on Twelve English Poems.* London: Routledge and Kegan Paul, 1962.

Waite, Arthur Edward. *Lives of the Alchemystical Philosophers.* London: George Redway, 1888.

Webster, Brenda S. *Yeats: A Psychoanalytic Study.* Stanford University Press, 1973.

Whitaker, Thomas. *Swan and Shadow: Yeats's Dialogue with History.* Chapel Hill: University of North Carolina Press, 1964.

Wilson, F.A.C. *W.B. Yeats and Tradition.* New York: Macmillan, 1958.

―――. *Yeats's Iconography.* New York: Macmillan, 1960.

Index